BLOCKCHAIN BASICS + NFTS FOR BEGINNERS + CRYPTOCURRENCY DEFI INVESTMENT GUIDE - 3in1:

Blockchain Wars & Nft Revolution-
How to Defi and Make Money with
Non-Fungible Tokens &
Decentralized Finance after Bitcoin
and Ethereum

By

Satoshy Nakamoto

D1361823

BLOCKCHAIN BASICS BIBLE

Non-Technical Beginner's
Introduction to Cryptocurrency.
The Future of Bitcoin & Ethereum
Crypto Technology, Non-Fungible
Token (NFT), Smart Contracts,
Consensus Protocols, Mining, &
Blockchain Gaming

By

Satoshy Nakamoto

DISCLAIMER

© Copyright 2021

Table of contents

INTRODUCTION

WHAT IS BLOCKCHAIN?

Individuals can collectively uphold a database without having to depend upon a central authority via Blockchain. Aimed for our unified future, Blockchain is prototypical for sharing and reconciling information.

Information has been traced through a ledger for a long time which is a simple sequential list of data. Ledgers have been used to track heaps of wheat, deaths from epidemics or from curses, basically any thing man can think of.

Ways of tracking and syncing data have extended with the development of the scope of human activity. With the development of computers and other digital resources in the previous century, our information also became electronic and the ledgers were now recorded on computers. The number of prospects and databases increased, and with the invention of new methods of improved, interconnected, electronic ledgers, it was suddenly easy to search, sort, share, and transport information.

Today, almost every digital service is reinforced by databases. But the practicality of database is being restricted, and its universality is being questioned due to it being originated in the pre-internet and pre-global world. Databases are sustained by a dominant authority that has complete power over the information the database contains. For instance, Facebook could change your Instagram to be just pictures of pretty flowers if it wanted to, and you'd have no choice but to accept it. Similarly, if a bank wanted to they could easily take $100 from your checking account. You'd clearly notice this and complain. But what if they only took a dollar per day?

We need something more irrepressible and cooperative, something that is wide-ranging but not subjected to a single dogmatic ideology, private intentions, or corporate incentive to manage our data since the world and our interactions have become more linked, and more digital.

Blockchain, invented in 2009, is exactly what we needed.

Blockchain can keep data coordinated across numerous, liberated stakeholders. Blockchain allows a collection of unrelated entities, having an enticement to modify their shared data, to agree on and maintain a unified dataset. In contrast to the blockchain, a traditional database is better equipped for tracking the records of a single entity.

So far, Blockchain has been the most convenient for tracking money because the reason to edit data in your own favor is very strong in financial systems. The basic idea of how blockchain works are given below.

The Basic Idea Behind Blockchain

First, by running the same blockchain software, computers wanting to share data join together on a network. The data is assembled together into "blocks" for authentication as it is coming into the network; for instance through people spending and receiving money. The computes vote on the current block of data systematically, typically every few minutes or even every few seconds, deciding whether it all looks good or not. The computer votes on the overruled current block again when the next block is submitted. When the computer agrees about the validity of the data it holds, the current block is accepted, and then added to the system's complete past history of authenticated data blocks. Hence, the data is "chained". A long chain of information is formed as a result.

Every computer on the network stores the chain, cryptographic functions are used to carry out the appending, hence making it easy to tell if any past transaction has been changed even in the slightest. So with the addition of each new block of data, the whole network confirms the authenticity of all preceding data.

Let's say if you have more money than you're supposed to and wanted to cheat and, say, modify any past transaction, you'd have to change the histories across all the computers on the system working independently. Or have sufficient new computers join the network that could vote your cheats into "fact." Such an attack is called a 51% attack. Such an attack would be ridiculously costly if you're a part of a large system like Bitcoin because you'd have to run too many computers. Such attacks are unmanageable, by design, on Stellar. You can't even submit bad data instantaneously because ultimately the network will approve the right data and your self-seeking objective will be voted down.

As expected, a reasonable amount of technical detail goes into all this. We highly recommend reading the primary paper describing the first blockchain system, because it is rather ingenious.

Important Blockchain Products

Blockchain is not looked at as a competition at Stellar. There's a lot of good software out there! If you are looking to gain better information and knowledge of blockchain technology, you can resort to the following resources.

Bitcoin

Almost a decade ago the yet unidentified "Satoshi Nakamoto" created Bitcoin; a foundation and inspiration for essentially all blockchain systems. The up-front offshoots of BTC include popular platforms like Litecoin and Dogecoin. Even though much of its fundamental principles are the same, Stellar doesn't use the same technology.

This is a good rudimentary technical/conceptual Bitcoin primer.

This is another good indication which draws in some of what inspired the creation of the technology.

One of the plus points of a decentralized currency is presented by this Op-Ed by Meridian speaker Carlos Hernandez. Bitcoin has a tangible use case as an economic sanctuary in many parts of the world, despite it being a curiosity for Americans. Stellar anticipates building something that is as dominant but more accessible and like-minded with the present monetary system.

Ethereum

The second-largest blockchain platform is Ethereum. Even though it is somewhat similar to Bitcoin, it was thought of as something more multi-purposed than being just a currency like Bitcoin. Designed to become another Internet-style network or "world computer", Ethereum has its own programming language (Solidity) that ideally enables you to create any type of program inside the Ethereum network. These programs are known as decentralized applications or "dapps", and would even be ideally sturdy to government control and inaccuracy.

The Ethereum blockchain network has smart contracts as one of its main elements. Smart contracts are a type of contract that works automatically. These tokens are issued via Solidity. At this point, the spirit of Ethereum surpasses its capabilities. This is a reason that the Ethereum network is pretty slow. The intricate nature of Solidity is making it easy to exploit and it adds to the problem as well. It has its flaws and defects but is still considered to be one of the best examples of programming models.

A basic and ideal up to a certain level is Ethereum primer.

The DAO – the "Digital Autonomous Organization" was one of the firsts and ideal Ethereum projects that superbly went sideways.

Stellar

The creation of Stellar happened in the year 2014. It was after the bitcoin but before the creation of Ethereum. Stellar was created in order to facilitate remittances and payments. Stellar works on an environment-friendly syncing mechanism. No platform worked on such mechanism. Stellar is like a cashlike which causes short suspensions in between the transactions. Similar to that of Ethereum you can issue other assets and then trade them with great ease on Stellar.

Stellar can be connected to real-world endpoints. This is something that allows people to convert their digital money into the form that they can spend. This is something that you cannot do on every blockchain system. The growth of this network is something that the Stellar Development Foundation is working tirelessly on.

The Stellar community site which goes by the name Lumenauts.com has a lot of great Stellar interpreters. They have come up with a course that provides detailed information regarding the entire platform.

A few other projects worth checking out

Z-Cash

Z-Cash's tech is derived from Bitcoin. It is altered so it is able to guard and secure the users' privacy. Unlike the Ethereum Blockchain network that stores all the information on a digital ledger that can be traced by anyone, Z-Cash keeps some of the information of the transactions anonymous.

Basic Attention Token

This is an Ethereum-based project which is considered as an example. They aim to re-evaluate the working of internet advertising by building a resourceful and proficient "attention economy" using their token and their Brave browser.

0x

0x is a decentralized exchange protocol that lets people trade their coins peer-to-peer and not have any exchange on its own in the middle. It is something that happens in the CoinBase. It is a project by Ethereum. An example of this can be RadarRelay.

CHAPTER NO 1

THE HISTORY OF BLOCKCHAIN TECHNOLOGY

Blockchain technology is a decentralized, distributed ledger that records information on the transactions. The in-built design does not allow any data to be altered on the blockchain. It makes it a genuine disruptor for industries like payments, cybersecurity, and healthcare. This guide will help you understand how can it be used and what is its history.

Blockchain is also known as Distributed Ledger Technology (DLT). The digital ledger technology allows the history of any digital asset unable to change. It is kept transparent by using decentralization and cryptographic hashing.

Google Docs is a great way to understand Blockchain technology. Whenever a document is created on Google Docs, it can be shared with people. You see that the document that was created is distributed and not copied or transferred. This helps create a decentralized distribution chain that provides everyone access to the document simultaneously. No one has to wait for somebody else to make the changes that they want to make. All the changes that are made to the document are recorded instantaneously. This makes the whole process transparent.

Yes, blockchain is pretty complicated in comparison to a Google Doc, but the correspondence is appropriate because it demonstrates three critical ideas of the technology.

Risk reduction is one of the great factors that makes Blockchain a promising and groundbreaking technology. It is a great way to eliminate any fraudulent situations and ensures transparency in an accessible way for a myriad of uses.

How Does Blockchain Work?

Blockchain is used so that people can share important data in a secure, tamperproof way. — MIT Technology Review

The three important concepts that blockchain consists of are: blocks, nodes, and miners.

Blocks

Each of its chains is a composition of multiple blocks. Each block further has three basic elements.

The data in the block.

Nonce is a 32-bit whole number. It is randomly generated whenever a block is created, which in turn generates a block header hash.

Hash is a 256-bit number linked to the nonce. It needs to start with an enormous number of zeroes (i.e. be extremely small).

Nonce is a cryptographic hash that is generated when the first block of the chain is created. The data in the block is deliberated, signed, and forever tied to the nonce and hash till it is mined.

Miners

New blocks of data are formed by the miners on the chain. This process is termed mining.

Unique nonce and hash are a part of every block that is a part of the blockchain. Not just that but the nonce and hash that are used in the previous blocks in the chain are mentioned as well. This shows that mining a block is not something easy, particularly on large chains.

Miners use special software that is used to solve the extremely complex math problem of finding a nonce that generates an accepted hash. The size of nonce is 32 bits and that of hash is 256. This means that there are approximately four billion nonce-hash combinations that must be mined before the right one is initiated. After this, the miners are said to have established the "golden nonce." Once done that block that they just created is added to the chain.

You need to re-mine the block in which the change is made as well as all those blocks that come after that. This is done when changes are made in the blocks early. This makes blockchain technology very hard to influence. Think of it as "safety in math." That is because finding golden nonce entails a lot of time and power of computation.

All the nodes that are in the chain recognize and accept the changes that are made once a block is mined. This is a great way for the miners to earn some extra money.

Nodes

Decentralization is considered to be one of the most important concepts that you need to understand regarding blockchain technology. The chain is not owned by a specific organization or a computer. It is a distributed ledger by the nodes linked to the chain. Any electronic device that retains the copies of the blockchain and keeps it running at all costs is known as a node.

Every node that is part of the network owns its own copy of the blockchain. It is significant for the network to algorithmically accept any block that is mined for the chain to be updated, trusted, and verified. Blockchains are transparent. Everything that happens in the ledger can be checked and viewed with ease. In order to display the number of transactions, every member is given an ID that is alphanumeric and unique in nature.

The combination of the checks-and-balances system and public information helps the blockchain maintain the integrity and creates trust among its users. Blockchains are a great way to gain trust through technology.

Cryptocurrencies are a popular application of blockchain technology. Cryptocurrencies are also known as digital currencies (and sometimes tokens) such as Bitcoin, Ethereum, or Litecoin. These digital currencies are used to buy goods and services. It is said to be cash, but in a digital form. You can use crypto to purchase everything. Crypto is based on a blockchain system that is both a public ledger and an improved cryptographic security system. This is something that is not their cash. The transactions are recorded and kept secure.

There are 6,700 cryptocurrencies in the world to date with a total market capitalization of around $1.6 trillion. Bitcoin has a major value. These tokens have become extremely prevalent for a few years. The worth of a bitcoin is equivalent to $60,000. But why have people started to notice cryptocurrencies all of a sudden? Here are a few reasons for that:

Theft and fraud get difficult because each cryptocurrency has its own indisputable and recognizable number that is committed to one owner. This is a plus point of Blockchain security.

Crypto has decreased the want for individualized currencies and central banks. Crypto can be directed anywhere due to blockchain technology. That too, without any requirement for exchanging currency and with no central banks interfering in the matter.

Cryptocurrencies have the ability to make people earn more. Investors have been fueling the Crypto's price, especially Bitcoin. The people who adopted this technology in their initial days have now become billionaires. Whether this is actually a positive has yet to be understood as some retractors believe that investors do not have the long-term profits of crypto.

The majority of the large corporations have started to accept the idea of a blockchain-based digital currency for payments. Tesla has already made an investment of $1.5 Billion into Bitcoin back in February 2021. They have accepted it as payment for their cars.

There are multiple points of view regarding the digital currencies that are based on the blockchain. The crypto market is not much regulated. Many governments jumped onto the crypto bandwagon, but few have a firm set of codified laws regarding the crypto market. Due to its investors, the crypto currencies are highly volatile. In 2016, Bitcoin was estimated to be around $450 for each token. It then soared to $16,000 per token in the year 2018. Then it plunged to around $3,100. An increase was seen and it got to $60,000. This absence of stability has triggered some people to get very rich, while a majority has lost thousands.

If we state the prerogative that cryptocurrencies are the future will be something ahead of time. For now, the swift rise in blockchains is preliminary to take essence in reality than buildup. Blockchain still looks like a promising field as compared to Bitcoin.

Applications of Blockchain in the Music Industry:

The growth of technology and the internet has paved the way for the music industry. It has gone huge over the past few years. It has been noted that that there has been a significant increase in music streaming websites and platforms. Artists, labels, publishers, songwriters to the streaming service providers all are being influenced negatively in the music industry due to this. Music royalties are determined by an intricate process but the internet has made it even more worse by giving rise to the demand for transparency in the royalty payments by artists and songwriters. This is where blockchain technology comes into play. It maintains an all-inclusive, precise distributed database of music rights ownership information in a public ledger. Furthermore, the rights to ownership information, royalty splitting as determined by "smart contracts" could be made a part of the database. The relationships between the different stakeholders can be programmed by the use of smart contracts.

Dropbox and Google Drive are Decentralized Storage Cloud file storage solutions that are seeing growth in popularity. They are used to store documents, photos, videos, and music files. Notwithstanding their popularity, cloud file storage solutions characteristically face challenges in areas such as security, privacy, and data control. One of the biggest issues that one comes across in these scenarios is that you have to trust a third party with one's confidential files. Storj provides a blockchain-based peer-to-peer distributed cloud storage platform that permits users to transfer and share data without trusting a third-party data provider. This lets the people share the internet bandwidth that is not used as well as extra disk space in their devices. This is something that would help those people who are considering storing large files in return for micropayments based on the bitcoin. Lack of central control removes data failures that are more conventional. This also considerably increases security, privacy, and data control. Storj platform can occasionally cryptographically check the integrity and availability of a file, and offer direct rewards to those maintaining the file. Micropayments that are based on the incentive and payment are served in a separate blockchain. That is used as a datastore for file metadata.

Beyond Bitcoin: Ethereum Blockchain

The extremely transparent ledger system for Bitcoin that it works on, and blockchain have been linked with cryptocurrency. But then again the transparency and security of the technology have been flourishing in a number of zones. The majority of this can be traced back to the development of the

Russian-Canadian developer Vitalik Buterin in the late months of 2013 who published a white paper. The white paper projected a platform that combines the working of traditional blockchain with a major alteration: the execution of computer code. This gave birth to the Ethereum project.

Ethereum blockchain allows the developers to create sophisticated programs that have the ability to communicate with each other on a blockchain.

Tokens

Tokens are created by the Ethereum programmers to signify the digital assets. Not just that, but coming up with trajectories to find who owns the assets as well, and execute its functionality according to programming instructions.

Tokens can be anything from music files, contracts, concert tickets, or even a patients medical records. Nowadays the popularity of the Non-Fungible Tokens (NFTs) has increased multiple folds as well. NFTs are exclusive tokens based on blockchain technology that are used to collect digital media or art. NFTs have the capability to prove and authenticate the past history and sole ownership of the piece of digital media. NFTs have greatly helped the artist in selling their digital artworks and also get proper credit and a fair share of profits.

The applications of blockchain have expanded the likelihood of the ledger technology to saturate other areas like media, government, and identity security. Several companies are working on developing products and ecosystems that run completely on the rapidly increasing technology.

Blockchain is inspiring the existing state of affairs of novelty. They are allowing the companies to experiment with revolutionary technology like peer-to-peer energy distribution or decentralized forms for news media. This is pretty much how Blockchain is defined. With the evolution of technology, the evolution of the ledger system would happen too.

History of Blockchain

Despite being a new technology, blockchain already claims a rich and interesting history. A lot of important events occurred in the past and in order to distinguish events that led to the development of blockchain are given below.

2008

In 2008, a book called "Bitcoin: A Peer to Peer Electronic Cash System" was published by Satoshi Nakamoto - the identity of whom is not known.

2009

In 2009, the first effective Bitcoin (BTC) transaction took place between computer scientist Hal Finney and the mysterious Satoshi Nakamoto.

2010

The first-ever purchase using a bitcoin – two Papa John's pizzas, was made by Florida-based programmer Laszlo Hanycez. A total of 10,000 BTC's worth $60 at that time, were transferred by Hanycez. Today it holds a value of $80 million.

Within the same year, the market cap of Bitcoin publically surpassed $1 million.

2011

The cryptocurrency was given equivalence to the US dollar with 1 BTC being equal to $1 USD.

Bitcoins started being accepted as donations by organizations such as Electronic Frontier Foundation, Wikileaks.

2012

Blockchain was introduced into pop culture when renowned TV shows like The Good Wife mentioned cryptocurrency and Blockchain.

Early Bitcoin developer Vitalik Buterin launched Bitcoin Magazine.

2013

BTC's market cap exceeded $1 billion.

The value of Bitcoin equivalent to dollar reached the value of $100 BTC for the first time.

"Ethereum Project", the paper suggesting that blockchain had other possible uses besides Bitcoin, like smart contracts,was published by Buterin.

2014

Bitcoin has started being accepted as payment by gaming company Zynga, The D Las Vegas Hotel, and Overstock.com.

Buterin's Ethereum Project was crowdfunded through an Initial Coin Offering (ICO) which raised over $18 million in BTC and increased opportunities for blockchain.

A group called R3 was formed to discover new ways of implementing blockchain in technology. This group comprised over 200 blockchain firms.

Bitcoin integration was announced by PayPal.

2015

The number of merchants accepting BTC exceeds more than 100,000.

In order to test the technology for trading shares in private companies, NASDAQ and San-Francisco blockchain company Chain teamed up.

2016

A blockchain strategy for cloud-based business solutions was announced by the tech giant IBM.

The validity of blockchain and cryptocurrencies was recognized by the Japanese government.

2017

For the first time, Bitcoin reached $1,000 BTC.

The cryptocurrency market cap crossed $150 billion.

Jamie Dimon who is the Chief Executive Officer of JP Morgan specified his belief in blockchain as a future technology which gave the ledger system a vote of confidence from Wall Street.

Bitcoin reached its unsurpassed high at $19,783.21 BTC.

It was announced by Dubai that by 2020 its government will be powered by Blockchain.

2018

Facebook pledged to start a blockchain group and also suggested the possibility of creating its own cryptocurrency.

A blockchain-based banking platform was developed by IBM and great banks like Citi and Barclays signed on.

2019

Blockchain was publicly embraced by the Chinese president Ji Xinping as China's central bank announced it is working on its own cryptocurrency.

Twitter & Square CEO Jack Dorsey announced that Square will be hiring blockchain engineers to work on the company's future crypto plans.

The creation of Bakkt, a digital wallet company that comprises crypto trading was announced by the New York Stock Exchange (NYSE.)

2020

By the end of 2020, Bitcoin almost reached $30,000.

It was announced by PayPal that they would allow users to buy, sell, and hold cryptocurrencies via Paypal.

"Sand Dollar", the first central bank digital currency, was launched by the Bahamas, hence becoming the world's first country to do so.

Due to securely storing medical research data and patient information, Blockchain became a key player in the battle against the Corona Virus.

CHAPTER NO 2

HOW DO CRYPTOCURRENCIES RISE UP?

Just like a band, cryptocurrency is a digital currency that can be exchanged between two persons directly without the involvement of a third person. It shows the financial amount without disclosing the identities of the people carrying out the transaction, hence enabling consumers to digitally connect directly through a transparent process. In order to confirm a cryptocurrency exchange and prevent replication of the very transaction, the network consists of a chain of computers. This form of a transaction has the likelihood to reduce scams because of its transparency.

A cryptocurrency exchange is fairly analogous to PayPal, with the exception that the currency being exchanged is not traditional money. To guarantee the security of transactions, cryptocurrency uses digital safeguards. A process known as mining a digital public ledger, called a blockchain, must confirm each transaction.

How do Cryptocurrency Exchanges Work?

In order to clear up any confusion let's discuss the following words:

Transaction: The transfer of currency between two digital wallets is known as a transaction. Before the give-and-take can be settled, a transaction is submitted to a public ledger to await authorization. During a transaction in demand to show ownership, an encrypted electronic signature based on a mathematical formula is obligatory. People called miners carry out the process of confirmation.

Public Ledger: A public ledger called a blockchain store the transaction after a miner confirms it. The confirmation of the ownership and guarantee of the validity of recordkeeping is carried out by the public ledger.

Mining: Before being added to the public ledger, the transactions are confirmed by a process called mining. In order to prevent misuse of cryptocurrency mining, a miner must know how to solve "proof of work"; a computational puzzle. Before the transaction block is added to the blockchain, anyone can authorize the transaction, hence mining is open source. For their work in cryptocurrency miners receive a fee.

In short, a cryptocurrency exchange using blockchain practically works in the following ways:

1. "A" desires to send cryptocurrency to "B."

2. The exemplification of transactions online is known as a block.

3. Everyone on the network receives the block.

4. A miner within the network will approve the validity of the block.

5. The newly created block becomes a part of the public ledger or blockchain.

6. Then the currency moves from "A" to "B."

In traditional banking systems, intermediaries must be trusted by the sender and receiver to assist centralized transactions. Not only does this kind of demand cost great fees, but it takes hold of the private data of individuals while doing so. Conversely, cryptocurrency exchange safeguards individual identities whilst providing a decentralized, transparent mechanism for transferring value at a lower cost.

This guide will enable us to better understand the time when the cryptocurrency market was at its best. It will also allow us to gain some knowledge regarding the ICOs as well as the different types of cryptocurrencies.

The Rise of the Cryptocurrency Market

Largely anonymous to the world's wide-ranging population, ten years ago cryptocurrencies were an academic concept. This was all revolutionized in 2009 with the creation of Bitcoin. People may not be aware of how the system works, but today mostly know of cryptocurrencies.

The grip of the cryptocurrency market has become strong. Various aspects of government, business, and other personal financial activities are covered using cryptocurrencies:

— For the assessment of how the transaction mechanism, specifically blockchain technology, can be adapted to exchange value, government and large corporations are now looking into the cryptocurrency market.

—In order to evaluate the likelihood of incorporating this technology into their businesses many companies have begun blockchain projects.

— Just like the internet connects people from all over the world and facilitates data exchange, blockchain technology is considered to be the second type of internet by experts: the internet of value.

People today rely more on technology to provide secure services in a more well-organized and profitable manner. Financial service providers in particular are looking at cryptocurrency. Before considering the probable growth of the cryptocurrency market, let's talk about the start of it all:

The advent of Bitcoin as a standard in the market:

— Using centralized control many people tried to create digital currencies in the 1990s, but they all failed due to numerous reasons.

— A peer-to-peer cash system, called Bitcoin was developed in late 2008 by Satoshi Nakamoto. For the very first time, someone was able to build a protected, decentralized digital cash system.

—Double spending was prevented by Satoshi Nakamoto's system, conventionally something that only a centralized server could achieve. The foundation of cryptocurrency was based on Nakamoto's innovation.

— A decentralized network functions on a system of checks and balances, where every unit within the network checks to see if there is any attempt to spend the same currency twice. With the advent of bitcoin, it became easy to reach consensus without a central authority when no one deemed it possible.

For issuing currency, processing exchanges, and verifying transactions, Bitcoin uses peer-to-peer network and blockchain technology since it is a decentralized currency. Due to this, it is free of government meddling or manipulation; contrasting to a fiat currency, which is managed by a country's central bank.

The current rate of creation of Bitcoins via the mining process is 25 Bitcoins every 10 minutes. It is expected that in 2140 the number of Bitcoins in circulation will be stopped at 21 million. The disadvantage to cryptocurrency exchange is that the currency's value depends upon the demand from investors, and with the drop of the market, the value of Bitcoin drops as well.

Moreover, unlike money can in traditional banking systems, debts are not represented in cryptocurrencies. It is hard currency; as treasured as holding gold coins. As stated, the volume of Bitcoin is set at 21 million, so there's a limit set on the supply of cryptocurrency tokens.

The Transactional Characteristics of Cryptocurrencies

A number of characteristics of cryptocurrency transactions contrast from customary banking.

It is anonymous. It is not necessary for both the parties that are a part of the transaction to know and recognize each other but still the transaction is transparent. This has grabbed the attention of U.S. Federal agencies such as the FBI and the Securities and Exchange Commission (SEC), who are apprehensive about the prospect of money laundering.

It is secure. The person who owns the private key that allows them to access the funds can exchange cryptocurrencies, and the funds are safely locked in a system.

It is fast and worldwide. Geographical location is not a hindrance to allowing a transaction since the network operates worldwide. It takes only a few minutes for transactions to be mined and confirmed, making them faster than traditional banking systems.

It is irreversible. A transaction cannot be reversed after being confirmed and added to the blockchain. There is no alternative in the event that cryptocurrency is sent in error.

It does away with red tape. For using the cryptocurrency exchange system one does not need permission. It is free to download and use.

The Future of Cryptocurrencies

If the success of Bitcoin is any hint, the cryptocurrency market has an optimistic future even though it is not probable to foresee the future prospects of all of the cryptocurrencies.

— Price of bitcoin gradually increased from over $280 in July of 2015 to a mark of $1000 in January of 2017.

— Since then, remarkable growth has been recorded in cryptocurrency. The worth of Bitcoin got $17,000 by early December 2017. The price of "Ether", another cryptocurrency, has also continued to increase recently.

Initial Coin Offerings (ICOs) have played an important part in creating interest in the cryptocurrency market. Coins or tokens similar to a company's shares are used by ICO which are then vented to those who invested in an (IPO) transaction. IPO refers to Initial Public Offering. Equated to crowdfunding, ICO uses cryptocurrencies as a source of capital for startup companies. A cryptocurrency crash is anticipated by market experts at some point. It is foreseeable that a regulator like the SEC will want to intervene by providing guidance and putting into effect actions where necessary, when market conditions are so unstable.

ICO's will further be talked about later in this guide.

Types of Cryptocurrency

Since cryptocurrencies are protected investments and free of political sway, they are considered "digital gold." Peer-to-peer transactions are involved in cryptocurrency exchange. One person can pay another through a computer or mobile device using a downloaded or browser-based app to begin and verify the transaction and transfer the funds. Popularity is being gained by mobile payments which are somewhat similar to cryptocurrency exchange, and are predicted to reach $142 billion in the U.S. by 2019.

Investors and speculators have provided access to a dynamic and fast-growing market by cryptocurrencies, apart from their value as payment mechanisms. Exchanges like Okcoin, Poloniex, and ShapeShift have benefitted greatly from this. In order to fund startups through ICOs, cryptocurrency market has also been used for crowdfunding projects.

The Top Five Cryptocurrencies

Apart from Bitcoin, there were over 1,300 cryptocurrencies on the market by the end of November 2017.

Below we shall discuss the leading five cryptocurrencies by market capitalization:

Bitcoin.

Bitcoin is one of the most commonly used cryptocurrencies to date. Bitcoin was also the first cryptocurrency that was created. Bitcoin has a market capitalization of $180 billion and stands the highest among all the other cryptocurrencies. Bitcoin is considered the gold standard for this industry.

Ethereum.

The second most popular cryptocurrency is Ether. Ethereum blockchain network is powered by a token called Ether. It has a market capitalization of over $18 billion. Ethereum was created back in the year 2015. Ethereum is a Turing-complete programmable currency. This property allows the developers to develop different apps and technologies. This is where Ethereum competes with Bitcoin. Ethereum has the capability of processing complex contracts and programs as well as transactions.

Ripple.

Ripple was created back in the year 2012. Ripple is said to have a market capitalization of $10 Billion. Banks like UBS and Santander have been operating using the Ripple. It is being used because it allows tracking transactions.

Litecoin.

Litecoin is similar to Bitcoin. Litecoin was developed after the creation of Bitcoin. There is a mining algorithm that is used to make the payments fast and process more transactions. These new innovations were a part of the development of Litecoin. It has a market capitalization of $5 billion.

Monero.

Monero is an open-source cryptocurrency that was developed using less transparent CryptoNote Protocol. The algorithm that was used to create this has enhanced security and privacy features over Bitcoin. Being based on an open-source model, consumers have not liked it much as it can help the actions of fraudsters and scammers disguise themselves. Monero has weak growth.

There are a number of cryptocurrencies that exist and these mentioned here are just a tiny part of it. There are signs suggesting that industries have started to consider the development of their own cryptocurrencies. They are doing so as to enable more secure and faster transactions. Let's consider Dentacoin. It has been developed just a while back as the first blockchain platform for the dental industry worldwide.

Understanding Initial Coin Offerings (ICOs)

Initial Coin Offerings (ICOs) has now become widespread. They provide a way to evade the complex and regulated procedure of raising capital from banks or speculating capitalists. ICO is often compared to the crowd funding process as it lacks regularity. In the ICOs, promoters of a startup are pre-sold their cryptocurrency. This is done in exchange for legal tender or other established cryptocurrencies like Bitcoin.

How Does an ICO Work?

The working of an ICO can be better understood by its comparison to the conventional methods. In the conventional methods, the start-up companies raise capital from investors.

Conventionally, a startup company will sell shares to investors in an Initial Public Offering (IPO) transaction.

In the cryptocurrency market, a startup generates coins or tokens. These tokens are used to bargain with the investors in an Initial Coin Offering (ICO) in exchange for legal tender or digital currency.

IPOs deal with investors while ICOs deal with ardent sponsors of their project. This is very similar to crowdfunding.

The cryptocurrency company that comes up with a startup while beginning an ICO campaign makes a plan that sketches the goal that they are trying to achieve in the project. Not just that but it also states all the financial details and how much money they acquire for the project. All the information regarding the sponsors and investors, currency information, and the length of the ICO campaign are mentioned too. When the time for which the campaign was supposed to run ends and the company is not able to increase enough money that is required for the project, the money which the sponsors invested goes back to them.

ICO Success Stories

Ripple is considered to be the first cryptocurrency that raised funding through an ICO. 100 billion XRP tokens were created in order to develop the payment system for Ripple. Those tokens were later sold so that the development of the Ripple platform gets funded.

The most noticeable platform that is involved with ICO funding is Ethereum. Ethereum came up with a smart contract system. In that system, a simple token may be transacted on the Ethereum blockchain. Successful ICO projects were launched through this standard. A few examples of successful ICOs on Ethereum include:

Augur.

In order to fund the development of Augur, the money was raised by selling almost eighty percent of REP tokens. About $5 million of funds were raised which at this time are worth $100 million.

Melonport

Melonport's main objective is to create a platform that would manage the Ethereum-built blockchain assets. MLN tokens were sold for more than 2,000 Bitcoin back in 2016.

Golem.

The main aim behind Golem was to develop a supercomputer. This supercomputer would enable contributors to sell its power. The ICO was limited to 820 million tokens, and the developers received over 10,000 Bitcoin. Today the market share of Golem market share stands at 50,000 Bitcoin.

Singular DTV.

Singular DTV plans to amalgamate with Ethereum, smart contracts, and the production and streaming of videos. The number of Bitcoins that were raised for the purpose was 12,000. These funds were raised through an ICO and now have a worth of 40,000 Bitcoin.

ICONOMI.

ICONOMI is a platform where one can manage and look after their asset. Around 17,000 Bitcoin was collected by the developers who managed to sell eighty-five million ICN tokens in the ICO movement. The market cap today stands over 40,000 Bitcoin.

If you want to see the potential that an ICO has , understand that it virtually knows no bounds. That is because it allows both the companies and individuals to release tokens that can be traded to raise funds. Cryptocurrencies and exchange pose a great influence on the future of financial transactions all across the world. The cryptocurrency model has the capability of security and is able to exceed geographical boundaries. This helps it keep pace with today's digital world but also be a chief motive of innovation.

CHAPTER NO 3

WHAT ARE THE IMPACTS OF CRYPTOCURRENCIES ON THE ECONOMY OF DEVELOPING COUNTRIES?

According to the description of the World Bank, the number of people who live their lives under the poverty line is incredibly high. This shows that the welfare and aids that help the economy grow are distributed disproportionately among different regions and countries. Along with these incidents of economic chaos, civil war, governmental collapse, and plague are developing in regions (Prahalad & Hammond, 2002). Besides, poverty is mainly driven by economic factors which include limited access to financial services (Beck & Demirguc-Kunt, 2006) and high inflation rates (Aisen & Veiga, 2006). Moreover, studies have argued that a low level of trust (Barham, Boadway, Marchand, & Pestieau, 1995) and corrupt government institutions harm economic development (Olken, 2006).

Crypto currencies could provide a significant benefit by overcoming the lack of social trust and by increasing the access to financial services (Nakamoto, 2008) as they can be considered as a medium to support the growth process in developing countries by increasing financial inclusion, providing better traceability of funds, and to help people to escape poverty (Ammous, 2015).

Before we move on to an overview of the cryptocurrencies and their usage in developing countries, it is important that we understand what are the advantages and disadvantages of the cryptocurrencies delivered for users in comparison to the central bank-issued fiat currencies, identical to the Euro or the US dollar. Not just that but also their deliberate emergence from the fundamental technology. The majority of the cryptocurrencies function using blockchain technology. Basically, blockchain is distributed on different nodes that are a part of the network. The entries of the blockchain are stored in form of blocks.

Bitcoin is the first-ever digital currency that works on an algorithm. The transactions that take place on a decentralized peer-to-peer network are recorded and kept track of. All the participants of the network are able to see and monitor these transactions. The first digital currency that was ever invented is bitcoin. The market cap of bitcoin is over $189 billion.

Satoshi Nakamoto is the inventor of bitcoin. He invented bitcoin in the year 2008 when he published his white paper "Bitcoin: A Peer-to-Peer Electronic Cash System" (Nakamoto, 2008).

Ethereum is an open-source and decentralized platform. Ethereum is based on a blockchain network. It is also a computing platform for smart contracts. Additionally, it backs the improved version of Satoshi Nakamoto's consensus mechanism. Ether is the cryptocurrency that powers the Ethereum blockchain network. Ether is said to be the second-best and popular currency; the first being bitcoin. It has a market cap of $18 billion.

General advantages and disadvantages of crypto currencies

Now, let's discuss the positives and negatives of the cryptocurrencies in comparison to the fiat currencies issued by the central bank and discuss their emergence from the underlying technology. Additionally, we will also draw a comparison to the solutions that exist already. These solutions provide to display the real-world importance of crypto currencies.

One of the top advantages of cryptocurrencies is the combination of creating trusts like accountability and transparency. It lets the users have unrestricted and free exchanges among both parties. The basic technology that runs the blockchain uses consensus mechanisms, hash functions, and public and private key encryption to control transactions. In such scenarios it is not essential for both parties to have trust in each other. Conversely, the user has to trust the network and the underlying blockchain. This is vital so as to secure the blockchain against fraud and attacks.

The currencies that have been issued by the World Bank basically establish trust by third party people. An agent is engaged so as to keep a track of the transactions that happen in a fiat currency. Transactions that are done by intermediaries or third parties are time-consuming and have high costs of the transaction. This results in risking premium for its user.

Decentralized cryptocurrencies have a lot of advantages, one of them being the decentralization of cryptocurrencies that governments cannot cope with. Cryptocurrencies are traded all around the world and cannot be constrained to a specific area. Bitcoin allows low-cost money transfers, principally for those who are looking to transfer lesser amounts of money somewhere internationally like remittance payments (Scott, 2016). Cryptocurrencies lets the transfer of money all around the world without any intermediary. The speed with which the money is transferred increases as there are no third parties that could intervene in the transaction.

However, there are some negative aspects of the broader independent payments which are important to address. One distinguishing aspect is the simplification of the transfer of money that is generated from any illegal activity or by that it makes it easy to transfer money from illegal activities or investing in terror activities. Also, the odds of getting caught or any government interference are next to nil. If you compare conventional money transfers to digital transfers you would conclude that the user in the Bitcoin system is pseudonymous. Opposing a user who uses a bank account, they do not have to get through a "Know Your Customer" (KYC) process. It is a process in which the user has to identify himself in order to have the right of entry to the Bitcoin market.

Furthermore, the decentralization and bitcoin's highly rigid supply schedule lead to instability in its price. The issue of price instability is not faced by bitcoin only, but in fact it is an issue that the majority of the cryptocurrencies have to face. This is a major reason why is storing money difficult and also making contracts in crypto.

The absence of stability in the supply schedule of the Bitcoin symbols in high price volatility.

An additional key feature of cryptocurrencies is that the sustenance of financial presence. That is because they do not require any extraordinary standards of technology. It also allows you to have the right of entry to the internet and a digital device (for example a smartphone) to involve in transactions (Dow Jones Institutional News, 2018).

No institution can impact the supply of crypto-currencies. That is because the supply is well-defined in the core protocol of the crypto- currency (Nakamoto, 2008). Consequently, no state can influence the flow of money, which restricts the power of government.

The forfeiture of power for the government as well as the peril of terror financing has led to a majority of the countries putting a ban on the usage and trading of cryptocurrencies. Indonesia has put a ban on cryptocurrencies due to the same reason. The Central Bank of Indonesia in a press release on the 13th of January 2018 published that it "forbids all payment system operator [...] in Indonesia [...] to process transactions using virtual currency" (Bank Indonesia, 2018, p. 1). This accomplishment represents that some states consider crypto currencies as a danger. This danger overshadows all the advantages that these cryptocurrencies make available for such countries.

Developing countries and poverty

This section conveys a definition of developing countries. Not just that but it will also help in providing an impression that which countries are classified as developing countries. We shall focus on those countries in this section.

A country is said to be a developing country in which the development of the Human Index is low. The industrial base relative to the other countries develops not as much. (O'Sullivan & Sheffrin, 2003). There is no arrangement in which we can say which countries are the developing countries. But the majority of the countries are considered developing countries. These countries have a lot in common and that is something that can define the criteria for the developing countries. These resemblances are scarce supply of food for enormous groups of the population, low per capita income and poverty, absence of educational prospects, a shortage of admittance to quality health care. This is also a reason for the high infant mortality rate and low life expectancy. These factors contribute to a higher ratio of unemployment in these countries and a poor standard of living in general. Additionally, the prevailing assets in developing countries are distributed disproportionately.

"World Economic Situation and Prospects" is a research study that was conducted back in 2018, showing the UN delineate trends and dimensions of the economy of the world. According to this study, all the countries of the world are categorized into three classes. These classes are: developed economies; economies in transition; and developing economies. The arrangement of these groupings anticipates reflecting the economic conditions in these countries (United Nations, 2018). Still, the majority of the countries cannot be categorized as a single category. That is because they have individualities that could divide into multiple categories. The groups that are created by the UN are mutually exclusive. Appendix A contains the list of all the countries that are considered by the UN as developing countries and their classification over geography.

Here, we shall discuss the leading issues that these developing countries have to face. It is not meticulous and there are several other problems that they face like a low educational level and inadequate medical care. One of the major reasons that contribute to poverty is inadequate access to financial services (Beck & Demirguc-Kunt, 2006). A lot of studies show that financial inclusion is vital in order for a country to develop. For example, Honohan (2018) perceived in his study that poverty and access to financial services are associated with each other. Partial access to financial services is a substantial problem on its own. Financial services can be of great help to people because they have the ability to ensure defense at odds with any dearth of money.

Financial intermediaries are of great significance to individuals and companies alike. (Gorodnichenko & Schnitzer, 2013). That is because of the provision of jobs and the ability to release loans. Moreover, it could be made obligatory for the firms to a suboptimal behavior. However, if financial frictions are severe the companies face an unfavorable and harmful situation due to this (Gorodnichenko & Schnitzer, 2013). That is when they are not given a right to financial intermediaries due to which they cannot acquire aid for the innovation, which leads to the creation of competitive disadvantages in comparison to the companies overseas. In addition to that, they cannot abuse the possible complementarities between the innovation and export activities, which results in an increase in the gap in its productivity. (Gorodnichenko & Schnitzer, 2013). Due to this the companies and firms that operate in developing countries are unable to produce the desired revenue. Consequently, backing the local economy less through fewer jobs, lower salaries, and an overall lower tax volume.

Another issue that contributes to the restricted access to financial services for companies and individuals is that they are unable to involve themselves in worldwide trade. This is because they require a bank account with an international transaction identification. Those firms that do not have any bank accounts are not a part of this extensive range of international services and are slowed down in selling their products outside their region (Scott, 2016).

Social trust is another issue that is being faced by developing countries. This is because the economy is improved and developed due to social trust. (Barham, 1995). Social trust and equality, economic equality, and equality of opportunities are connected to each other on a deeper level. The majority of the developing countries struggle with developing social trust. These countries are unable to come out of this situation because they are trapped. The reason for such a situation is that social trust will decrease as long as there is high social inequality. Though, public policies that are able to cure this problem cannot be defined because there is no trust. (Rothstein & Uslaner, 2005).

Corrupt government institutions are another reason why these countries are struggling with development. Corruption results in a loss of welfare as the opportunities are not proportionately distributed among all the citizens. The majority of the people suffer as a consequence of a small number of people who get the advantage of bribes. These people struggle with their government's income. There have been cases of corruption that prevail over the welfares of redistribution programs, such as Olken (2006) presented for Indonesia.

Opportunities through crypto currencies in developing countries

As per the investigation of the economic complications faced by the developing countries, crypto currencies can hasten the process of developing a number of fields. It holds true that innovations are strategic solutions for the catch-up process of developing countries as explained by Chudnovsky and Lopez (2006).

In order to benefit from the advancements that are offered by crypto, people need to have the internet. It means that those people who have the internet can do trading of crypto currencies whereas those who would not be able to do so. Aiming at this reason, it has been seen that the practice of the internet in developing countries has improved intensely over the past decade (Aker & Mbiti, 2010; Tapscott & Tapscott, 2016).

With no cryptocurrencies, the fiat currency needs to be exchanged to those currencies that are widely used like the US Dollar or the Euro. Then it has to be re-converted into the economy which is being used. Subsequently the majority of the time there is no liquid market could be used to exchange the fiat or local currency to the target fiat currency. Optimization of this could be done using crypto- currencies. It would end up making the process faster and cheaper (Ammous, 2015).

Let's consider an example of an Indian worker based in Chicago. This worker can use a local service provider that exchanges US Dollars into Bitcoins in order to transfer money to his family living in India. There the family can deduct Rupees at a local service provider that would change Bitcoins back to Rupees. This process results in making companies like Western Union indisposed. It is still conversely important to have a liquid market that could interchange the Bitcoin with US Dollar and to Rupee, so as to maximize its proficiency. There have been a few startups that were founded for the sole purpose of creating a liquid market for Bitcoins. For instance, BitPesa was founded in Kenya. BitPesa provides liquid markets for some specific currency passageways, e.g. for the direct exchange of Kenyan Shilling to the US Dollar.

Cryptocurrencies can help with getting involved in trading internationally without having a bank account. Bitcoin is a cryptocurrency that can help with the facilitation of businesses and individuals to get involved in international trade on a smaller level. These businesses and individuals can use Bitcoins in exchange for trading goods. This helps in evading traditional e-commerce systems (Scott, 2016), which requires the creation of a bank account.

The financial situation of the developing countries can be improved by using crypto- currencies, which means that cryptocurrencies can help the developing countries to serve as a quasi-bank account. That is because everyone who has access to the internet is able to download a Bitcoin wallet (Honohan, 2008). Bitcoin wallet can be used as a quasi-bank account. This is where people can conduct savings and daily transactions (Scott, 2016).

The high costs that are faced by the transactions can help with increasing the odds for microcredits. This comes at a cost of reducing the transaction costs. If these costs are eradicated there are high chances that international financing could bloom. People from developed countries are able to send money to people in developing countries, all this is possible due to cryptocurrencies as well. As these are small transactions they would be of less money but that could have a lot of impact on the life of a person in a developing country.

At this point in time microfinance transactions like such can cost a lot of money due to the borrowing and then repaying of transactions, which face transaction high fees. This transaction fee is sometimes as much as the money that is being transferred. However, when transaction costs are enormously minimized or disregarded completely, it can make it possible for loans like such to become more popular and such loans could become more widespread (Ammous, 2015).

Additionally, an amalgamation of the crypto currencies and smart contracts can prove to be a defining factor for the solidification of social trust as well as battling corruption via a system that is more transparent. It would become possible for the common citizens to use the data of the cryptocurrencies that are available publically in the blockchain to observe the way in which the funds from the state are utilized. The governments could also benefit from this as they would be able to track and monitor the total expenditure of their money and in what ways they can improve their budget provision. (Schmidt Kai Uwe, 2017).

On the basis of the literature analysis, here we shall focus on the qualitative analysis that is centered around the interviews of experts. Social sites such as Xing and LinkedIn were used to choose an interview partner. The experts that are a part of this differ hugely considering the information and knowledge that they have. They may be representatives of some start-up, a lecturer, or an ambassador at consultancy companies. Another reason that makes them different from one another is their geographical location. As per the region they live and work in, they differ considerably. An overview of this is provided in Appendix B.

Crypto currencies and local fiat currencies

Money has three main functions.

- Money has to be acknowledged and recognized as a medium that can be used in exchange for trading goods and services.
- Money essentially needs to be appropriate as a medium that can store value for saving wealth.
- Money must perform as a unit of account. It can be used to measure and compare the value of goods (Ammous, 2018).

Gold is considered to be the oldest form of money. Cryptocurrencies are matched to the fiat currencies that are issued by the Central Bank as well as gold.

It is of notice that the conventional types of money that are considered to be gold and fiat money achieve all characteristics of money. Cryptocurrencies are actually more appropriate as the exchange medium. That is because the crypto currencies are divisible and can be transferred on a global level. (Ammous, 2018).

One of the major benefits that gold has is that it is the best-collateralized form of money. That is because the medium of exchange has value in contrast to the notes issued by the bank or digital money. Cryptocurrencies are a decentralized form of currency whereas the fiat currency is issued by the Central Bank under the rules of the government thus making it completely centralized. This is a basic difference between fiat currencies and crypto currencies.

The reason which can be regarded for the high instability of the cryptocurrency is that of its decentralization for crypto and the lack of security. So, it destructs the store of the value function and the unit of account function.

One of the major issues that come with crypto-currencies is the instability in their price. Due to this reason during the value transfer, no huge fluctuations in the financial aspect can be seen (Expert 1, 2018). In order to attain a price that is more stable and fluctuates less, the majority of the crypto currencies progress in the direction of a currency that is regulated enough (Expert 5, 2018). Furthermore, a trend in the majority of the crypto currencies is observed to vary from a complete decentralized system to a system that is more centralized. In this centralized system, the players have the power to maximize any possibilities of development. The majority of the cryptocurrencies in use transition from a decentralized system to a centralized system. They do so despite all the odds. This transitioning may lead to a decrease in value. There can be a reduction in the stability of its price through centralization and support provided by economic policy decisions. Cryptocurrencies can develop significantly (Aisen & Veiga, 2006).

Cryptocurrencies have to be restricted to the national boundaries in order to attain political support. This way the governments will have the power and will be able to control the economic parameters so as to retain financial dominion (Expert 6, 2018). However, this would be a way that would completely reduce the pros of the cryptocurrencies and would result in a system that would be centralized.

At this point, we cannot say that the crypto currencies are not a replacement for the currencies that are issued by the government. Additionally, this has given the national authorities a reason to describe crypto currencies as digital assets and not currency. This way it makes it similar to gold. It is also undecided as it needs to be regarded as an asset or as a form of money. It is safe to say that

— Bitcoin is a digital token that can be exchanged by two parties in a transaction.
— If you compare this token to fiat or national currencies, you would see that it has a worth.
— You can use it to exchange for something tangible. It is used occasionally in trivial amounts.

Improvement of financial inclusion in developing countries

A paramount advantage of crypto currencies is the betterment of financial inclusion for the people living in developing countries (Darlington, 2014). The time and cost of the transactions can be reduced by the crypto-currencies. It will act as some sort of bank account that permits people to make their daily transactions as well as save. (Honohan, 2008; Scott, 2016).

Cryptocurrencies can help in making fast and less expensive transactions in comparison to conventional money transfers through bank accounts like the SWIFT process. It can be achieved by eliminating third parties involved, thus resulting in cost reduction and an increase in the speed of transactions (Tapscott & Tapscott, 2016).

If you consider the remittance payments, cryptocurrencies can prove themselves significantly important in the said field as well. Reduced costs of transactions by the usage of crypto currencies will influence microcredits. That is because of the decrease from every transaction in the conversion fee of the banks. The lending process presently is limited to small amounts only, especially for those people who earn a low income. That is because the items that they own are problematic and result in collateralizing with the old-fashioned tools for the money. For instance, if someone uses livestock as collateral, it would be strenuous for the banks to release the loan in this case.

Cryptocurrencies also greatly help in the creation of access to the world market for businesses in order to develop. The customers of these companies pay companies from other countries in cryptocurrencies. The firms need to have an account in a bank with an international identification number. If they do not have this that would be a hindrance in the payments. For instance, you can hire a person in a developing country to do work for you and then you can pay with bitcoins or other cryptocurrencies.

Restrictions and additional prospective capacities of cryptocurrencies

Cryptocurrencies are used to enhance cross-border payments presently because of the minimized costs and less time per transaction. The Libra project that was started by Facebook intends to drastically decrease the cross-border payment fees. This is done so by using blockchain technology. (Groß, Herz, Schiller, 2019). At this time cryptocurrencies are used mostly for cross-border payments. But we can say that in the upcoming future it can be influenced by peer-to-peer lending through a far-reaching market because peer-to-peer lending helps in taking care of the problems caused by liquidity in developing countries. Besides, the collateralization issue could be solved partly by community trust as Expert 6 (2018) has stated.

Crypto currencies also influence the central systems in large organizations or governments. This would greatly help the credibility to a point that the systems used presently cannot help with.

Ethereum can be used helpful in the case of smart contracts because cryptocurrencies are essential to conduct smart contracts as a model that is incentive so people could operate the blockchains and the underlying infrastructure. Ether is majorly used in the services for making payments. On the basis of smart contracts, there are a number of applications that these contracts are an indispensable factor for the future use of cryptocurrencies (Wood, 2014).

Social security is another important application of smart contracts. At this time, numerous layers of bureaucracy handle payments like unemployment benefits and society needs to pay the fee of commission for that. These costs of bureaucracy can be gotten rid of with the help of smart contracts. The social benefit payments could be well-defined in a smart contract.

All of these potential areas require low price instability (Expert 2, 2018; Darlington, 2014). Furthermore, the use of cryptocurrency depends upon the regulatory framework. A relatively sloppy regulatory system would increase price instability. This could prove to be a reason for the mismanagement of the cryptocurrencies for illegal transactions. For example, money laundering. Conversely, a regulatory framework that is too rigid would weaken the advantages of crypto currencies.

In general, crypto currencies can have a substantial influence on developing countries. This can be achieved by maximizing the financial inclusion of individuals and companies. Reduction in the transaction fee and time, cross-border payments can be improved significantly in specific. (Scott, 2016). This is favorable for remittance payments, peer-to-peer lending, and international trade. The battle against the menace of corruption can be fought with technology. This can be done so by having a tracking system that is transparent for the use of funds (Darlington, 2014).

In order to enjoy the benefits that the crypto currencies provide, it is important for the public to adopt and switch to cryptocurrencies. This will help in achieving the basic functions of money. It does not exist presently due to the extreme price instability. The absence of backup and centralization does not support a stable price level (Ammous, 2018). If there are resilient regulation policies and more political support for the cryptocurrencies it would become possible to achieve a high stable price. Cryptocurrencies can however only get political support if the government or central banks get the right to control them. (Jaag & Bach, 2015). However, this would reduce many benefits of the crypto currencies.

Presently, the growth and development of cryptocurrencies are restricted for developing countries in a number of ways. The introduction of cryptocurrencies could help develop the future of developing countries.

CHAPTER NO 4

HOW TO MINE THE CRYPTO

Crypto mining is a way that can help you with receiving cryptocurrency without any investment. You might think, "How are bitcoins and other cryptocurrencies created, and how can you get them without buying them on a crypto exchange?" Initially, the majority of people showed interest in bitcoin and other cryptocurrencies because their prices climbed high. Cryptocurrencies like Bitcoin, Ether, and Dogecoin very much interested people in the early months of 2021 . Crypto exchanges are where you can buy cryptocurrencies as well as trade them. But you can create or mine these tokens on your own PC.

The promise of getting paid with Bitcoin is a major lure for many miners. To be clear, you do not need to be a miner to possess bitcoin tokens. You can buy cryptocurrencies with fiat currency, trade them on an exchange like Bitstamp with another cryptocurrency (for example, Ethereum or NEO to buy Bitcoin), or earn them by shopping, writing blog posts on platforms that pay users in cryptocurrency, or even setting up interest-earning crypto accounts.

What is Crypto Mining?

Crypto mining is a process in which cryptocurrencies are minted by solving complex mathematical equations and puzzles by using high-power computers. In this process, blocks of data are validated and recording the blocks on a digital ledger. A Digital ledger is referred to as a blockchain. Complex mathematical techniques are used in order to keep the blockchain protected.

Cryptocurrencies use the decentralized way in which help in the distribution and confirmation of transactions that take place. Cryptographic algorithms are used for this purpose. Here there is no central governing authority that looks over the transaction. Also, there is no central ledger.

In order to receive new coins, complex mathematical puzzles are solved in order to help in the verification of digital currencies. All this information is added to the decentralized ledger. The miners receive pay for this whole process. New coins come into circulation due to this mining process.

Working of The Process:

In the process of mining, complex mathematical equations are solved using high-power computers. The one who is able to crack the code has the authority over the transaction. The miners receive a small amount of cryptocurrency for the process of mining. After the miner is able to validate the transaction, it is then added to a public ledger on a blockchain.

How Can You Start Mining?

For your crypto mining, you need a high-power computer. Not just that but you will also need a digital wallet to store your cryptocurrencies and trade them as well. You can become part of a mining pool where you will get more opportunities for earning profit. Mining pools are basically groups for miners where they are able to improve their mining power. The money that is made from the mining process is distributed equally among all those members that are a part of the pool. Through these mining pools, miners get a chance to work together and fight more efficiently.

The algorithm acquires several cryptocurrencies including Bitcoin, Ethereum, and Dogecoin. It guarantees that no single authority becomes so powerful that it starts to run the show. This process done by miners is a crucial part of adding new blocks of transaction data to the blockchain. A fresh block is only added to the blockchain system if a miner appears with a new winning proof-of-work. This occurs after every 10 minutes in the network. Proof-of-work aims to prevent users from printing extra coins they didn't earn, or double-spending.

Mining the bitcoin can be pretty interesting and profitable as well. The majority of the countries are not really into the crypto space because the mining process can be pretty expensive. But there are a few countries that support crypto mining and you will come across great opportunities for your crypto mining. But where do you start? Below is a list of a few countries where you can begin your journey of crypto mining.

But before we dive deeper into that, let's take a look at some of the factors that make a country an excellent spot for mining.

Key drivers for profitable crypto mining operations

There are lots of factors to be considered if you want to try your hand at crypto mining, but here are some of the most common ones you need to be familiar with:

Advanced and specialized mining machines

As we mentioned earlier, crypto miners dig BTC's digital cave to collect fractions of this digital coin. If gold miners use hard rock equipment to dig up nuggets of precious metals; Bitcoin miners assemble their very own mining machines that consist of expensive specialized software and powerful mining rigs.

Crypto miners use this equipment to solve highly complex mathematical problems that are impossible to answer through pen-and-paper and mental approaches. After finding the solution, BTC miners will be rewarded with a newly minted coin and amounts from the transaction fee—but that's a story for another time.

Fast and reliable Internet connection

Besides the costly and powerful equipment, you'll also need a high-speed and stable Internet connection to run the mining operations. Of course, this service also comes with fees which depend upon the part of the world that you live in.

Cheaper electricity costs

It takes up a lot of electricity to mine crypto. This is why some countries do not agree to have activities like such taking place in their border perimeter . If you plan to mine cryptocurrencies, go for a country where the electricity is available at cheaper costs.

Suitable climate conditions

You need to find a country that has an overall cooler climate. That is because the machines that mine crypto run 24/7. A place with cooler climates would help in avoiding the overheating of these machines. It also minimizes the cost of electricity that is consumed by systems that are used for cooling the machines.

Country's economic situation

The economic condition of a country is crucial if you are looking for a country to mine crypto. This can help you in determining how cheap or expensive mining operations for the cryptocurrencies will be. You need to have expensive equipment and skilled professionals to help you monitor them as well. The money that they get in return for their work is calculated on the basis of the country's cost of living. Moreover, you will have overhead expenditures. The place that you would require to place your machines would add up to your total costs.

Government's stance on crypto-related activities

The resources required for the mining of cryptocurrencies affect the environment as well as the power consumption rate of the country. Some authorities remain cynical about digital coins. This is a reason you need to look for those countries that do not find it offensive to mine cryptocurrencies and regard it in a positive way.

Ideal spots to mine cryptocurrencies

There are a few countries that are great to mine crypto and provide you with numerous opportunities alongside as well. The countries that are ideal for mining crypto are mentioned below:

1. Georgia

Georgia is a country that is both cryptocurrency and blockchain technology-friendly. It ranks 109th in October 2020. It has a broadband download speed of 26.80 Megabits per second (Mbps). The price of electricity in Georgia is 0.056 USD per kilowatt-hour (kWh). Also, its temperature is enough to cool the mining machines.

2. Estonia

Estonia ranks 50th in the global ranking list. It has a broadband download speed of up to 74.73 Mbps. The price of electricity in Estonia is 0.174 USD per kWh. Not just that, but there are hundreds of blockchain and crypto companies in the country. It looks at crypto as "value represented in digital form."

3. Canada

Canada ranks 17th on the list. It has the best broadband download rate of 149.35 Mbps. The price of electricity in Canada is 0.174 USD per kWh, Cryptocurrency mining grew in Canada back in 2018 because of the cheap electricity prices and its cold weather. They do allow the usage of digital currencies but they aren't considered legal tender in the country.

4. Norway

Norway closely follows Canada and ranks 18th on the list. Norway has an Internet speed of 146.53 Mbps. In Norway, electricity is generated using hydropower. It snows mostly and the weather is generally cold. It makes it an apt place to cool the equipment used for mining.

Norway neither prohibits nor recognizes crypto. On the contrary, the Norwegian Financial Supervisory Authority (FSA) imposed regulations of money laundering on people who provided virtual currency exchange locally.

5. Kuwait

Kuwait ranks 34th on the list. Kuwait has an internet download speed of up to 110.33 Mbps. The price of electricity in Kuwait is 0.029 USD per kWh. It includes the cost of power, distribution, as well as taxes. Kuwait has problematic regulation issues.

The Ministry of Finance of Kuwait does not recognize cryptocurrencies and the Central Bank of Kuwait prohibits crypto trading for official transactions. In the year 2018, CBK announced issuing an e-currency that they will monitor. If you do consider Kuwait for Bitcoin mining, you have to keep tabs on its regulatory policies.

6. Iceland

The rank that Iceland is on the list is undefined but the positive thing is that Iceland generates its electricity from geothermal resources. That is because Iceland has over 200 volcanoes and abundant hot springs. This provides tons of underground water to be converted for power generation.

7. Switzerland

Switzerland ranks 4th on the list. It has an internet download rate of 186.40 Mbps. This is the fastest among the list of countries mentioned here. The electricity price in Switzerland is 0.228 USD per kWh which is a little costly. In Switzerland, the regulations regarding cryptocurrencies are pretty relaxed. They are categorized as assets or properties. Switzerland is a country that supports crypto.

8. Finland

Finland ranks 35th on the list. It has an internet download rate of 108.84 Mbps. The price of electricity in Finland is 0.183 USD per kWh. Finland has an overall cooler climate.

9. Sweden

Sweden ranks 14th on the list. It has a download speed of 158.73 Mbps. Electricity prices in Sweden are 0.179 USD per kWh. However, these prices vary from area to area and depend upon where you live in.

10. Latvia

Lastly, Latvia ranks 35th on the list. It has a download speed of 115.22 Mbps. The price of electricity in Latvia is 14.2 euro cents per kWh. This cost is said to be the lowest price in Latvia since the year 2014.

Coin Mining in India

In the past few years, mining of the Bitcoin has significantly increased. There are a number of companies that do provide facilities for crypto mining as well as blockchain development in India. However, the mining of Bitcoins in India is an overpriced and risky business. The reason for that is that in India the fight for coins is high and complex. In order to mine Bitcoins successfully, high computational power is essential. For this purpose, high electricity is required and the costs of electricity in India are pretty high.

The electricity price in India ranges between Rs 5.20-8.20 per kilowatt-hour. That is approximately equal to 7-11 cents. Now the total power that is required to mine the coins is 67.29 terawatt-hours a year. This is as per the approximation of the Cambridge Bitcoin Electricity Consumption Index.

Not just that but there is a lack of equipment in India too. In order to have the complete equipment required to mine Bitcoins, it has to be imported from China. This further increases the expenses and reduces profit. Besides that, India also does not have any clear rules for cryptocurrencies. Due to these reasons, India is a risky place to invest in.

The government of India and the central bank have an unclear association with cryptocurrencies. GOI did suggest launching their digital coin in the intervening time. In 2017, India put a ban over the import of ASCI machines. These machines are specifically designed to mine Crypto which pushed Bengaluru-based blockchain technology company AB Nexus to put mining Bitcoin and Ethereum on a halt.

Setting foot on crypto's digital cave

From all this information provided, if we have learned one thing is that there is a lot of research and knowledge required if you are planning to get involved in the field of crypto mining. Explore the information that has been discussed here and see if mining Bitcoin makes financial sense for your crypto needs.

It can be perplexing to fight the right equilibrium between the factors listed above, but just like for the attainment of any goal you need lots of tolerance and persistence for crypto mining. This is one of the initial and chief methods to make profits in the crypto sphere. So, in order to procure sufficient rewards, be certain to prepare the needed resources and let loose your inner crypto genius!

CHAPTER NO 5

WHAT IS BITCOIN?

Bbitcoin was created by Satoshi Nakamoto back in the year 2009. Bitcoin is a digital currency that is decentralized by nature. Pseudonymous Satoshi Nakamoto in his whitepaper talked about Bitcoin. To date, no one knows exactly the person's name who created Bitcoin and its underlying technology. In comparison to the conventional systems of trading, Bitcoins provide a lower fee for the transaction. Contrasting to the currencies issued by the government, digital currencies function by means of decentralized authority.

Cryptography is something that keeps Bitcoin secure and protected. There is a digital ledger that uses blockchain technology to record the history of transactions that take place. This is so to keep the whole process of transactions more transparent and clear. Physical Bitcoins do not exist. Blockchain verifies all those transactions that are added to it. An enormous amount of power of computation is required in order to verify the transactions. This process is known as "mining." Bitcoins are digital currencies and they are not supported and issued by the governments or any banks. Not just that but an individual bitcoin is not considered to be as valuable as a commodity is. Notwithstanding being legal tender in most parts of the world, bitcoin is very popular and has activated the launch of a huge number of other cryptocurrencies. These cryptocurrencies are jointly referred to as "altcoins." Bitcoin is commonly abbreviated as "BTC".

- As per the market capitalization, Bitcoin is considered to be the largest and most popular cryptocurrency. It was launched in 2009.
- Bitcoin uses a decentralized ledger to store, mine, distribute, and trade it. This ledger is referred to as the blockchain.
- The price of Bitcoin and the Bitcoin market is highly unstable. Bitcoin has been seen to have gone through numerous cycles of boom and bust over a very short span of time.
- Bitcoin is the very first digital currency of its kind and has paved the way for other cryptocurrencies.

Understanding Bitcoin

A group of computers also known as nodes or miners is used by the bitcoin system. It runs the code of Bitcoin and is used to store its information on the blockchain. Symbolically speaking, a blockchain can be considered as a collection of blocks. Every block is basically a collection of transactions. Since all the computers that run the blockchain have a similar list of blocks and transactions they can clearly understand these blocks are being filled with new bitcoin transactions so no one is able to rogue the system.

The transactions that happen on the Blockchain network can be viewed by everyone. A fraudster would require to have 51 percent of the computing power that creates the bitcoin to get done with any immoral activity. Bitcoin had about 11,300 full nodes by September 2021. This figure is gradually increasing continuously which makes it difficult to do launch such attacks.

If there were chances that an attack would be launched, those people who are supposed to be a part of the Bitcoin network with their computers or oftentimes referred to as miners would highly likely divert to a new blockchain. This means that the attack that the fraudster was supposed to launch would go to waste.

Two keys are used to store the balance of tokens of Bitcoins. They are the private and the public keys. Private and public keys are strings of numbers and letters that are interconnected via the mathematical encryption algorithm that was used in their creation. The public key which is often compared to a bank account number is basically the address that is available to the world. If anyone wants to send their bitcoins they can use this address for this purpose.

The private key is often compared to an ATM PIN. It is used to authorize the transactions that are happening over the blockchain. You need to keep your private key private and not share it with anyone. Don't mix up the concepts of Bitcoin keys and bitcoin wallet. Bitcoin wallet is a physical or digital device that simplifies the trading of bitcoin and allows users to track ownership of coins. In this context, the word "wallet" may confuse people. Bitcoin is a decentralized currency and does not need to be stored. Rather, it is distributed on a blockchain network.

Peer-to-Peer Technology

Bitcoin was the first cryptocurrency that operated on peer-to-peer (P2P) technology in order to ease instant payments. Those individuals and companies that govern the computing power are referred to as miners and they have the charge of the processing of the transactions that happen on the blockchain. They are driven by the rewards which are the release of new bitcoin and the transaction fees paid in bitcoin.

The job of these miners is to make sure that the credibility of the bitcoin network is ensured. Not just that but they act as a decentralized authority for this network. New Bitcoins are launched at a rate that is deteriorating periodically. The number of bitcoins that can be mined is 21 million overall. It is being said that there are 18.8 million Bitcoins that exist as of September 2021. There are less than 2.25 million bitcoins left to be mined.

This shows how bitcoins and other cryptocurrencies work differently from fiat currencies. In a banking system that is centralized, the currency is released at a rate that matches the growth in goods. This is a system that is anticipated to maintain the stability of the price. An algorithm enables the decentralized system to release the rate in advance.

Bitcoin Mining

The process through which the bitcoin is circulated is known as Bitcoin mining. In general, we can say that there is a lot of computational power required to solve the puzzles to discover a new block. This block is then made a part of the blockchain network.

Verification of the records of transactions over a network is added by Bitcoin mining. Miners are compensated with some bitcoin; the reward is halved after every 210,000 blocks. In 2009, the block reward was said to be 50 new bitcoins. On the 11th of May in the year 2020, the third halving took place which brought down the reward for each block discovery to 6.25 bitcoins.

Bitcoin can be mined using a wide range of hardware, however, some return higher rewards than others. A few computer chips, called Application-Specific Integrated Circuits (ASIC), and more advanced processing units, like Graphic Processing Units (GPUs), have the ability to return abundant payments. "Mining rigs" are these intricate mining processors.

One bitcoin can be divided up to eight decimal places which are roundabout 100 millionths of one bitcoin. This is the smallest unit and is known as a Satoshi. Bitcoin can be divided further into even more decimal places if the miners participate and agree to it.

Early Timeline of Bitcoin

Aug. 18, 2008

The domain name bitcoin.org is a registered domain. This domain is "WhoisGuard Protected." That means that the identity of a person who is registered in the domain cannot have their information publically available.

Oct. 31, 2008

An individual or a group of people that uses the name Satoshi Nakamoto announces to the Cryptography Mailing list at metzdowd.com: that a new electronic cash system that is peer-to-peer and with no intervention from a third party in works. The whitepaper published on bitcoin.org, which was titled, "Bitcoin: A Peer-to-Peer Electronic Cash System" would become a great charter for the working of bitcoin today.

Jan. 3, 2009

January 3, 2009, is the date when the first bitcoin was mined and "block 0" was generated. Block 0 is known as a "genesis block" and comprises the text: "The Times 03/Jan/2009 Chancellor on brink of second bailout for banks." This was proof of the fact that the mining process was completed successfully on the date mentioned or after that.

Jan. 8, 2009

Cryptography Mailing list announces the very first bitcoin software.

Jan. 9, 2009

9th January 2009 was the date when the first block was mined. It kick-started bitcoin mining in earnest.

Who Is Satoshi Nakamoto?

No person exactly knows who created the first bitcoin categorically. However, the name Satoshi Nakamoto is linked to the person or a group of people who worked on the Bitcoin software and released the original bitcoin whitepaper in 2008. The bitcoin software was released in the year 2009. Ever since then the majority of the people claimed to be Satoshi Nakamoto, but no one knows who Satoshi is convincing. The identity of Satoshi remains unknown to date.

Although it is alluring to believe that Satoshi Nakamoto is an introverted, idealistic genius who invented bitcoin out of thin air as per media, innovations like bitcoin do not normally happen in a vacuum. The majority of the discoveries made by science were based on previous researches, no matter how new and innovative they may seem.

There are predecessors to Bitcoin. Adam Back's "Hashcash" which was invented in the year 1997 followed by Wei Dai's "b-money", Nick Szabo's "bit-gold", and Hal Finney's "Reusable Proof of Work." The white paper that was presented regarding Bitcoin indicates Hashcash and b-money and numerous other works covering quite a few fields of research. Maybe many of the individuals behind the other projects named above have been speculated to have had a role in the invention of bitcoin.

There may be a few reasons as to why the person or the group of people who invented Bitcoin are keeping themselves disguised and not revealing their identity.

- One of the reasons is that of privacy. Bitcoin was able to garner a lot of fame and that fame made it become a worldwide spectacle. This would lead to a lot of media and government attention towards Satoshi Nakamoto.
- Apart from this, another reason may be the potential for bitcoin to create a huge uproar in the present banking and monetary systems. If in case, bitcoin was to achieve public acceptance, this system has the power to exceed the fiat currencies issued by the governments. This move would have led to the governments taking legal action against the person who invented bitcoin.

- One of the other reasons could be that of safety. In the year 2009 alone, the number of bitcoins mined was that of 32,489 blocks. At the reward rate of 50 bitcoins per block the total overhead in 2009 was 1,624,500 bitcoins. This could lead to the conclusion that in the year 2009, Satoshi and his team were busy mining the bitcoins because they are the ones who own a majority of the bitcoins mined.
- Anyone who owns that much of the bitcoin could get targeted by criminals and thieves. Bitcoin is more like cash and less like stocks. The private keys are needed to approve spending could be printed out and literally kept anywhere.

The one who invented the bitcoin must have taken precautions, but staying anonymous is a great way to reduce publicity.

Special Considerations

Bitcoin as a Form of Payment

Bitcoin can be used to pay for products that are sold and to provide services. Nowadays physical stores also display signs for accepting bitcoin "Bitcoin Accepted Here." These transactions can be controlled with the necessary hardware or address of the wallet. It can be done via QR codes and touch screen apps. An online businesses can also accept bitcoin as a form of payment through credit cards, PayPal, etc.

The first country that officially accepted Bitcoin as a legal tender is El Salvador.

Bitcoin Employment Opportunities

You do have an opportunity to earn money through bitcoin. Those people who are self-employed can generate revenue through the jobs linked to bitcoin. You can earn through bitcoins in several ways like generating an internet service, and to pay for that you can simply add your bitcoin wallet address for payment to the site. A number of websites and job boards allow users who work with digital currencies.

Cryptogrind is a website that helps in bringing together job seekers and potential employers to one place.

Jobs are featured on the Coinality website. Freelance, part-time and full-time job offers. These jobs pay in bitcoin, as well as other cryptocurrencies like Dogecoin and Litecoin.

BitGigs

Bitwage allows you to pick out a percentage of your work paycheck to be converted into bitcoin. That is directed to your bitcoin address.

How to Buy Bitcoin

The majority of people regard that digital currency as the future. The people who use bitcoins consider this facility as a faster, low-fee payment system for transactions all around the globe. You can exchange cryptocurrencies for any kind of fiat currency as it is not supported by any government or a bank. Actually, the exchange rate of the cryptocurrencies against the dollar appeals to prospective investors and traders. It is deliberated as a fundamental and basic reason for the growth of digital currencies like bitcoin. These cryptocurrencies can be used alternatively with national fiat money and traditional commodities like gold.

IRS released a statement in March 2014 and stated that digital currencies like bitcoin, Ether, etc. are to be taxed as property and not as a currency. All types of transactions that use bitcoins or other digital currencies will be taxed. Be it mining of the bitcoin or purchasing from someone else.

Similar to the other assets, the principle of trading high applies to bitcoin as well. Purchasing a bitcoin through an exchange can help you greatly in increasing your currency. However, there are numerous other ways through which you can earn bitcoins.

Risks Associated with Bitcoin Investing

The price value of bitcoin increased dramatically in May 2011 and then for the second time in November 2013. It interested a lot of investors to jump into the bitcoin market even though bitcoin was not designed as an equity investment. Bitcoin is basically a medium that can be used for exchange. But people do not regard it as a medium of exchange and purchase it for its value of the investment.

Nevertheless, there are many risks that come built-in with the bitcoins. Many investor warnings have been delivered by the Securities and Exchange Commission (SEC), the Financial Industry Regulatory Authority (FINRA), the Consumer Financial Protection Bureau (CFPB), and other agencies.

Bitcoins have seen a rise in investments but still, it is a concept that is new. The market is still highly volatile. If you compare the investments in the virtual currency to the conventional investments, you would realize that bitcoin investment is still a risk as there is no history of credibility to back it. These cryptocurrencies are still in the phase of development. CEO of Digital Currency Group, Barry Silbert said that this is a very "highest-risk, highest-return" investment that can be made. Digital Currency Group constructs and capitalizes in bitcoin and blockchain companies.

Regulatory Risk

Bitcoin is an opponent to the currency that is issued by the government. The odds that they may be used for black market transactions, money laundering, illegal activities, or tax evasion are pretty high. Due to these reasons, the governments may end up regulating it, restricting, or banning it for the use and trade of bitcoin. The New York State Department of Financial Services in 2015 settled the regulations for the companies and individuals that are dealing and trading cryptocurrencies. All buy, sell, transfer, or storage of bitcoins to record the identity of customers, shall have a compliance officer, and maintain capital reserves. If any transaction increases more than $10,000. It shall be reported.

As there are no proper regulations regarding bitcoin and other virtual currencies it increases questions over their longevity, liquidity, and universality.

Security Risk

The majority of the owners of bitcoins have not gotten their tokens via mining operations. Instead, these people trade bitcoin and other digital currencies on any of the popular online markets known as bitcoin exchanges or cryptocurrency exchanges.

Bitcoin exchanges are digital and this is the reason that there are so many threats from hackers and malware to this virtual system. Bitcoin theft has increased a lot recently. If the hard drive of any bitcoin owner is hacked by a hacker, he will be able to steal the bitcoin through the private encryption key and then transfer it to some other account. This would result in the owner losing his bitcoin to theft. In order to prevent such frauds and thefts the owner should store the private encryption key over a computer that has no internet connection. Or note down the addresses on a paper and keep it somewhere safe.

Bitcoins are stored in a bitcoin wallet. There are cases recorded where the fraudsters and scammers are able to hack the bitcoin exchanges and then gain access to the digital wallets of the users. For example, in 2014 a really serious occurrence happened in Japan where Mt. Gox was hacked and bitcoins worth millions of dollars got stolen. Afterward, they asked the people who ran the exchange to close down forcefully.

Transactions that happen on a bitcoin network and that involve the trade cannot be reversed. They are permanent. You cannot do anything. No third party can help you get your payment back once you have sent it. It is only possible to get the payment back if it is refunded by the person to whom you sent it. You basically cannot do anything here if you come across a problem. Be very specific and vigilant when you carry out your bitcoin transactions.

Insurance Risk

No federal or government program ensures bitcoin exchanges or bitcoin accounts. In 2019, SFOX states that it will offer bitcoin investors FDIC insurance. However, it would only be provided to the portion of transactions that involves cash. SFOX is one of the leading trading platforms and a prime dealer of cryptocurrencies.

Fraud Risk

There have been cases reported where fraudsters sell people fake bitcoins although verifications of the owners and the registration of the transactions function over the usage of the private key encryption. For example, SEC took legal action over a Ponzi scheme related to bitcoin in July of 2013. Besides that, there have been occurrences of bitcoin price manipulation. Bitcoin price manipulation is also a common type of scam.

Market Risk

The values of bitcoins can swing a lot like in any other investment. In its short life bitcoin has seen a lot of swing in its price. Focusing on the maximized volume of trading on exchanges, it has a high sensitivity to any event that is worthy of the news. As per the CFPB, the price of bitcoin was reduced by 61% in one day in 2013. In 2014, the price drop of a single day was about 80%.

This digital currency is going to lose its value and become worthless if a majority of the people disregard bitcoin as a currency. There has an assumption that the "bitcoin bubble" had burst when the price decreased from its all-time high during the cryptocurrency increase in late 2017 and early 2018.

If you consider the competition in the market, you will find that it's a lot. There are a number of other cryptocurrencies but bitcoin is on a leading front. That is due to its brand recognition and venture capital money; a technological innovation by introducing an improved virtual coin is always a danger.

Bitcoin reached its highest price of $64,863 on April 14, 2021.

Splits in the Cryptocurrency Community

Ever since bitcoin launched, there are a number of instances in which dissimilarities between factions of miners and developers stimulated splits across-the-board in the community of cryptocurrency. The majority of cases in these groups of bitcoin users and miners have changed the protocol of the bitcoin network itself.

The creation of any new kind of bitcoin with a new name is done through a process called "forking". This split can be a "hard fork." In a hard fork, a new coin shares transaction history with bitcoin up until a decisive split point, at which point a new token is created. Instances of cryptocurrencies that are invented as an outcome of hard forks also include: bitcoin cash which was invented in August of 2017; bitcoin gold which was invented in October of 2017; and bitcoin SV which was invented in November 2017.

A "soft fork" is a change to the protocol that is still compatible with the previous system rules. For example, bitcoin soft forks have added functionality like segregated witness (SegWit).

Why Is Bitcoin Valuable?

Yes, bitcoin is valuable. Its price has increased dramatically from $1 to more than $50,000 in just over a decade. The high value of bitcoin is due to a number of reasons comprising of its scarcity, market demand, and negligible production cost. Bitcoins are impalpable but have a market capitalization of $1 trillion as of 2021.

Is Bitcoin a Scam?

Bitcoins are very real. You may be unable to touch them as they are virtual but they are real. It's been ten years now since the first bitcoin was created. The code that is used to run the system is open-source and downloadable. Anyone can evaluate the code for bugs, or evidence of immoral intent. There are chances that there may be some mishaps but these are not because of the bitcoins but human flaws or due to any third-party application that is being used.

How Many Bitcoins Are There?

The overall Bitcoins to be mined by the year 2140 is going to be 21 million. Presently there are more than 18.8 million (almost 90%) of the total bitcoins have been mined. Researchers say that approximately 20 percent of the mined bitcoins have gone missing. There are a number of reasons for that to happen. Death of the owner; forgetting the private key; or sending the bitcoins to addresses that are no longer in use are a few reasons for those bitcoins being lost.

Should I Capitalize the 'B' in Bitcoin?

While talking about a Bitcoin network, system, or protocol you have to use a capital "B" by convention. When talking about individual bitcoins or as a unit, you have to use a small "b" by convention.

Where Can I Buy Bitcoin?

You can purchase bitcoins from online exchanges. Now the Bitcoin ATMs have also become a common sight all around the world. Kiosks connected by the internet can also help you purchase bitcoins using a credit card or cash. You can also purchase bitcoins directly from someone you know.

CHAPTER NO 6

THE ETHEREUM COIN

Ether is the cryptocurrency that powers the Ethereum blockchain, and Solidity is the programming language of the Ethereum blockchain.

In order to verify and record transactions, a decentralized blockchain network, Ethereum, is used. Applications can be created, published, monetized, and used by users on the Ethereum platform and the payment is made through Ether cryptocurrency. According to insiders, dApps are decentralized applications on the network.

- As of May 2021, Ethereum had the second-highest value in the market and was closely following up to Bitcoin on first.
- Ethereum is said to be an open-source platform that is based on blockchain which creates and shares business, financial services, and entertainment applications.
- To use dApps Ethereum users pay fees called "gas." They vary with the extent of computational power necessary.
- Ether or ETH is the cryptocurrency running the Ethereum blockchain.
- Ethereum holds the second-highest value in the market and is second only to Bitcoin.

Understanding Ethereum

The main purpose of the creation of Ethereum was to enable developers to build and publish safe and secure smart contracts and distributed applications (dApps), hence enabling users to use them without the dangers of interruption, scam, or interference from a third party.

As defined by Ethereum itself, it is "the world's programmable blockchain." Being a programmable network serving as a safe and secure marketplace for financial services, games, and apps. The payment can be done in Ether, which makes Ethereum unique from Bitcoin.

Ethereum's Founders

A small group of blockchain devotees including Joe Lubin, founder of blockchain applications developer ConsenSys, and Vitalik Buterin launched Ethereum in July of 2015 with Vitalik Buterin being attributed with coming up with the Ethereum concept and now functioning as its CEO and public face. Buterin, born in 1994, is sometimes described as the world's youngest crypto billionaire. Although designed to be used within the Ethereum network, Ether is now an accepted form of payment by some merchants and service vendors including online sites like Overstock, Shopify, and CheapAir.

What Is Ether (ETH)?

Operations on the Ethereum network are eased by the transactional token, Ether. The programs and services that are associated with the Ethereum network need computing power which is not free, and payment is made to execute operations on the network through Ether.

Ether is considered as the cryptocurrency powering the Ethereum blockchain, but it can be accurately referred to as the "fuel" of this network. Each and every transaction in the network is tracked and facilitated by Ether. This is not how an average cryptocurrency works but Ether still has a few properties similar to those of other cryptocurrencies like bitcoin.

Operations on the Ethereum blockchain are powered by the transactional token, Ether.

To change the storage of consumer data like financial records, blockchain development is used by Ethereum technology which is used by third-party internet companies.

As of 2021, Ether is the world's second-largest virtual currency, second only to Bitcoin, by market capitalization.

In 2017 work began to shift the Ethereum network from a proof-of-work (PoW) system to a proof-of-stake (PoS) system, known as Ethereum 2.0, which is not yet fully developed and released.

Understanding Ether (ETH)

To change the storage of consumer data like financial records, blockchain development is used by Ethereum technology which is used by third-party internet companies. A blockchain is an exceptional type of database which stores data in chronologically arranged blocks, formerly used to record bitcoin transactions but presently, it serves as a basis for most major cryptocurrencies.

The Ethereum model intends to create a safer and secure environment for users by protecting their personal data from being hacked. Even though similar to other cryptocurrencies, Ether is a medium of exchange, however, it distinguishes it from other cryptocurrencies by its ability to be used on the Ethereum network to enable the computation of dApps. In contrast to being able to substitute other cryptocurrencies for Ether tokens, you cannot exchange Ether with the other digital currencies in order to provide the computing power that is required for Ethereum transactions.

The building and running of digital, decentralized applications called dapps is supported by Ethereum. You can use Ether tokens to pay for the computational resources mandatory to perform these operations.

Ether acts as a medium to allow payments made by a developer building Ethereum applications who needs to pay in order to host and execute the applications on the Ethereum network, and a user using the application who needs to pay in order to use it.

The number of Ether tokens paid by a developer depends upon network resources used in the creation of an application. This is analogous to how an ineffective engine requires more fuel—and an effective engine consumes less fuel. Data-hungry applications need more Ether for processing transactions. The Ether fee charged to complete the action depends upon the computational power and time needed by an application, for instance, the more computation power and time needed by an application. The fee that is charged in order to complete the transaction is pretty high.

How Is Ether Different from Bitcoin?

As of 2021, Ether is the world's second-largest virtual currency, second only to Bitcoin, by market capitalization. Ethereum blockchain was launched on July 30th,2015 while Bitcoin was first released on Jan. 3, 2009. As opposed to Bitcoin, the number of Ethereum tokens varies and increases constantly according to demand and does not have a specific limit. It is rather limitless hence making the Ethereum blockchain considerably larger than the bitcoin and is expected to continue to overtake bitcoin in the time yet to come.

Another significant difference is the creation of "smart contracts." These can be created when more codes are built into the transactions by contributors to the Ethereum blockchain, hence the network contains executable code. This is not possible in the Bitcoin blockchain since it is simply a ledger of accounts and the data connected to bitcoin network transactions is mainly used for keeping records.

Another difference is the time taken to build a new block which happens in seconds in the Ethereum blockchain while it takes minutes for the bitcoin correspondent to confirm. And most crucially, the biggest comparison is the difference in overall aims and purposes of the networks. Bitcoin offers a safe and protected peer-to-peer decentralized payment system, created as a substitute to traditional currencies. On the other hand, with Ether as a medium to carry out transactions, the Ethereum platform was created with an aim to allow and ease contracts and applications, and it was never planned for it to be an alternate currency or to substitute other mediums of exchange. Rather, the purpose of its creation is the facilitation and monetization of the operations of the Ethereum platform.

Since Ethereum actually supports bitcoin and due to their different reasons for developing, it makes no sense for these two cryptocurrencies to compete with each other from a functional perspective, but they do so for investor dollars because they have both enticed huge amounts of investments from investors.

Plans for Ether

In 2017 work began to shift the Ethereum network from a proof-of-work (PoW) system to a proof-of-stake (PoS) system, known as Ethereum 2.0. The main reason to upgrade to Ethereum 2.0 is to make the underlying network faster and more secure. Advocates of the planned upgrade say that the number of transactions taking place every second increases drastically.

In a PoW system, to authenticate transactions the alleged "miners" compete with each other to solve hard mathematical problems through their computers. In the new PoS system, for the processing of transactions, instead of depending upon miners the Ethereum network will use "stakers" already having some Ether tokens. On

Ethereum 2.0 a transaction could be validated when Ether tokens are deposited in a cryptocurrency wallet by a staker using a smart contract - a contract on the Ethereum blockchain that is automatically executed using code.

In a proof-of-stake system, a substantial amount of computational power is not used by stakers because they're randomly chosen and are not competing with other miners. Instead of mining blocks, stakers create blocks upon their selection, and upon rejection they validate those blocks through a process known as "attesting". Participants involved in the process of attesting can receive rewards for proposing new blocks as well as for attesting to ones they've seen.

A game plan for the release of Ether 2.0 was provided on December 2, 2020, by the founder of Ethereum, Vitalik Buterin. The Ethereum 2.0 road map significantly stated that full enactment of the new version would take some time although, the first block of the new Ethereum blockchain was created on December 1, 2020. Despite officially switching to Ethereum 2.0 the network is still contingent upon miners for computing power.

The Ethereum Business

According to Gartner Research, in the category of businesses investing in a blockchain software platform, Ethereum's main rivals, include Bitcoin, Ripple, IBM, IOTA, Microsoft, Blockstream, JP Morgan, and NEO.

At the end of May 2021, the market value of ETH became $2,236.

Disjointedly, Ether is a contender in the highly unstable cryptocurrency market. In May 2021, second, only to Bitcoin, Ethereum was the second-largest cryptocurrency, with its market cap as estimated by Analytics Insight at $500 billion in comparison to that of bitcoin at $1.080 trillion.

Binance Coin, Dogecoin, Cardano, Tether, XRP, Internet Computer, Polkadot, and Bitcoin Cash comprise the other eight on Analytics Insight's list of Top 10.

Ethereum-Based Projects

Quite a few projects are underway to test the claim made by Ethereum regarding its platform's ability to be used to "codify, decentralize, secure, and trade just about anything."

Microsoft is partnering with ConsenSys to offer Ethereum Blockchain as a Service (EBaaS) on the Microsoft Azure cloud. It is envisioned to offer Enterprise clients and developers a cloud-based blockchain developer environment at a single click.

A joint project for creating a network of data centers built on the Ethereum network was announced by Advanced Micro Devices (AMD) and ConsenSys in 2020.

Ethereum's Continuing Evolution

The possibility of using blockchain technology for purposes other than secure buy-and-sell of virtual currency was first seen by the founders of Ethereum. In order to have a secure payment medium for apps built on the Ethereum platform, the cryptocurrency ETH was created.

Since the Ethereum network is safe and protected from hackers, it has now opened up new avenues for the blockchain to be used for storing confidential information such as healthcare records and voting systems. Furthermore, since it depends upon cryptocurrencies, it can be used by programmers for the creation of games and other business applications on the blockchain network.

The Hard Fork

Futile attempts have been made to hack blockchains even though a blockchain may be impenetrable to hacker attacks. In 2016, $50 million worth of Ether had been stolen by a malevolent actor that had been collected for The DAO. It is a project in which a third party has to develop the smart contracts and originate from Ethereum's software platform. A third party developed was held responsible for this efficacious attack.

A "hard fork" was created by the community of Ethereum in order to reverse the robbery which annulled the present blockchain and created a second Ethereum blockchain. The original is known as Ethereum Classic.

Ethereum 2.0

Recorded in May of 2021, the value of Ethereum as a virtual currency was the second-highest in the market, behind only Bitcoin. Back in 2018, the number of ETHs in circulation surpassed 100 million.

Contrasting Bitcoin, an endless number of ETH's can be created.

Presently, Ethereum is being upgraded to Ethereum 2.0, which is anticipated to allow the network to function better and solve the overcrowding glitches that have slowed the network in the past. For instance, in 2017, transactions on the platform were singlehandedly slowed down by a game called Cryptokitties.

Ethereum with its wider aims and ambitions wants to be a platform for all kinds of applications that can store information safely.

Criticisms of Ethereum

 Ethereum is subjected to the same criticism as any other cryptocurrency:

Bitcoin price action is imitated by the prices of all cryptocurrencies including Ether. Although this has been obvious for a long time it can barely go unnoticed anymore. For instance, the value of bitcoin fluctuated between about $900 and about $20,000, and then in April 2021 hit a high of around $63k and stayed at around $30k in July 2021. Cryptocurrencies can be subjected to having both highs and lows and remain highly hypothetical and unpredictable.

A large amount of energy is being consumed by every one of these networks. A large amount of computing power is allocated by cryptocurrency miners chiefly to the process of validating transactions. All-encompassing crypto coin mining operations drain fossil energy which is one of the reasons why China is repressing cryptocurrency.

Perhaps, the introduction of Ethereum 2.0 can withstand the criticism that Ethereum had to face due to its fee.

What Is Ethereum in Simple Terms?

Ethereum is an information database, like any other blockchain with Ether being the cryptocurrency used to facilitate transactions on the Ethereum blockchain.

A blockchain organizes data "blocks" of information that are arranged in a chronological "chain." For example, when a transaction is made through an Ether token, it is verified and recorded as an additional block on the Ethereum blockchain. The main reason why a blockchain is often equated to a ledger is this process of sequential verification of transactions.

Apart from storing Ether currency's transaction records, the Ethereum blockchain also permits the creation and marketing of decentralized applications called dApps. Those users want to be benefitted from the comparative absence of dangers that come with storing sensitive information on the internet.

What Is ETH Trading?

Quite a few digital currency trading platforms such as Coinbase, Kraken, Bitstamp, Gemini, Binance, and Bitfinex are used by investors to trade Ether. Investing apps like Robinhood and Gemini also trade in cryptocurrencies.

The prices of cryptocurrencies are extremely unstable and the people trading crypto is making efforts to benefit from this instability. In July of 2021, the value of one ETH, which had surpassed $4,000 in mid of May and was at $231 a year before was fluctuating between $1,800 and $2300.

Is Ethereum Better Than Bitcoin?

In order to provide cryptocurrency support, the bitcoin blockchain was invented. In contrast, the wider-aiming Ethereum blockchain was created as an in-house currency for dApps or any other kind of applications storing information safely.

Regardless of their dissimilarities, Ethereum and Bitcoin are the creators of rival virtual currencies in the investing world. And virtual currencies are nothing but coins without a physical existence. Instead, they are represented by a string of codes that a buyer and seller can exchange at a price agreed.

How Does Ethereum Make Money?

In order to use dApps users are required to pay a fee called "gas" that is conditional on the amount of computational power used.

As recorded by the Ethereum Gas Report at the beginning of 2021, the intermediate fee for gas had crossed $10 per transaction.

How much time is required to mine an Ethereum?

Hashrate, consumption of power, electricity cost, and fees paid to a mining pool associated with the mining operation are some of the factors which affect the time taken to mine Ethereum and obtain mining rewards. The cost-effectiveness and upsurges in mining difficulty, targets, and the general price performance of the crypto market are also affected by these factors. As assessed by the default calculations of an Ethereum mining calculator, it takes 51.8 days to mine ETH.

CHAPTER NO 7

WHAT IS NFTS?

What is a Non-Fungible Token (NFT)?

Non-fungible tokens or NFTs are cryptographic assets on the blockchain. NFTs have unique codes for identification and metadata that differentiate them from each other. You can exchange cryptocurrencies with cryptocurrencies or fiat currencies, but in the case of the NFTs you cannot exchange one with another. That is because NFTs are unique and differ from one another, unlike cryptocurrencies.

WHAT YOU NEED TO KNOW

- NFTs are tokens that are cryptographic. They are unique and reside on a blockchain. You cannot duplicate these tokens.
- NFTs are used to signify real-world items such as artwork and real estate.
- "Tokenizing" these real-world physical assets provide them with an opportunity to be bought, sold, and traded proficiently and resourcefully so as to minimize the possibility of a scam.
- NFTs can also be used to symbolize the identities of people. Not just that but also their properties rights etc.

Every NFT is designed in such a way that it can be used for multiple purposes. For instance, you can use the NFTs to represent physical assets in a digital medium. The physical assets can be anything; be it artwork or real estate. Also, there are no third parties involved in the trading of NFTs. That is because of the underlying technology that powers it. NFTs are based on blockchain networks that simplify and facilitate transactions between two parties. As well as create new markets.

Beeple was able to sell NFTs worth $69 million in March.

This was one of the most expensive transactions that took place via the NFTs. These art pieces are the most expensive art pieces sold ever.

Beeple's first 5,000 days of work were compiled together in a collage and this was the artwork that was sold.

The NFT market generally deals with collectibles such as digital artwork, sports cards, and rarities. NBA Top Shot is the most talked about and famous platform that deals with collecting on-fungible tokenized NBA moments in a digital card form. These digital cards have been sold for millions of dollars. Lately, Twitter CEO Jack Dorsey tweeted a link to a tokenized version of the first tweet ever written where he wrote: "just setting up my twttr." The NFT version has by this time has been bid up to $2.5 million.

Understanding NFTs

Cryptocurrencies are fungible similar to fiat currencies. They can be exchanged with one another. You can trade them easily. An example of this can be that a dollar bill will always be equal to what a dollar bill is worth even if the serial number on both the dollar bills is different. Similarly, you can trade one bitcoin in exchange for another one of equal worth and value. Likewise, one Ether is equal in value to another. This characteristic makes cryptocurrencies an appropriate way to use as a safe and protected medium of transaction in the digital economy.

One NFT can never be equal to another one. That is because the NFTs shift the crypto standard. This ends up making every NFT unique thus making it impossible for two NFTs to be equal. Each NFT is differentiated from another by means of a unique, non-transferable identity. NFTs are basically the symbolization of digital assets. However, you can combine two NFTs and come up with a third NFT. This NFT will be unique as well.

Similar to Bitcoin, NFTs also hold details of ownership so that identification and transfers are stress-free among token holders. For instance, tokens that are demonstrating coffee beans can be classified as fair trade. Artists are capable of signing their artwork by using the stored metadata.

The evolution of the ERC-721 standard gave birth to NFTs. ERC-721 standard was developed by a group of people who were involved in the development of the ERC-20 smart contract. ERC-721 standard describes the minimum interface, ownership details, security, and metadata. All these details are mandatory to be shared so that the exchange and distribution of gaming tokens are made possible. This concept is further taken forward by 1155 standard. This standard minimizes the transaction and storage costs that are a prerequisite for NFTs and batching multiple types of non-fungible tokens into a single contract.

CryptoKitties is regarded as the most famous use case for NFTs. CryptoKitties was launched in November of 2017, and is a digital representation of cats with unique identifications on Ethereum's blockchain. All the "Kitties" are different from one another and each of the Kitty has a different price in Ether. These Kitties give birth to new Kitties. The newly birthed Kitties have different attributes and valuations. CryptoKitties was able to gather a huge fan base that spent $20 million worth of Ether purchasing, feeding, and nurturing them soon after it was launched.

CryptoKitties may be of minor or inconsequential importance but there are several others that have more serious uses in business. For example, NFTs are used in private equity transactions and real estate deals as well.

It insinuates empowering many types of tokens in a contract. This is the capability to deliver trust for different types of NFTs, from artwork to real estate, all into a single financial transaction.

Why Are Non-Fungible Tokens Important?

The evolution of the cryptocurrencies concept has given birth to the NFTs. Contemporary finance systems comprise refined trading and loan systems for various types of assets that range from real estate to lending contracts to artwork. NFTs are a step towards the future of facilitating the digital representations of physical assets.

All these little concepts are merged together into smart contracts on a blockchain network. Representation of physical assets digitally or using a unique identification is not a new concept.

Market efficiency is considered to be one of the most important advantages of NFTs. Converting a real-life or a physical asset into a digital asset modernizes processes and eliminates any third parties involved. All the details of the transactions are recorded on a blockchain and this eliminates the need for involving any third party or an intermediary. Owners can directly make a contact with the buyers and finalize a deal. Business deals can also be greatly improved using this concept. For instance, an NFT for a bottle of the vine will make it easier for various members that are a part of the supply chain to interact with it and also be able to track where it originated from, produced, and sold. Ernst & Young has come up with such a solution for their client.

Identity management is greatly enhanced by the use of non-fungible tokens. Let's consider the example of physical passports. You need to display your passports at every entry and exit point. If these passports are converted into the NFTs each with their own unique identification number it would greatly help in simplifying the process of entry and exits for the concerned authorities. NFTs can also be used in digital identity management.

NFTs provide investors to make an investment in a new market and increase their investment opportunities. Suppose there is real estate that is distributed into a number of pieces. Every piece of land has its own distinctive features and types of property. One piece of land might be next to a beach, the other one in an entertainment complex, and another one is a residential district. If you look at the features of all these places you would see that every piece of land is unique and thus will have a different price. Every piece of land will also be represented by a different NFT.

This concept has already been put to use by a platform that goes by the name Decentraland. Decentraland is a virtual reality platform on the Ethereum blockchain. With the rapid evolution that is happening in this field that day is not far when it would become possible to apply the same concept of tokenized pieces of land, differing in value and location, in the physical world.

The internet of assets

One of the few problems that exist on the internet presence can be easily solved by the NFTs and Ethereum. Everything is being digitized due to which there feels a need to duplicate the properties of physical items like scarcity, uniqueness, and ownership proof. For example, you cannot sell an iTunes mp3 again after you have bought it, or exchange the loyalty points of the company for the credit of some other platform even if it is in demand. You can't exchange one company's loyalty points for another platform's credit even if there's a market for it.

NFT examples

NFTs are still considered a new concept and the NFT market is a risky one. NFTs are tokens that represent ownership of assets. Below is a list of examples that will help you understand better.

- Unique digital artwork
- Unique sneaker in an unrepeatable fashion line
- Any in-game item
- An essay
- A digital collectible
- A domain name
- A ticket that allows you for an event or a coupon

POAPs (Proof of attendance protocol)

You can ask for entitlement of the POAP NFT if you donate to ethereum.org. You can use these collectibles and show that you were a part of these events. POAPs are used in the Crypto congregations as a form of a ticket to their events.

ethereum.eth

Ethereum.eth has an alternative domain name that is driven by NFTs. The .org address is handled centrally by a DNS provider. On the other hand, ethereum.eth has been listed on Ethereum using the Ethereum Name Service (ENS).

How do NFTs work?

ERC-20 tokens, such as DAI or LINK are not the same as NFTs. In the DAI and LINK, every token is completely unique and is not divisible. NFTs are a representation of the ownership over a digital asset. It is a unique piece of digital data, that can be tracked by using Ethereum's blockchain. An NFT is a representation of digital objects as a claim of ownership rights of digital or non-digital assets.

For example, an NFT could represent:

- Digital Art
- GIFs
- Collectibles
- Music

- Videos
- Real-World Items:
- Deeds to a car
- Tickets to a real-world event
- Tokenized invoices
- Legal documents
- Signatures

These are not the only ones. In fact, there are a lot of other options as well.

Each NFT is to have one owner at one time. Ownership is handled by uniqueID and metadata. These characteristics are unique to every token and cannot be duplicated. NFTs are minted via smart contracts that allocate ownership as well as manage the transfer of one NFT to another. The creation of an NFT means that the code that is stored in the smart contracts is triggered and executed. It obeys different standards, such as ERC-721. This information becomes a part of the blockchain where the NFT is being managed. Let's walk you through the steps of creation or minting of an NFT below.

- Creation of a new block
- Validation of information
- Recording information into the blockchain

Below are a few special characteristics of an NFT:

- Each token that is created or minted has its own unique identifier that is directly linked to a single Ethereum address.
- They cannot be interchanged openly with other tokens 1:1. For instance, 1 ETH is the same in worth as another ETH. This is not something that NFTs are concerned about.
- There is an owner of each token and this information can be verified with ease.
- They reside on Ethereum. The buying and selling can be done using any NFT market that is Ethereum-based.

In other words, if you own an NFT:

Proving ownership over an NFT is not a difficult process but a pretty easy one.

You can easily prove that you have ether stored with you in your account as you can prove that you own an NFT.

This denotes that when you purchase an NFT, the unique token that comes with it is then stored in your wallet using your public address.

That unique token is proof that you own the original piece.

The private key you have is proof that you own this authentic piece.

The public key that the creator of content has access to basically certifies the genuineness of a specific digital artifact.

The public key of the creator is basically a permanent part of the token's history. The public key of the creator is a demonstration that the token you now own was created by a so and so.

You can prove your ownership over an NFT in several ways, one of them being messages that are signed to show that you are the owner of the private key on a specific address.

The private key that you have access to is a proof that it is original. This is a way to show that private keys behind a specific address control the NFT.

No individual has the ability to influence it one way or the other.

In case you sell it and receive the royalties of the creator who created the art originally.

If you don't wish it to sell, you can keep it with you for as long as you want to. It will be stored in your wallet on Ethereum safely.

If you are able to mint an NFT:

- Proving that you are the one who created this art would become easy.
- Scarcity can be decided by you.
- Through the royalty scheme, you would be able to earn a percentage of money each time your art is sold.
- Any peer-to-peer market can be used to sell the art without getting any third parties involved.

Scarcity

The scarcity of an NFT is determined by the original creator.

An example below would give you more understanding regarding this topic. Suppose there is a sports event happening. It is only for the organizer of the event to determine how many tickets to sell for the event. Similarly, only the original creator of the asset has the right to determine how many copies he wants to create. Often times the copies are an exact replica of the asset. Other times a number of them are created with a minute difference. In other cases, the creator may want to create an NFT where only one is minted making it one unique and rare collectible.

In the cases explained above each NFT would still have a unique identifier with a single owner. It is the decision of the creator to determine the scarcity of an NFT. It is something that matters. In order to maintain scarcity the creator can create the NFTs completely different from each other. If he wishes, he can also come up with a lot of copies. All this is publically known.

Royalties

If your NFT has a royalty scheme programmed into it, every time your art is sold you will be able to receive your share automatically. This concept is still under works but it is one of the best ones. The ones who own EulerBeats Originals receive an 8% royalty whenever the NFT of their art is re-sold. Platforms such as Foundation and Zora back royalties for their artists.

The whole royalty process is automatic and stress-free. This is so that the artists who created the art originally don't have to go through a hassle and can earn from their art every time it is sold again. Presently, there are a lot of issues in the whole royalties scheme as it is manual. Due to this reason, a majority of the artists are not paid. If you pre-define that you will receive a percentage of money as royalties from the artwork in your NFT, you can keep earning from that art piece.

What are NFTs used for?

Below are a few more famous and widely known use-cases for the NFTs on the Ethereum blockchain network.

Digital content

Gaming items

Domain names

Physical items

Investments and collateral

Maximizing earnings for creators

NFTs are widely used in the capacity of digital art. The reason for that is that the digital art industry has a lot of issues that need to be fixed. The platforms that they sold on would end up swallowing their earning and profits generated thus letting the artists suffer financially.

An artist puts up his work on a social network site and makes money for the platform that sells ads to the followers of the artists. This gives the artist the publicity but exposure and publicity don't make any money for him.

The new creator economy is powered by the NFTs. In the creator economy, the original creators don't pass on the ownership of their content to the platforms.

Every time these artists make a sale, all the revenue generated by the sale goes to them directly. The one with whom he sells his art becomes the new owner. Whenever that owner would sell the art piece further, this would give the artist to have an opportunity to generate some revenue from the sale through the royalties' scheme.

The copy/paste problem

Some people fail to understand the concept of NFTs and claim them to be of no use. The main statement that they pass over such a scenario is that if you can screengrab something and get it for free then why do you have to spend millions of dollars over it?

- If you screenshot or google pictures of a painting by Picasso it doesn't make you the owner of it.
- If you own a real and genuine thing, that means that you won something valuable. The more an item becomes viral, the more in demand it is.
- If you own something that is verified it will definitely have more value.

Boosting gaming potential

NFTs are commonly used in the industry of digital art but they are also very applicable in the game development industry. The developers in the industry use the NFTs to claim ownership over the in-game items. It can help with the in-game economies as well as benefit the players in multiple ways.

You purchase items in almost every game that you play. If the item that you purchase is an NFT, you can end up making money from it outside the game. It can also become a source of profit for you if the item is in demand.

The people who developed the game are the ones who issue the NFTs. This means that they have the right to generate revenue through royalty schemes every time an item is sold again. In such cases, there is a benefit for both the parties (i.e. the players and the developers.)

The items that you have collected in the game are now yours and that the game is not handled by the developers anymore.

If there is no one to handle the game the items would still be yours and you will have complete control over them. Whatever you earn in the game can have a lot of worth and value outside of the game.

Decentraland is a VR game that allows you to purchase NFTs that symbolize the virtual parcels of land that you can use as per your liking.

Physical items

If you compare the tokenization of digital assets and physical assets, you will realize that the tokenization of digital assets is more advanced. There are several projects that are working on the tokenization of real estate, rare fashion items, etc.

In the near future, you will be able to purchase cars, houses, etc. all with the NFTs. This is because the NFTs are basically deeds and you can purchase a physical asset and then get a deed as an NFT in return. With the advancements in technology it will be real soon that your Ethereum wallet would become the key to your car or home. You will be able to unlock your door with cryptographic proof of ownership.

NFTs and DeFi

The NFT space and the DeFi world are beginning to work together closely in several interesting ways.

NFT-backed loans

There are DeFi applications that allow you to borrow money using collateral. For instance, you collateralize 10 ETH so you can scrounge 5000 DAI. If the one who borrowed the money is unable to pay back the DAI the lender will be able to get his payment back. However, not everyone can afford to use crypto as collateral.

Presently, the projects have started the exploration of using the NFTs as collateral. Suppose you purchased a rare CryptoPunk NFT awhile back with a present worth thousands of dollars. That means that if you put this up as collateral you will be able to access a loan with the same ruleset. If you are not able to pay back the DAI, your CryptoPunk will be sent to the lender as collateral. Ultimately, you would be able to see that it can work with anything you tokenize as an NFT.

It is not something that is difficult on Ethereum. That is because both of these share the same underlying technology and infrastructure.

Fractional ownership

NFT creators have the ability to create "shares" for their NFT. Due to this the investors and the fans have a chance to own a share of an NFT and not purchase it as a whole. This is a great way for both the NFT creators and collectors to have more opportunities.

DEX's like Uniswap can help with the trade of fractionalized NFTs. The total price of the NFT can be defined by the price of each fraction.

Fractional NFTs are still a new concept and people are still experimenting with them.

NIFTEX

NFTX

This means that you would be able to own a piece of a Picasso in theory. This is like you would become a shareholder in a Picasso NFT. You would be sharing revenue with every partner that is a part of the NFT. It is highly likely that owning a fraction of an NFT will move you into a decentralized autonomous organization (DAO) for asset management.

The organizations that are powered and backed up by Ethereum permit strangers to become global shareholders of an asset. This would allow them to manage everything securely. They don't have to trust each other necessarily. In these systems, no one is allowed to spend a dime unless approved by every member of the group.

As we have been discussing, this is just the beginning.NFTs, DAOs, and fractionalized tokens are all developing at their own pace. However, their infrastructure has already been built and all these technologies can work in close correspondence to each other as they are all backed up by Ethereum.

HOW ETHEREUM IS RELATED TO NFTS

Ethereum and NFTs

Ethereum makes it likely for NFTs to work for a number of reasons:

You can prove your ownership over an asset by verifying the history of transactions and token metadata.

No one has the authority to steal and falsify the data and ownership of an asset after the confirmation of a transaction.

You can trade the NFTs without the involvement of a third-party platform or application. This helps in the reduction of overhead expenses.

All those products use the Ethereum blockchain as the underlying technology and due to this reason all these products can comprehend each other well. This is why the NFTs can be transferred easily. You can purchase an NFT on one product and sell it on some other one easily. Ethereum is always running and that makes your token available for trade all the time.

The environmental impact of NFTs

NFTs are becoming more and more famous with every passing day and people have started to pay attention to it as well, but they are also subjected to a lot of inspection over their carbon footprint.

To provide a clear overview:

The increase in the carbon footprints of Ethereum may not be due to the NFTs.

Ethereum may use a strenuous way to secure the funds and assets but its improvement is in the works.

Upon improvement, the carbon footprint of Ethereum will be 99.95% better. This would make it more energy-efficient than many existing industries.

In order to have a better understanding, let's discuss some technical aspects of this:

NFTs do not need to be blamed for it.

Due to the decentralized and secure nature of the Ethereum network, the whole system of NFT is up and running.

Decentralized means that you or anyone who owns something can be verified and proven. You would not require any third party to enforce any rules and regulations. You will be able to do everything on your own. This means that the NFTs can be transferred across markets.

No one can copy and paste your NFT as it is secure.

Ethereum has multiple qualities that make it unique and make it possible for you to own digital assets at a justified price. But it comes at a cost. And that is that blockchains like Bitcoin and Ethereum are energy-intensive at this point in time. That is because it requires a lot of energy to function. If it was easy to rewrite the history of Ethereum history to steal NFTs or cryptocurrency, the system collapses.

The work in minting your NFT

Upon minting the NFTs, the following things would take place.

It is important that you authenticate your asset on the blockchain.

It is mandatory for the owner to update his account balance in order to take account of the asset. Due to this, you will be able to trade and own the asset.

The transactions that are validated and verified are to be added to a block and "immortalized" on the chain.

Every person who is part of the blockchain network has to confirm that the network is correct. This block needs to be confirmed by everyone in the network as "correct". This agreement eliminates the need for any third-party application to become a part of the process because everything is recorded on the blockchain and it shows that you are the owner of the NFT. It is publically available and hence everyone is able to view it. This is a great way for the creators to generate extra revenue.

Miners are in charge to do all these things. These miners are supposed to let everyone on the network know about the real owners of the NFT. Mining is a task that demands a lot of responsibility. That is because if it's not done carefully, anyone could claim that they own the NFT who actually do not. There are numerous encouragements to ensure that the miners do their job with honesty.

Securing your NFT with mining

A lot of computing power is required in order to create new blocks in the blockchain. This makes the mining process pretty difficult. The creation of blocks is done at all times. They are not created when there is a need for it, but every 12 seconds a new block is created and added to the chain.

The Ethereum network is safe and secure and this one quality among many is the reason for the existence of the NFTs. The security of the chain is directly proportional to the number of blocks added to the chain. The addition of more blocks to the chain makes it more secure. If a hacker wants to steal your NFT by altering your data on the block, this would lead to the change in all the other blocks and that would make it possible for those who are running the software to instantly detect it and then stop it from happening.

Computing power has to be used at all times in order to keep the chain secure. The block with no NFTs would still have the same carbon footprint as would the one with NFTs. Other non-NFT transactions will fill the blocks.

At this point, blockchains are energy-intensive.

Every block has its carbon footprint associated with it and this is a problem for the bitcoins too. The NFT's are not the only ones at fault for this.

Mining requires the usage of a huge percentage of renewable energy sources. Not just that but people have also been arguing that NFTs and cryptocurrencies are becoming a problem for the industries due to high carbon footprints. But just because prevailing industries are bad it doesn't mean we shouldn't work hard for the better.

But again we are working for a better future. Making Ethereum more energy efficient is the plan and this has always been the plan.

It's not that we are defending the effects mining has on the environment. As an alternative, we will discuss the changes that can help in making things better:

A greener future

Ever since Ethereum has been developed, the developers are trying hard to focus and make things better. They have been constantly around energy consumption due to the mining process. Developers and researchers alike have put this area under focus and trying their best to solve this issue. And the dream has always been to replace it as soon as they can.

A greener Ethereum: ETH2.0

Ever since the development of Ethereum, researchers and developers have been trying to solve the energy-consumption problems. Due to that, there have been several upgrades in the works. The upgraded ETH2.0 is soon to replace the mining process with staking. Staking will reduce the power of computation as a way to enhance security. This would result in minimizing the carbon footprint by ~99.95%. ETH2.0 would work on stakers committing funds rather than using the power of computation to make the blockchain safe and secure.

The energy cost that Ethereum has will be converted into the cost of running a PC. This is multiplied by the number of nodes that are integrated with the network. Let's suppose there are 10,000 nodes in the network and the cost that is required to run a home computer is approximately 525kWh per year. That would make about 5,250,000kWh each year for the whole network.

This power can be used in comparison to compare ETH2.0 and global services like Visa. 100,000 Visa transactions consume 149kWh of energy. In ETH2.0, the number of transactions would cost around about 17.4kWh of energy or ~11% of the total energy. Here, in this case, we are not bearing in mind the optimizations being worked on in equivalence to ETH2.0, as in rollups. It can be as less 0.1666666667kWh of energy required for 100,000 transactions.

This is important because it helps in the improvement of energy efficiency. Energy efficiency is enhanced as well as the decentralization and security of the Ethereum network are maintained. There may be blockchains that operate on staking but in the case of Ethereum the number of stakers required will be a lot. It can go up to thousands. If you want to make the system more secure, decentralize it as much as possible.

CHAPTER NO 9

WHAT IS BLOCKCHAIN GAMING?

Presently, the gaming industry has been flourishing like never before. The gaming industry is currently valued at $173 billion with very high chances that it will exceed the $300 billion mark in five years' time. The reason for the growth in the gaming industry recently is due to the increase in new players, specifically in mobile games. This has made the gaming industry more sustainable.

The gamers have realized that they have been working more and earning less. They know that they are making big investments but the revenue that is generated is far too less. This has pushed them to discover and explore new ways of earning online. They are coming up with different ways in which they can use their hobby for making more money. This has led to increased growth in the game development sector.

Nowadays the blockchain games are on a rise. These games are providing an opportunity for the players to be the main decision-makers regarding finance, and not the developers. Play-to-earn (P2E) crypto gaming is a trend that should not be overshadowed. Let's have a discussion below on how all this works.

What are blockchain games?

A blockchain is a form of ledger technology that functions as a recording and storing system for information. It is one of the safest and secure technologies because it cannot be hacked nor can any data be modified. The history of the transactions that happen over the network is available publically and everyone can see it. Cryptocurrencies are powered by the Blockchain. Bitcoin and Ethereum are the two leading cryptocurrencies right now and they are creating multiple opportunities for people. Game developers have realized the opportunities it can provide them with.

Normally, in video games or mobile games when a player purchases avatars or other game items like assets, etc. they are not owned by the player. It doesn't matter even if the player is spending real cash to get the assets for the game. That is because these games are built using centralized systems in which the whole control of the dynamics of the game is in the hands of the one who developed it. Everything that happens within the game is controlled by the game developer and the player has zero control. Players do not really own any game assets or accounts, etc. This is not the only issue with this system. Another issue is that the system is not completely transparent and there are high chances for manipulations in the game mechanics.

Fair virtual markets were introduced for the first time using the blockchain. The markets have also become decentralized and players have gained more control over the game mechanics. Blockchain not only works in gaming but also powers virtual economies.

Real ownership: Games that are based on the blockchain make the players be in complete ownership of the in-game assets and other items that they purchase. Assets are typically represented by unique non-fungible tokens (NFTs).

Metaverses and interoperability: The tokens that are used to purchase the in-game assets can also be used to trade on the different platforms on a blockchain.

Fair experience: Games that are based on blockchain technology provide more transparency. That is because blockchain enables the creation of open, distributed, and transparent networks. This has given more control to the players than the gaming companies. Players are the ones who control the game dynamics. Not just that but if they want something to be changed in the game, they can vote in favor of the changes.

Unlimited creativity: Traditional games only ran as long as the developer wanted. That is because those games were run on a centralized server. However, the blockchain-based games run on a decentralized and distributed server and this provides the players to keep playing for as long as they want. It doesn't matter if the developers are involved or not. This helps in expanding the range of assets and boost creativity.

CryptoKitties is the first game of its kind. It is a blockchain-based game and was launched in 2017. In the Cryptokitties game, you can trade and create various kinds of Kitties in the form of NFTs, or non-fungible tokens. This makes each virtual kitten into a unique NFT. The rarer the kitten, the higher the value it holds. One of the most expensive Cryptokittens was sold for $172,000.

This encouraged the virtual market to flourish and expand even more.

Can you earn money from blockchain games?

Blockchain games have two unique features that are:

- Incorporation of cryptocurrencies that can be used for in-platform payments
- The use of NFTs

NFTs allow the users to claim ownership over unique assets. Those assets can be traded with other players within the same game or transferred between platforms as well. You can use these blockchain-based games to make money from the marketplaces in the blockchain games.

Enthusiastic players do have the option of producing physical rewards. It also helps the players earn digital collectibles if that is something that interests them. There is huge potential in this field and this is just the beginning.

People have started to regard this as a full-time job. Others think of it as a prospective investment sector.

How to get started with blockchain games?

If you are looking to get involved in blockchain games, here is what you need to do. First, you need to have a device. It can either be a computer or a mobile phone. After this, you need to choose a cryptocurrency exchange. This platform will help you in converting your money into cryptocurrencies. There are a number of exchanges available but you have to research well and look for the one that is well-suited as per your needs. As the majority of the blockchain-based games are using the Ethereum blockchain, it is advised that you use Ether as it is what powers the Ethereum blockchain network. Next, you need to store your Ether or any other digital currency that you have chosen somewhere safe and secure. You can store your Ether in a digital wallet. There are many digital wallets to choose from. Choose the one that is easy for you to use. Then you have to opt for a game and start playing. Ta-Da! You are good to go!

Top Blockchain Games 2021

If you compare the two types of gaming industries, you would realize that blockchain-based gaming is still a new technology and has not developed much. Although there are a lot of blockchain games available and this number is increasing. These games have racked up millions of players and created a lot of money as a result.

Below are the movers and shakers of the crypto gaming industry:

Axie Infinity

Axie Infinity is considered to be the champion amongst all the crypto games. Axie Infinity has taken NFTs to a new level. It has a Pokemon-like experience and the game is inhabited with Axies. Axies are digital creatures. Each Axie is an individual NFT (or digital creature), with each being an NFT. Players can buy, exchange and breed Axies, and also use them to battle other players or teams in seasonal tournaments. The Axies that are not so commonly available have a very high worth. Awhile ago they were sold for thousands of dollars. In-game tokens like Smooth Love Potion (SLP) and Axie Infinity Shard (AXS) are seeing a huge rise that can go up to 5,700%. This has led to an enormous increase in the virtual economy of the game. This is what differentiates this gaming platform from the others. Players are given an opportunity to cash out in the Axie Infinity game which is a feature that is particular to Axie Infinity only. Also, you can exchange the fiat currencies with the AXS. Axie Infinity proved to be a huge hit in a lot of countries.

Blankos Block Party

Mythical Games marked its entry into the crypto gaming industry with Blankos. In Blankos you are allowed to create your own characters. These characters are created from vinyl toys. These designs are completely customizable. Users are given a chance to collect unique 'Blankos', join quests and be a part of team games ("Block Parties").

Upland

Upland is a blockchain-based game that allows users to buy, sell and trade virtual land mapped to the real world. There are "digital landlords" that build properties and then earn through the UPX coins. The project has mapped the cities of San Francisco and New York and lets you buy virtual properties for sale linked to real-life addresses in both these cities.

Mobox

Mobox is free-to-play. It is a combination of gaming with decentralized finance (DeFi). It runs on the Binance Smart Chain. People who developed Mobox say that this will bring gaming closer to GameFi. It will become such a platform where both the players and investors can access games from different blockchains in one single place. One of the key objectives of this game is to let the players take part in the NFT games with ease and be able to make money just by playing the game. Processing of transactions, staking and governance can be done through the MBOX tokens. This would greatly help in encouraging development and allocating the resources inside the MOBOX ecosystem. Presently the number of games that are available on the platform is three and more will be released soon.

Lightnite

Lightnite was developed by the same team that worked on the Bitcoin arcade game portal "Satoshi's Games." Lightnite is a battle royale game. In this game the players are given prizes in the form of bitcoin if they shoot other players in the game. Lightnite is a multiple-player game. The more people you shoot in the game the more bitcoins you yield as a prize. Players who are shot are punished by losing their bitcoins. The in-game assets can be tokenized and used as NFTs. These can be sold and traded via an NFT marketplace.

Gods Unchained

Magic was the basic motivation behind this game. Gods Unchained is a blockchain-based game. In this game, the users create decks and then play cards among themselves in order to fight the opponents. Being a blockchain-based game, it allows the users to have complete control over their cards. Not just that but in case a player wins, he can sell and trade the cards as well. The cards that are rare in the game are worth thousands of dollars. There is a free-to-play option for those players who may be confused and not want to go all-in.

CryptoKitties

CryptoKitties is the first game of its kind. It is a blockchain-based game and was launched in 2017. In the Cryptokitties game, you can trade and create various kinds of Kitties in the form of NFTs, or non-fungible tokens. This makes each virtual kitten into a unique NFT. The rarer the kitten, the higher the value it holds. One of the most expensive Cryptokittens was sold for $172,000. The user interface of the CryptoKitties game is pretty simple. It is highly addictive and you won't be able to stop once you start playing it! The problem with CryptoKitties is that breeding and purchasing the Kittens usually costs a lot and can you may have to spend a lot of Ether on that.

Splinterlands

Splinterlands is reminiscent of Pokémon, Yugi-oh, and Magic The Gathering. Splinterlands is one of the most successful examples of a card fighter experience with a player-driven economy. All the cards that are involved in the game are of real value. You can trade them if you want to. Splinterland is a relatively easy game. There is an in-game shop from which users can purchase cards. There are multiple updates for Splinterland and due to these expansions a huge number of people have started to join the game as players. Rare cards are more tempting for the players to join the game.

Sandbox

Sandbox is a metaverse in which a player can own land, build, play, and take part in virtual experiences. The Sandbox is a video game where players use the Ethereum blockchain to monetize their experiences.

SAND is a cryptocurrency that is used as a usage fee for the game. It is a kind of utility token. A web-based marketplace that lets users upload, publish and sell creations made in VoxEdit, a 3D voxel modeling package, as NFTs. Game mechanics can be easily changed using the scripted behaviors after the creations are published and purchased. An editor can be used to place on land parcels. These in turn make changes to the game mechanics.

Cryptopop

Cryptopop is a game that is similar to the widely popular game Candy Crush. Players can receive points by matching the symbols of cryptocurrencies. The more candies you match; the more points you receive. There is an in-game market through which players can earn extra money. Not just that but they can also trade with other players who are playing the game. Ether and Popcorn are the currencies that are used in Cryptopop.

Illuvium

Illuvium has not been released yet. The developers are planning to release it soon. Illuvium has become the talk of the town because as per the developers it is supposed to be the first game of its kind. It will be the first AAA game on the Ethereum network. It has caused quite an uproar and it is justified because this open-world fantasy battle game is built on the Ethereum blockchain and is populated by creatures called Illuvial. Each Illuvial has its own unique capabilities, classes, and categories. These Illuvials can be captured and then used in the fight in order to battle other Illuvials. Players can capture them and have them battle other Illuvials. These creatures can be sold in exchange for ILV tokens. The profits that are earned go all to the players and stakeholders of the game.

Why should you try crypto games?

The concept of the players earning from video games is not a new concept. Games that are based on the blockchain network provide an opportunity for the game developers as well as the players to earn from playing these video games. You will earn money through these in-game assets as well as you can claim ownership of these assets in the game. It also makes you a stakeholder by backing a community-driven ecosystem (DAO). The advantages that these blockchain-based games have were not possible in the conventional gaming methods that worked on centralized platforms.

CHAPTER NO 10

EVERYTHING ABOUT SMART CONTRACTS

Programs that are stored on the blockchain are known as smart contracts. These programs have a set of instructions that execute only when the condition is met. Smart contracts are used in the automation of the execution of a contract. In smart contracts, all the members that are a part of the contract are certain of the outcome without any third party getting involved. Whenever the conditions are met, it triggers an automatic workflow.

How smart contracts work

Smart contracts work using the "if/when...then..." statements that are written into code on a blockchain. Whenever a certain condition is met, the lines of code that are stored in the blockchain get executed. These actions could be anything from releasing funds to the appropriate parties, registering a vehicle, sending notifications, to issuing a ticket. When the transaction is over, the subsequent updates are made into the blockchain. This makes the transaction impossible to alter. Only those people who have the permissions will be eligible to view the results that are generated.

There are many conditions in a smart contract. The number of these conditions can be as per the needs of the user or how many satisfies him that the task will be completed reasonably. Terms and conditions are supposed to be provided by the participants. He should determine how transactions and their data are represented on the blockchain, agree on the "if/when...then..." rules that administer those transactions, explore all possible exceptions, and define a framework for solving any disagreements.

The developer would program the smart contracts as per the rules defined by the participants.

Benefits of smart contracts

Speed, efficiency, and accuracy

The execution of the smart contract begins at the very instant when a set of conditions are met. Smart contracts are digital and automated. Smart contracts do not involve any paperwork. In the manual system, there are a number of errors that may take time to resolve but as smart contracts are automatic, there is no time wasted in this regard.

Trust and transparency

Due to no intermediary being part of the whole process and sharing of the encrypted records amongst all the participants, it makes it difficult to make any changes for personal gains.

Security

Smart contracts are secure. That is because the transaction records that are stored on the blockchain are in an encrypted form makes it almost impossible to hack. Every record on the blockchain is linked to the previous and subsequent records on a distributed ledger. It would take the hackers to hack the entire change and make the changes.

Savings

Smart contracts eliminate intermediaries to handle transactions and, by extension, their associated time delays and fees.

Applications of smart contracts

Safeguarding the efficacy of medications

Sonoco and IBM are working on increasing the supply chain transparency so that it is easier to transport lifesaving medications. Powered by IBM Blockchain Transparent Supply, Pharma Portal is a blockchain-based platform that tracks temperature-controlled pharmaceuticals via the supply chain to provide trusted, reliable and accurate data to all the concerned parties.

Increasing trust in retailer-supplier relationships

Smart contracts are used to solve clashes with the vendors. The Home Depot uses smart contracts for this purpose. They are able to do so via real-time communication and improved visibility into the supply chain. This helps them in maintaining a good relationship with the suppliers. This is a great way for innovation.

Making international trade faster and more efficient

We.trade uses identical and standardized rules and simplified trading options so they are able to minimize the friction and risk while the whole trading process is easy. This helps in expanding the trade opportunities for the companies and banks that are a part of the network.

Smart contracts are automatic and execute on their own whenever certain conditions are met. Business automation applications run on a decentralized network such as blockchain.

Smart contracts are a great way to eliminate any extra expenses. This makes smart contracts one of the most interesting and attractive features of blockchain technology. Blockchain is a sort of database that helps with verifying transactions that may have happened. Smart contracts execute pre-determined conditions. The smart contract can be regarded as a computer executing on "if/then," or conditional, programming.

The whole process of smart contracts is pretty simple. What happens is that the conditions that are required to be met are coded in the smart contracts. When those conditions are met, the lines of code execute and goods arrive in a port. The parties that are involved in the transaction settle for an exchange in cryptocurrency. Transferring fiat money or the receipt of a shipment of goods that allows them to continue on their journey can be automated as well. The underlying technology used is the blockchain ledger that is used to store the state of the smart contract.

Understanding tokens and smart contracts

Let's consider an example of an insurance company. The insurance company could use smart contracts to automate the release of claim money based on events such as large-scale floods, hurricanes, or droughts. When the shipment reaches a port of entry and IoT sensors installed inside the container confirm the contents have not been opened and are stored properly throughout the journey, a bill of lading is issued automatically.

You can use smart contracts to transfer the cryptocurrency and the digital tokens through the network. ERC-20 and ERC-721 are the two tokens that are used in the blockchain network. Alongside tokens, they are smart contracts as well.

But this does not imply that all the tokens are smart contracts. As per Martha Bennet, you can have smart contracts running on Ethereum that trigger an action based on a condition without an ERC-20 or ERC-721 token involved." Martha Bennet is the principal analyst at Forrester Research.

Transfer of cryptocurrencies from buyer to seller can also be administered by smart contracts. Once payment is verified, bitcoin can be traded.

You see that majority of the blockchain networks do not use the tokens. All the rules for it are stated in the smart contract, from the token allocation process to conditions set for transfer.

"That still doesn't mean the token is the smart contract - it all depends on how the token has been constructed." Bennett said. "And tokens don't have to be about economic value; a token can simply be something you hold that gives you the right to vote on a decision; casting the token means you've voted, and can't vote on this decision again – no economic value associated."

How smart contracts mimic business rules

Smart contracts are basic rules for businesses that are coded into software. On the contrary, to the name smart contracts, they are not smart and not contracts legally as well.

"People often ask what makes smart contracts different from business rules automation software or stored procedures. The answer is that conceptually, the principle is the same; but smart contracts can support automating processes that stretch across corporate boundaries, involving multiple organizations; existing ways of automating business rules can't do that," explained Bennet.

She further clarified, "In other words, they're code that does what it's been programmed to do. If the business rules...have been defined badly and/or the programmer doesn't do a good job, the result is going to be a mess." Bennett said. "And, even if designed and programmed correctly, a smart contract isn't smart – it just functions as designed."

"Translating business rules into code doesn't automatically turn the result into a legally enforceable agreement between the parties involved (which is what a contract actually is). Although there are some initiatives aimed at making smart contracts automatically legally binding, that path, at least for now fraught with difficulty and risk." Bennett said. The reason for this that there's no decided standard definition of what is a smart contract.

"And what happens if the software has bugs and yields bad results? Is the resulting loss now also legally binding?" she further added.

The importance of good data, and 'oracles' in smart contracts

It is very important to ensure the quality of programming for smart contracts. That is because a smart contract would work better if the rules and regulations are properly coded to automate processes. The data that is to be added to the smart contract needs to be done vigilantly. Due diligence is required because once you code the smart contract you would not be able to make any changes to it. Not even the programmer could help you in this regard.

The smart contract would be unable to work properly if the data that is coded into it is wrong or false.

Blockchains have the data that triggers the execution of smart contracts. These happen from using external sources like data feeds and APIs. Direct fetching of the data cannot be done via a blockchain. The real-time data feeds for blockchains are called oracles. These oracles are kind of an intermediate layer that is present between the data and contract.

Oracle may be:

- Software-based
- Hardware-Based

A hardware-based oracle, for example, might be an RFID sensor in a cargo container that sends the location data to smart contract parties. A software oracle could be an application that feeds information through an API about a securities exchange such as changing interest rates or fluctuating stock prices.

Smart contracts run on one node. Unlike the blockchain, they are not decentralized and are able to run on a number of computers. The nodes that are part of the blockchain do not know the working of a smart contract. The number of companies that are involved has to trust the oracle for the information that is being added into the smart contract.

No company can know what is happening in the smart contract if your company is part of the blockchain network. There is absolutely no sustainability. In any case, you would have to trust the company that is working on the server that the information added to the blockchain is correct. The company works on the server on which lives the oracle and smart contracts.

"You have to go to one source, one table, one oracle for that data. There are no standard processes to verify the data is what it says it is and it's coming in properly. It's a central point of failure." explained Gartner Vice President of Research Avivah Litan.

"It's not mature yet." Litan continued. "I've talked to companies participating in a consortium and asked them how do you know what the smart contract is doing and they say they don't. If you have a contract running your life, wouldn't you want to know what it's doing?"

Potential problems with smart contract data

Oracles usually transmit data from a single source, thus the data is not to be trusted completely. As per Sergey Nazarov, CEO of Chainlink, an oracle start-up that uses multiple external sources of oracle data. Nazarov, in a white paper, talked about this and said that there are chances that the data may be "benignly or maliciously corrupted due to faulty websites, cheating service providers, or honest mistakes."

Development partnerships have occurred between the internet and financial services by Chainlink. These comprise of Google and the Society for Worldwide Interbank Financial Telecommunication (SWIFT). SWIFT runs one of the world's largest clearing and settlement networks.

Nazarov says the functionality of the smart contracts presently can be tricky. That is because one party may perform a task but the other party may choose not to pay. This would instigate a legal battle between both parties.

"Those contracts are not rigorously enforceable; they can't be enforced by technology the way a smart contract can." Nazarov said. "A smart contract is deterministic; it can absolutely be enforced as long as the events related to its contractual clauses happen".

"Smart contracts are contingent on events; they're contingent on market events, in insurance they're contingent on IoT data from cars, factories, or other equipment." Nazarov continued. "In trade finance, they're contingent on shipping data."

Let's consider an example, Chainlink made a smart contract for a media company. The company did not pay the search engine optimization (SEO) firm that was hired until news article URLs reached and then sustained search engine rankings for some time.

"That payment wasn't held by our client or the search engine optimization firm," Nazarov said. "It was held by this new technology (blockchain and the smart contract) that will programmatically enforce the contract as it was written. That's the fundamental difference."

"The emergence of new technologies and improvements in programming tools has made the creation of smart contracts easy in comparison to the past. These programming tools have helped in moving away from the underlying complexity of smart contract scripting languages, essentially enabling business people to pull together the basics of a smart contract." Bennett said.

"We're even beginning to see tools that allow business people to pull together the basics of a smart contract," said Bennett. "That's only the beginning, though, as some companies have already discovered it can be a challenge to ensure that every network participant runs the same version of a smart contract."

Edge computing, IoT and the future of smart contracts

The use of IoT devices has increased multiple folds. In the coming years there will be a high surge of IoT-connected devices that can shoot better use of smart contracts. Regarding the Juniper research, it is approximated that approximately 46 billion industrial and enterprise devices connected in 2023 will depend on edge computing. This would result in making standardization and deployment critical.

Eliminating any third party involved has increased the speed of the exchange of data and this could prove to be a standard for improving the exchange speed between the IoT devices. This could be made possible due to smart contracts. The server or cloud service that acts as the central communication spoke for requests and other traffic among IoT devices on a network is said to be a middle man or a third party.

Member of the Institute of Electrical and Electronics Engineers (IEEE), Mario Milicevic said, "Fundamentally, the idea is you don't have a central agent – no one approving and validating every single transaction. Instead, you have distributed nodes that participate invalidating every transaction in the network."

The time that is required for the IoT devices to exchange information and processing time has been significantly reduced due to the Blockchain ledgers.

"It could be in an automotive manufacturing plant. As soon as a certain part arrives, that part then communicates to other nodes at that destination which would agree that part arrived and communicate it to the entire network. The new node would then be allowed to begin doing its work," Milicevic said.

Blockchain experts from IEEE are of the view that merging together blockchain and IoT could prove to be a game-changer and would actually transform vertical industries.

At this point in time, the financial services and insurance companies are leading presently in the blockchain development and deployment, transportation, government, and utility sectors are now also becoming a part of it. There has been a huge focus on the opportunities due to process efficiency, supply chain, and logistics. These will most likely merge with the smart contracts in the coming years and that will make the whole process more universal.

CHAPTER NO 11

WHAT ARE THE BLOCKCHAIN'S CONSENSUS PROTOCOLS?

Satoshi Nakamoto was the first one to speak about bitcoin or cryptocurrencies in the white paper that he presented in 2009. After this, there were a number of other cryptocurrencies launched as well. All these digital currencies have been doing really well. Cryptocurrencies like bitcoin and Ethereum, etc. are decentralized currencies. Bitcoin has elevated blockchain technology to new highs and caught the attention of people ever since it was launched. Afterward, many cryptocurrencies and projects based on the blockchain sprung up. This resulted in blockchain becoming the talk of the town with everyone showing great interest. However, the technology on which blockchain works is not a new one. Blockchain is simply an amalgamation of cryptography, distributed system technology, peer-to-peer networking technology, and other famous and widely used technologies. Cryptocurrencies also use the blockchain network. The blockchain network acts as a secure framework for these cryptocurrencies. Due to this nobody can modify or falsify any information related to the transactions. All the nodes that are a part of the network are anonymously added to the network. This makes blockchain technology one of the widely used technologies in various fields, (e.g., financial field, medical systems, supply chain, and Internet of Things (IoT).)

Application of the blockchain technology could however result in a lot of challenges that need to be addressed. Designing the appropriate consensus protocol is also a problem. The consensus of blockchain is that all nodes maintain the same distributed ledger. Centralized servers in the past made the consensus protocol easy to implement. That is because all the nodes would be connected to one central server. This could however prove to be a huge problem in distributed systems because every node is both a host and a server. Both these nodes are supposed to exchange information with the other nodes to reach a consensus. The process of consensus could be disrupted due to offline and malicious nodes. Hence, an excellent consensus protocol can tolerate the occurrence of these phenomena and minimize the damage done so the result of the consensus remains unaffected. Another thing one needs to take care of in the consensus protocol is that you need to choose the consensus protocol that is suitable for the type of blockchain being used. Every type of blockchain has different application scenarios.

Here we shall discuss a few consensus protocols blockchain and investigate their performance and application scenarios.

Main consensus protocols

If you consider the distributed systems, you would conclude that there can never be a perfect consensus protocol for them. The consensus protocol needs to make a trade-off amongst consistency, availability, and partition fault tolerance (CAP). Here we shall discuss some popular blockchain consensus protocols that can effectively address the "Byzantine Generals Problem" in great detail.

PoW (Proof of Work): PoW protocol is implemented by Bitcoin, Ethereum, etc. PoW chooses one node to create a new block in every round of consensus by competition of the computational power. A cryptographic puzzle is required to be solved in order to become a part of the competition. A new block can be created by the node that gets done with the puzzle first. The flow of the creation of blocks in PoW is presented . The puzzle is very complex and difficult to solve. Nodes need to keep correcting the value of nonce to get the answer correct. This adjustment of the value requires huge computational power. PoW belongs to the probabilistic-finality consensus protocols since it guarantees eventual consistency.

PoS (Proof of Stake): In PoS, the creation of the new blocks by the nodes depends upon the held stake rather than the computational power. Despite this , the nodes are still required to solve a SHA256 puzzle: **SHA256(timestamp,previous hash...)<target×coin.** The basic difference between the PoW and PoS is that PoS solves this puzzle by adjusting the value of the nonce and PoS solves this puzzle by the amount of stake (coins). From this, we can say that the PoS is an energy-saving consensus protocol. It does not require a lot of computational power to reach a fair consensus. The flow of PoS is shown . Similar to that of PoW, PoS is also a probabilistic-finality consensus protocol. The very first cryptocurrency that applied the PoS to the blockchain is PPcoin. Another thing that helps in solving the puzzle along with the stake is the age of the coin. For example, if you have 10 coins for a total of 20 days, then the age of your coin is said to be 200. Whenever a node is able to create a new block, the age of the coin would drop down to zero. Additionally, Ethereum is planning its transition from PoW to PoS.

DPoS (Delegated Proof of Stake): DPoS operates on the principle that allows the nodes that hold a stake to vote to elect block verifiers or block creators. This provides the stakeholders with the right of creating blocks for the delegates they support instead of creating blocks on their own. This results in bringing their computational power consumption down to 0. The delegates are supposed to create blocks whenever it is their turn. If they are unable to do so, they would be eliminated and then selection of new nodes would take place by the stakeholders. In order to reach a fair consensus, DPoS uses the votes of the shareholders. In comparison to the PoW and PoS, DPoS is low in cost and has high inefficiency. Some of the cryptocurrencies are also approving DPoS such as BitShares, EOS, etc. The new version of EOS has turned DPoS into BFT-DPoS (Byzantine Fault Tolerance-DPoS).

PBFT(Practical Byzantine fault Tolerance):

PBFT is a Byzantine Fault Tolerance protocol with low algorithm complexity and high practicality in distributed systems. There are five phases in PBFT: request, pre-prepare, prepare, commit, and reply. The primary node sends the message that is sent by the client to the other three nodes in the network. If node 3 crashes, a single message has to go through all five phases to reach a consensus amongst these three nodes. In order to complete a successful round of consensus, these nodes reply back to the client. In every round of the consensus, PBFT makes sure that all the nodes that are involved preserve a mutual state and take stable action. The Absolute-finality of the PBFT protocol is that all the nodes achieve a mutual state and the protocol achieved what it was aimed for. Stellar is a new protocol. It is basically an improved version of the PBFT. Stellar adopts FBA (Federated Byzantine Agreement) protocol, in which nodes have the right to opt for the federation they trust to carry out the consensus process.

Ripple: Ripple is an open-source payment protocol. Transactions are commenced by clients and broadcast all over the network through tracking nodes in Ripple. In Ripple, the consensus process is done via validating nodes. Every validating node has a list known as UNL (Unique Node List). All the nodes in the UNL have the right to vote for those nodes that they are in support of.

Each validating node directs its own transactions fixed as a proposal to other validating nodes. When the proposal is received by the other validating node, it will look at each transaction in the proposal. In its local transaction set, if there exists the same transaction, the proposal would receive a single vote. The transaction would be able to enter into the other round if it was able to receive more than 50% of the votes. This number would increase for every other round. Those transactions that receive more than 80% votes will be added to the ledger. This makes Ripple is a consensus protocol that is able to achieve absolute finality.

Fault tolerance

PoW, PoS, and DPoS are probabilistic-finality protocols. The attackers would be required to gather huge computational power in order to create a long private chain to swap with a chain that is valid. In Bitcoin, an attacker would require to have a 50% fraction of the computational power to create a longer private chain. If the computational power of the attacker's fraction is more than or equal to 50%, it would destabilize the blockchain network. Like PoW, PoS and DPoS can only allow the existence of the stakeholder with less than 50% of the held stake. In PBFT, if there are a total of 3f+1 nodes in the network. The number of normal nodes must surpass 2f+1. This means that malicious or crashed nodes must be less than f. The fault tolerance of PBFT is 1/3. The fault tolerance of Ripple is only 20%, (i.e., Ripple can tolerate Byzantine problems in 20% of nodes in the entire network without affecting the precise result of consensus.)

Limitation

PoW may consume the highest computational power among these consensus protocols, and the transaction throughput per second (TPS) of Bitcoin adopting PoW is only 3–7. This speed limits the application view of PoW in real payment. PoS and DPoS also have similar inadequacies but they can help with bringing down the consumption of computational power. PBFT needs every node interacting with other nodes to exchange messages in each round of the consensus. PBFT has the highest requirements of performance for the network. There is no secrecy in PBFT as all the nodes have their identity revealed in the consensus. It requires a few seconds to finish a round of consensus Ripple. It is appropriate for the actual payment scenario. Ripple is organized and handled by some organizations which does not fulfill the decentralization nature of blockchain.

Scalability

PoW, PoS, and DPoS are relatively scalable. Although the TPS of them is not very high, there are some ways that can help improve the scalability. For example, in order to enhance its scalability bitcoin adopted a lightning network to deliver an off-chain payment. Ethereum chose sharding technology and Plasma. Both of these are layer 1 and layer 2 scaling solutions, respectively. As PBFT is appropriate for a network with fewer nodes and high performance the scalability of PBFT is inadequate. For networks that work on a large scale, Ripple can prove to be useful. TPS of Ripple is over 1500, hence Ripple has strong scalability.

Scenarios

The blockchain systems presently used can be divided into three categories. In a public blockchain, everybody has the right to be a part of the process and can view the distributed ledger. PoW, PoS, and DPoS can be applied to the public blockchain. Private blockchain and consortium blockchain fit the permissioned blockchain. Only those nodes can take part in the consensus process who have permissions. The identity of each node is known to the public in PBFT and Ripple, thus they are all appropriate for private blockchain or consortium blockchain. Private blockchains and consortium blockchains are not as decentralized. On the other hand, public blockchain is decentralized. Strong consistency and high efficiency of consensus have made them more suitable for some commercial and medical scenarios.

The steady operations of the blockchain systems are due to the consensus protocol. Via a consensus protocol, the nodes settle on a specific value or transaction. Some of the most widely used consensus protocols were discussed. Not just that but we talked about their strengths, weaknesses, and application scenarios through analysis and comparison. From the discussion above, we can conclude that it is important to design a strong consensus protocol that addresses not only good fault tolerance but also how to make it more useful in a suitable application scenario.

CONCLUSION

Blockchain technology is the new hot thing and it's here to stay. Nowadays everyone is deeply interested in blockchain technology. The majority of the investors have started to invest in this relatively new technology because they were intrigued. Computers running the same blockchain software and wanting to share data join together on a network. The data is assembled together into "blocks" for authentication as it is coming into the network. For instance, through people spending and receiving money. The computers vote on the current block of data systematically, typically every few minutes or even every few seconds deciding whether it all looks good or not. The computer votes on the overruled current block again when the next block is submitted. When the computer agrees about the validity of the data it holds, the current block is accepted, and is then added to the system's complete past history of authenticated data blocks. Hence, the data is "chained." A long chain of information is formed as a result. This process is known as the blockchain. Blockchain is also referred to as Distributed Ledger Technology (DLT). The digital ledger technology allows the history of any digital asset unable to change. It is kept transparent by using decentralization and cryptographic hashing.

Blockchains have a lot of applications in various fields. The music industry also relies a lot on this new technology. Blockchain technology is also one of the most used technologies in the game development field. There are a number of games that are based on the blockchain. These games provide the users with an opportunity to gain control over the game. Previously this was not possible as the conventional gaming industry was centralized and the whole control over the game dynamics was in the hand of the developers. Nowadays, there are multiple ways through which a player can earn from these games. Players can purchase the in-game assets as NFTs and then sell across the blockchain marketplaces. CryptoKitties, Decentraland, and Gods Unchained are a few of the most widely used blockchain-based games.

NFTs are tokens that represent your ownership over a digital asset. NFTs are becoming more and more famous with every passing day and people have started to pay attention to it as well, but they are also subjected to a lot of inspection over their carbon footprint. But NFTs are not the only ones to be blamed for this problem. However, Ethereum may use a strenuous way to secure the funds and assets but its improvement is in the works. Upon improvement, the carbon footprint of Ethereum will be 99.95% better. This would make it more energy-efficient than many existing industries.

Another important thing that you have to bear in mind is that the application of blockchain technology could result in a lot of challenges that need to be addressed. Designing the appropriate consensus protocol is a problem. The consensus of blockchain is that all nodes maintain the same distributed ledger. Centralized servers in the past made the consensus protocol easy to implement. That is because all the nodes would be connected to one central server. This could however prove to be a huge problem in distributed systems because every node is both a host and a server. Both these nodes are supposed to exchange information with the other nodes to reach a consensus. The process of consensus could be disrupted due to offline and malicious nodes. Hence, an excellent consensus protocol can tolerate the occurrence of these phenomena and minimize the damage done so the result of the consensus remains unaffected. Another thing one needs to take care of in the consensus protocol is that you need to choose the consensus protocol that is suitable for the type of blockchain being used. Every type of blockchain has different application scenarios.

You have to do your research well regarding all these protocols and other crucial things in order to choose a better consensus protocol. Blockchain technology at this point in time is blooming and there is a high chance that it will most likely be the next big thing in the future.

DECENTRALIZED FINANCE (DeFi)

Alternative To Central Banking For The Future Of Finance. How To Trade, Borrow, Lend, Save And Invest After Bitcoin & Ethereum In Cryptocurrency Peer To Peer (P2P). Lending, Yield Farming And Investing For Beginners.

By

Satoshy Nakamoto

DISCLAIMER

© Copyright 2021

Table of contents

CHAPTER

WHAT IS DECENTRALIZED FINANCE

A system that allows the availability of financial products on a public decentralized blockchain network is known as Decentralized Finance, or DeFi. This makes them open for use to anyone and there is no need for any third parties involved. In disparity to a bank account or a brokerage account, a government-issued ID, Social Security number, or proof of address are not compulsory to use DeFi. DeFi refers is a software system that allows the buyers and sellers, lenders, and borrowers to interact peer to peer. The only intermediary that may be involved in the transaction is software and not a company or a person. These software systems are based on blockchains. In order to attain decentralization a number of technologies and protocols are activated. For instance, a decentralized system is said to be a combination of open-source technologies, blockchain, and proprietary software. All these products are made available via smart contracts. Smart contracts are a piece of software that has a set of instructions that are executed after certain conditions are met. No matter which technology or platform is used these DeFi systems aim to eliminate any third parties.

This technology has numerous uses but still the DeFi technology is yet to develop properly while its infrastructure is still in the development phase.

- Decentralized finance, or DeFi, intends to practice technology in order to eliminate any third party that may be a part of the transaction otherwise.
- The elements upon which the DeFi is built are stablecoins. These stablecoins are considered to

be their use-cases. A software stack that helps in the development of applications.

- DeFi is still undergoing its development, the infrastructure and the use cases are developing with time.

The usage of technology in financial services is not a new concept. Technology is used in order to facilitate transactions in banks and other companies that offer financial services. But the role that the technology plays is limited to only helping in the facilitation of these transactions. A lot of companies are still struggling with the jargon of the authorities, they are competing with the financial markets, and different standards to make the transaction a success. DeFi has a stack of commonly implemented software protocols and public blockchains to construct them on. In the financial services industry, technology is placed at the forefront by DeFi.

DeFi is commonly positioned in the blockchain and cryptocurrencies domain. However, the scope of DeFi is not limited to this domain only. They are widely used. Decentralized finance is the future and in order to understand the need for such systems, it is highly important that we know the current situation of the finance sector.

The "Hub and spoke" model provides the base of the new financial infrastructure. Important economic centers of activity, like New York and London, operate as hubs for the financial services industry and influence economic activity at spokes. These are the regional centers sometimes referred to as financial powerhouses like Mumbai or Milan. These hubs may not be as important worldwide but they are considered to be important for their respective economies.

Economic prosperity or hardship goes beyond hubs to spokes. It is directed to move towards the international economy. This is a model of interdependency. This model of interdependency is recurrent for global financial services corporations to operate well. The headquarters are located in the hubs and local branches, partnerships, or investments all around the world. Expanding their operations funds the organization on its own. However, it is focusing on the set of laws regulations in every financial institution. These institutions have become important in order to expand the outreach of balance of the global economy. New financial services infrastructure would be birthed as a result.

This model worked the best in the past but now times have changed. Presently the financial crisis and, then, the Great Recession, exposed plenty of flaws in the architecture.

Centralized models were very commonly used in the past. Now slowly and gradually these models are being replaced by decentralized models. The models that are responsible for decentralized finance use the technology that eliminates any middlemen that may be a part of the transactions. This allows them to let anyone use the financial services anywhere no matter what the age, ethnicity, and cultural identity of a person is. DeFi services and apps are created on public blockchains, and they either duplicate the offerings that currently exist or they offer innovative services custom-designed for the DeFi ecosystem. This lets the users have more power and authority over their money. This power is given to them by the usage of personal wallets and trading services that overtly cater to individual users instead of institutions.

2

CHAPTER

WHAT ARE THE COMPONENTS OF DEFI?

If you consider the components of DeFi you will realize that they are all similar to the present financial ecosystems. This means that you need to have stable currencies and diversity of the usecases as well. Crypto exchanges, lending services, and stablecoins are converted into the DeFi components. In order for these services to work efficiently, it is required for smart contracts to deliver a framework. That is because the terms and conditions are all a part of the code that is written into the smart contracts. Let's consider an example here, a smart contract code has a set of programming instructions, this piece of code has those terms and conditions of loan between two parties. Collateral is liquidated if any of the terms are not met. This process takes place via a code and not manually.

A decentralized finance system is made up of different elements. These elements have their place in a software stack. Every component of the system is directed to perform a particular task in order to build the De-Fi system. Composability is a key feature of the stack. That is so because the components of each layer can be put together and then form a DeFi application.

Below are the four layers that make up the DeFi stack:

Settlement Layer: The settlement layer is referred to as Layer 0. That is because it is the base layer of the DeFi transactions. It comprises a public blockchain and the cryptocurrency that it uses. All those transactions that happen over the DeFi applications use this currency, this currency is not always traded in the market. An example that explains the settlement layer is Ethereum and its native token ether (ETH). ETH is used in trading at the crypto exchanges. There are tokenized versions of the assets in the settlement layer as well. For instance, the U.S. dollar, or tokens that represent the real-world assets in a digital form.

Protocol Layer: The protocols that are used to administer certain tasks and activities are known as software protocols. These software protocols are widely accepted as standards. The protocols that are implemented are considered to be interoperable. These protocols can be used by a number of entities simultaneously in order to design a service or an app. The protocol layer offers liquidity to the DeFi network. Synthetix is an instance of the DeFi protocol. Synthetix is a derivatives trading protocol on Ethereum. Synthetix is used in the creation of synthetic kinds of real-world assets

Application Layer: Looking at the name of this layer, we know that it is the layer that is closest to the consumers. On this layer, there are applications that are consumer-facing. The applications on the physical layer abstract underlying protocols into simple consumer-focused services. A lot of applications in the cryptocurrency network like the decentralized cryptocurrency exchanges and lending services reside on this layer.

Aggregation Layer: In order to provide a service to the investors, there are a number of aggregators that are found on the aggregation layer. These aggregators link together the applications from the preceding layer. For example, they would make the money transfer process smooth between financial instruments so the returns are maximized. If these were to happen in a physical environment it would take a lot of time to get done with the paperwork. A technology-based framework would make the whole process of investing rails seamless. This is done by permitting traders to move to the other services in a short span of time. An example of a service that exists on the aggregation level is the lending and borrowing service. Banking services and crypto wallets are other services that can be found on the aggregation level.

The Current State of DeFi

This technology of decentralized finance is relatively new and is constantly evolving as the technology does. As of March 2021, the overall value that is locked in DeFi contracts is more than $41 billion. The overall value that is locked can be calculated by multiplication of the total number of tokens that are inside a protocol with its worth in Dollars. The overall figure for DeFi may be extensive but it is significant to remember that because there is the absence of it adequate liquidity and volume for crypto trading in these DeFi tokens. Thus, it is hypothetical and estimated.

The number of hacks and scams that happen in the DeFi network. DeFi "rug pulls," are a common practice in which hackers ditch a protocol of funds and investors are not able for trading. Conversely, there exist a few protocols which can help with minimizing this risk.

The decentralized and distributed nature of the DeFi systems exposes it to a number of problems to the current financial regulation. The laws that are presently implemented use separate financial jurisdictions in which each has its own laws and rules. Borderless transaction over the DeFi system dispenses questions of important nature for this regulation. For example, who is guilty of a financial crime that occurs across borders, protocols, and DeFi apps?

Another sector that concerns the DeFi regulation is smart contracts. Besides the success of bitcoin, DeFi is considered as an example of the "code is law" thesis. In this, a set of rules are implemented via an immutable code. It represents the law. The algorithm on which smart contract is based is encoded with the essential concepts and terms of use to carry out a transaction. There may be a number of other reasons as to why the software systems fail.

CHAPTER

HISTORY OF DEFI POTENTIAL

From Inception to 2021 And Beyond

This content will prove helpful in making you understand what DeFi is, starting from its birth and how would the future look like for this technology.

Let's begin from the very start.

There is no specific date upon which we can say DeFi was invented. However, a few major developments led to the invention of the DeFi system.

Bitcoin

Bitcoin was the very first cryptocurrency invented back in the year 2009 by a *pseudo-anonymous alias Satoshi Nakamoto.*

The invention of bitcoin led to the overall cryptocurrency industry and decentralized finance is a portion of it. There are discussions over the topic if bitcoin can be categorized as DeFi or not.

Bitcoins lets its users send payments to any part of the world in a decentralized way. Payment is however a part of the finance industry, which advanced as DeFi.

Bitcoin led to the creation of Ethereum. Ethereum is the blockchain that has all the DeFi protocols.

Ethereum

You can send bitcoin to anyone in any part of the world but this is not the only thing. Every efficient financing system has a few important services to provide its users. These services include lending, borrowing, trading, funding, or derivatives.

Bitcoin used the programming language called script. This language limited the uses of bitcoin and made it inappropriate for these applications. This was the reason, Ethereum was created in the first place.

Ethereum was launched in the year 2015. Ever since the launch of Ethereum, it has been the talk of the town and has attracted a lot of investors and developers. These developers were interested in Ethereum so they are able to build decentralized applications from games to financial applications.

The programming language used by Ethereum is Solidity and the standard uses the ERC standard protocol. They created their own tokens and gave birth to a smart contract platform.

Maker

Maker is considered to be the oldest DeFi project on Ethereum.

DAI or a decentralized stablecoin can be created by using the maker protocol. The project was designed by Rune Christensen in the year 2014. Rune Christensen took inspiration from another project BitShares. Bitshares was created by Dan Larimer.

Maker was launched back in 2017. The funding that was required to develop the protocol was provided by Venture Capital. The first iteration of the protocol known as the Single Collateral DAI has sustained ETH as collateral. Another version was launched in late 2019 after the first version was extended to Multi Collateral DAI.

Even today, Maker is one of the most significant projects in the DeFi network as well as innovators of the entire decentralized finance space.

EtherDelta

EtherDelta is another project that was very famous back in 2019.

EtherDelta was one of the very first decentralized exchanges that were built on Ethereum. EtherDelta endorsed permission less in exchange for ERC20 tokens.

The security of the EtherDelta exchange was compromised after it was hacked in late 2017.

Unluckily, the exchange was hacked at the end of 2017. The hacker after accessing the frontend of the exchange website. Hackers directed the users to a phishing site and stole about $800k from them.

Not just that but in 2018 the person who founded EtherDelta was charged by the SEC. He was charged for running a security exchange that has not been regulated.

ICOs

ICO's are the first usecase of Ethereum. They became extremely popular in the year 2017.

The projects that were newly created back in the day began offering their self-created tokens and not ETH. Hypothetically decentralized fundraising was not entirely a bad idea it still ended up in a number of bad in theory, it resulted in multiple publicized projects. These projects raised a lot of money.

Some of the most noticeable and distinguished projects back in the times of ICO are as follows:

- Aave – This protocol can be helpful in the process of lending and borrowing
- Synthetix – It was known as Havven in the past. It is a protocol for derivatives.

- REN – REN was known as Republic Protocol in the past. It can be proved helpful in providing access to the liquidity between different blockchains.
- Kyber Network – This is an on-chain liquidity protocol
- 0x – This is a protocol that is used to enable the peer-to-peer exchange of assets. It is an open protocol.
- Bancor – This is also an on-chain liquidity protocol

This is a fascinating fact that the majority of the protocols and projects that were made during the time when ICOs had a bad reputation are now considered to be the top ones in the DeFi network.

One of the significant innovations that happened at the time was the notion of users interacting with smart contracts that had pooled funds from a number of users, rather than interacting directly with other users.

This gave birth to a new "user-to-contract" model. This model proved to be more useful for decentralized applications. That is because didn't need as many interactions with the underlying blockchain as the user-to-user model.

Post the ICO mania, the bear market came into action. DeFi had a comparatively quiet period. That is how everything looked on the surface. But in reality majority of the DeFi protocols were made during that time.

This is often referred to as a time "Before COMP".

Below are a few other important protocols that were built and other important incidents that took place discussed during that time.

Before COMP

The very first version of the Uniswap published to the Ethereum mainnet was back in 2018. The creator of Uniswap worked tirelessly over it for almost a year and was able to do what he intended. If you look at the DeFi network, you would realize that Uniswap is an important project in this regard. Unlike EtherDelta, Uniswap was built focusing on the concept of liquidity pools and automated market makers (AMM). The grant for the Ethereum foundation helped in the complete funding of the Uniswap.

The first liquidity was launched by Synthetix in July of 2019. It was considered to be one of the most important events that happened. But it did not stop here, Synthetix was able to launch their first liquidity incentive program soon after the first launch. This launch also helped with the DeFi Summer of 2020.

Not just that but there are a number of other protocols of DeFi projects launched as well. These projects launched their protocols on the Ethereum mainnet. This launch happened somewhere between 2018 and 2019. Compound, REN, Kyber, and 0x were included as well.

Black Thursday

A drastic drop in the price of Ethereum crypto currency was noted in March of 2020. It plunged by 30% in a time span of 24 hours. This drop in the price of ETH happened due to the fear that the pandemic instilled among people.

This was a major setback for the DeFi industry which is still an incipient one. There have been multiple other setbacks to the industry as well. Like the gas fee of Ethereum jumped through the sky and reached an all-time high. The Ethereum gas fee raised over 200 gwei. This led to a lot of users increasing their collateral in loans or trading between assets.

The protocol known as Maker was drastically affected by this event. The value of ETH dropped as well due to the liquidations instigated by the users. ETH collateral losing its value led to Keeper bots. These are external players that cause liquidations by being capable to bid 0 DAI for the ETH collateral that was auctioned. This resulted in a huge shortage of around $4M worth of ETH. This was then given accommodation by creating and auctioning additional Maker's MKR tokens.

Events like Black Thursday can be very disastrous but they are a way to make the DeFi system strong so it is not vulnerable.

This led to a time period where DeFi grew successively. This time period is known as the DeFi Summer.

DeFi Summer

The compound launched COMP tokens in May of 2020. This led to the liquidity mining program which resulted in the DeFi Summer.

Whenever the DeFi users lend or borrow using the compound, they are able to earn rewards in return. These additional motivations, which were provided in the form of COMP tokens led to the stock and borrow APYs for various tokens raising drastically. This also made it possible to create yield farming. That is because the users were provided with incentives to switch on and off between borrowing and lending different tokens in order to have the best yield.

After this wave, a lot of other protocols were made. These protocols would issue their tokens through liquidity leading to more opportunities for yield farming.

Compound governance was created as a result, where users with COMP tokens are able to cast votes for various changes that are suggested to be made in the protocol. Compound's governance model was then used again by several other DeFi projects.

Yearn Finance is another important and one of the major protocols of the DeFi.

Andre Cronje developed Yearn Finance in the year 2020. Yearn Finance is a protocol that deals with the optimization of the yield and increasing the abilities of DeFi by automatically switching between different lending protocols.

In order to decentralize Yearn Finance more, Andre handed out a governance token in July of 2020.

The token that was created was handed out through liquidity mining. It gave away no VCs, no funder rewards, no dev rewards. This model was very famous among the DeFi community as money was being collected in the incentivized liquidity pools topping $600M. This was the worth in locked value.

The price of the token started from around $6 when it initially got listed on Uniswap, to over $30,000. All this happened in under 2 months.

In similarity to the majority of the revolutionary and innovative projects in DeFi after Yearn's success, a lot of other similar projects were launched with little changes to make them different.

Ampleforth was another project that started gaining more power with every passing day due to the unique elastic supply model.

Yam which is a DeFi protocol was used for this model to be borrowed and reiterated.

Yam took 10 days of development and development and was launched on the 11th of August 2020.

YAM tokens were distributed in the essence of YFI. This led to this particular protocol being able to appeal to a lot of liquidity.

People who owned COMP, LEND, LINK, MKR, SNX, and YFI were remunerated for staking their tokens on the Yam platform. This was because the developers wanted the protocol to interest the DeFi community.

A day post the launch, a bug was discovered in the rebase mechanism. The total liquidity generated $0.5B of total value locked in the protocol. The bug affected only a share of liquidity providers in one pool only. The pool that was affected yCRV-YAM. This was the reason that people were no longer interested in Yam. However, they relaunched the protocol but still, Yam was not able to become successful.

Afterward came SushiSwap. SushiSwap was launched in the latter half of 2020. It was developed by a team that did not disclose its identity and chose to remain anonymous. A new concept was presented in SushiSwap. It was named a Vampire attack. It works on tapping the liquidity out of Uniswap.

SushiSwap was able to gather liquidity of $1B. This was so because the people who provided liquidity were given Sushi tokens in return.

Later, the ChefNomi who is said to be the main developer of SushiSwap sold all the Sushi tokens. Due to this, the protocol was able to take the majority of the liquidity of Uniswap to a new platform.

A number of other projects were launched with food names after Yam and Sushi. We had Pasta, Spaghetti, Kimchi, HotDog to name a few. The name used collectively for all these was food DeFi or food finance. Almost all of them were able to attract users for a day or two and then they would eventually lose interest. They all failed.

There were a lot of events that happened during the DeFi Summer. One of them was the launching of the Uniswap token. It was called UNI. All those users that used Uniswap and the liquidity providers of Uniswap were rewarded with a reviewing airdrop, the worth of which was $1k. Uniswap also began its program for mining liquidity. This interested a lot of people who were able to collect more than $2B in liquidity. The majority of this liquidity was taken back from SushiSwap.

The important and significant metrics of the DeFi network enhanced greatly in the DeFi Summer.

The monthly volume of Uniswap raised went from $169M in April 2020 to over $15B in September 2020. This raised over a hundred folds.

The overall worth of the locked-in DeFi went from $800M in April to $10B in September. This increased almost 10 folds.

Bitcoin also saw a great increase. The expanse of Bitcoin progressed to Ethereum went from 20,000 in April to about 60,000 in September. This increased 3x.

DeFi Winter

DeFi saw a great increase. It climbed higher but that was not something that could have sustained for long. Soon after the change in the market sentiment, the majority of the top tokens of the DeFi tokens lost their worth. The yields from liquidity mining that are consequent to the value of the tokens that were handed out also started to fall and became lower with every passing day. The DeFi Winter has come.

The negative sentiment of the market spanned for almost 2 months. The months of September and October brought no good news for the DeFi market. All this while the developers were working continuously on designing more protocols.

In the month of November, the DeFi market reached its rock bottom. A few of the protocols were being traded with a loss of 70-90%. It was hard to believe that these are the same protocols that were on a high just two months ago.

Post a speedy recovery of over 50% the DeFi market started climbing high again.

All throughout the DeFi Winter, the volume of Uniswap continued abundantly higher in comparison to early 2020. The whole value that is locked in DeFi kept climbing up and was able to cross $15B.

There were major setbacks that the DeFi industry faced in the year 2020. Yet there were some like bZx, Harvest, Akropolis, Pickle, Cover, and others to name a few of them.

It was observed that in the late months of 2020, that the worth of bitcoin had gotten to an all-time high breaking all its previous records. This indicated that a parabolic run was soon to be expected for the DeFi.

Future

If you consider the future of bitcoin, well, it looks bright.

DeFi developers are constantly working on the development of new projects.

Ethereum 2.0 is also in the works which would make the whole system much more scalable. Layer 2 solutions and several other blockchains are in the works as well. This will let more and more people become a part of the DeFi ecosystem.

Competition between DeFi on Layer 2, DeFi on Ethereum 2.0, DeFi on Bitcoin, and DeFi on other chains will as well prove to be a defining factor. Interoperability protocols and cross-chain liquidity may gain a lot of importance as well.

Exploration of areas like credit delegation and under-collateralized or non-collateralized loans is also on a rise.

You will soon be able to understand all this in the future.

CHAPTER

DEFI VS TRADITIONAL FINANCE

You can see the true potential that the DeFi holds only if you know and understand the prevalent problems.

- Not everyone is granted access to set up a bank account or benefit from using financial services.
- The deficiency of access to financial services can stop a lot of people from being usable.
- You can get blocked from getting paid by the financial services.
- You have to provide your personal data as a charge to these financial services.
- Governments and centralized institutions have the authority to shut down the markets whenever they wish.
- You can only trade during business hours of a specific time zone.
- As these processes are all conducted by humans, it may take time for your money transfers to be a success.
- You have to pay extra money so the intermediaries get paid as well.

Comparison between DeFi and traditional finance:

DeFi	Traditional finance
You are in charge of your money.	Companies are in charge of your money.
You are in control of your money and it's up to you where you spend it.	The companies are in control and you have to trust them with your money.

Funds transfers happen within minutes.	Payments can take days due to manual processes.
Transaction activity is nameless.	Your identity is known and it is ensured in all Financial activities.
Anyone can use DeFi.	Not everyone can have used it. You need to apply first.
The markets are running 24/7.	Markets close because employees need breaks.
It is a transparent network	Such systems have little to no transparency.

It started with Bitcoin...

Bitcoin in the majority of ways was regarded as the first DeFi application. Through bitcoin, you can own and have complete control over the currency and can send it all across the globe. This helps by providing a way for a huge number of people to come to an agreement on a ledger of accounts with no third party involved. All these people may not trust each other as well. No one has the right and authority to modify any of the rules of bitcoin, that is because it is openly available. These rules are written into blockchain technology. The rules include its scarcity and open nature among others.

Ethereum builds on this. Similar to that of bitcoin, everyone has access to Ethereum and thus the rules can't change on you. Via smart contracts, you can program this digital currency and not just store or send it only.

Programmable money

Programmable money is the default and built-in characteristic of tokens run on Ethereum. Programming the payments into logic makes the money programmable and absolutely anyone can do this. This allows you to have the control and security of Bitcoin diversified with the services that are provided by financial institutions. This enables you to do those things with it that you are unable to do with the bitcoin. It allows you to lend and borrow money, schedule payments, etc.

What can you do with DeFi?

The majority of the financial services have replacements that are decentralized. Ethereum produces chances for the creation of financial products that are entirely new and innovative. This list keeps expanding.

- Send money around the globe
- Stream money around the globe
- Access stable currencies
- Borrow funds with collateral
- Borrow without collateral
- Start crypto savings
- Trade tokens
- Grow your portfolio
- Fund your ideas
- Buy insurance
- Manage your portfolio

Send money around the globe quickly

Ethereum is a great way of carrying out transactions globally. These transactions are a safe and secure way to transfer funds internationally. Bitcoin and Ethereum have made sending money across the globe a very easy and hassle-free process. Provide the ENS name of your recipient or their account address from your wallet and your payment will go directly to them all within a very short span of time. A wallet is essential if you wish to send or receive payments.

Stream money around the globe...

Streaming money over Ethereum is now a common practice. This makes you able to pay their salary. This is possible at that very instant when you provide them with access to money that is yours. You can provide them with this access whenever they require it. Streaming ETH can modify its value a lot. If you don't want to do that you can use stablecoins.

Access stable currencies

The major problem for the majority of financial products is the instability of cryptocurrencies. This problem has been solved by the DeFi community by introducing stablecoins. Their value stays fixed to some other asset.

Coins such as DAI or USDC have worth that remains within a few cents of a dollar. That is why these coins are impeccable for earning or retail. Using stablecoins is a brilliant way to protect and secure their savings. People of Latin America have implemented this and used stablecoins when the currencies issued by the government faced uncertain situations.

Borrowing

You can borrow money from the vendors who deal with the decentralized money in two ways:

- Peer-to-peer, is when the borrower will borrow directly from a specific lender. The process is direct with no intermediary involved.
- Pool-based where lenders offer funds or liquidity to a pool. The ones who want to borrow the money can borrow from the pool.

Using a decentralized lender has many benefits.

Borrowing with privacy

Presently, lending and borrowing money are all about the people who are a part of it. Even in the banks, you are not granted a loan till the bank is gets satisfied that you are capable of paying back the loan.

In a decentralized exchange of money or goods, you don't have to make your identity known. The borrower will have to settle for collateral in case the borrower is unable to repay and that collateral will automatically be received by the lender. You can use NFTs as collateral as well. NFTs are a representation of the ownership of digital assets.

This way you can lend and borrow money without giving away any of your personal information.

Access to global funds

You have access to all the funds that are globally deposited. They are not restricted to only those funds that are in the custody of the bank or institution. Due to this, the loaning process has become much easier. Also, there has been a great improvement seen in the interest rates.

Tax-efficiencies

Tax efficiencies are improved as you don't have to sell your ETH in case you need money. You can simply borrow it as a loan. ETH is a taxable entity. If you wish to have a stablecoin loan, ETH can be used as collateral for that. With this, you are able to retain your ETH and also get some money to keep everything running. Stablecoins don't swing in worth and value as Ethereum does, so it is better to have some stablecoins when you are in need of money.

Flash loans

In flash loans, you can loan money without any collateral or by sharing any personal information.

Within the same transaction, the loan can be borrowed as well as paid back. This is the concept upon which flash loans work. If the one who borrows is not able to return the loan to the lender, the transaction returns.

There are big pools of funds that can be used for borrowing money from. This helps those people to borrow money from the pool in case of need. In flash loans, borrowers can loan money from the liquidity pools and then repay the loan back at the same time.

Flash loans can also be used to borrow asset at one exchange and then sell it for higher money in some other exchange.

Below are the steps that happen in every transaction of a flash loan.

- X amount of $asset at $1.00 is loaned by you from an exchange A
- X $asset is sold by you on an exchange B for $1.10
- The loan is paid back by you to the exchange A
- You retain the profit generated; this does not include the fee of the transaction.

The transaction would not be successful in case the supply of exchange B plunges low and the user is not able to pay back the loan originally taken.

You would be required to have a large sum of money if you want to become able to the example explained above. Those who have a lot of wealth presently can take advantage of these strategies for money-making. Flash loans are an instance of a future where having money is not automatically required to make money.

Start saving with crypto

Lending

You can also lend your crypto currencies if you are looking for ways to expand your funds. Interest rates are climbing higher and you will get more than what your banks are giving.

Below is an example to better understand this:

You loan your 100 Dai. Dai is a stablecoin, to an invention such as Aave.

- You get 100 Aave Dai (aDai) in return. This is a token that denotes the loaned Dai.
- The aDai in your possession will upsurge centered around the rates of interest. At this point, the balance that is stored in your wallet will rise. Reliant on the APR, your wallet balance will show 100.1234 after some days or maybe hours.
- You will have the complete right to take out an amount of regular Dai which is equal to your aDai balance at that particular instant.

No-loss lotteries

PoolTogether is no-loss lotteries are an innovative new way to save money.

- Using 100 Dai tokens you purchase 100 tickets.
- In return, you receive 100 plDai. These represent the 100 tickets you purchased.
- If the ticket you possess is elected as a winner, your plDai balance will upsurge by the volume of the prize pool.
- If you are unable to win, the pIDai that you had gotten in return will move to the draw happening in the subsequent week.
- You can take out an amount of regular Dai equals your plDai balance at all times.

Exchange tokens

There are a huge number of tokens on the Ethereum platform. You are allowed to trade your tokens whenever you want via decentralized exchanges. You will have complete authority over your assets. The DeFi markets are always open. There will always be someone available to accept the trade in a decentralized market, unlike conventional transactions.

For example, you will have to require a token as Dai and USDC in order to use the no-loss lottery PoolTogether. You can interchange your ETH tokens for those tokens and back again when you're finished using DEXs.

Advanced trading

If some trader wants to have more control, for that purpose there are options for that. Everything can be done from Limit orders, perpetual, margin trading, etc. Trading in a decentralized environment will grant you access to global liquidity. The benefits are that the market is open 24/7 and you have control over your assets at all times.

The assets in the centralized exchange are at risk because after you deposit them over there, you have to trust the exchange to look after them for you and not misuse it.

Grow your portfolio

Products for managing your funds will help you in expanding your portfolio based on a strategy. This is an automatic process and everyone can use it if they wish to. There will be no third party involved wanting to get paid for the profits you generate.

Let's consider the example of the DeFi Pulse Index fund (DPI). DPI is a fund that balances your funds automatically ensures your portfolio always includes the top DeFi tokens by market capitalization. You don't have to manage all the information.

Fund your ideas

If you consider crowdfunding, Ethereum is considered to be the ideal platform.

Ethereum and the tokens that come with it are open and thus, investors from all across the globe can use it.

The whole system is transparent and you can track everything. All the funds that have been spent can be tracked using the system.

Automatic refunds can be set up as well. An example of this can be a specific deadline and minimum amount that isn't met.

Quadratic funding

Ethereum is open source software and the community has funded a lot of work it has done. This helped in the expansion of a model known as quadratic funding.

Quadratic funding is a way to ensure that those projects get the most funds that are in demand and of a unique nature. Below is how the project works.

Matching pools of funds are donated.

A round of public funding starts.

The demand for a project can be shown by donating money.

Once the round gets completed, the matching pool is spread among the projects. A matching pool is given to those projects that have a high demand.

This shows that Project A with 100 donations of 1 dollar could end up getting more funds in comparison to Project B with one donation of 10,000 dollars

Insurance

The main objective of decentralized insurance is to make insurance cheaper, faster to pay out, and more transparent. If the insurance process is made automatic that would make the coverage more affordable and pay-outs are faster.

Ethereum may have bugs that can be exploited by scammers. That is why these insurance products are used to make sure that the funds of the users are protected. However, there are projects that are starting to build out coverage for everything that can happen.

Aggregators and portfolio managers

This space is always buzzing. In order to make sure everything is coordinated and done right you need a way to help you with all this. You will also require an approach to keep track of all your investments, loans, and trades. There are multiple products that can help you with managing all your activities and investments in the DeFi network. The open architecture of the DeFi network is also a great help in this regard. Teams create interfaces where you are able to keep a track of all your balances across the products but you can use the features they provide too. Exploring and understanding the DeFi more will make it more useful for you.

CHAPTER

UNDERSTANDING DECENTRALIZATION MYTHS

According to the Netflix documentary, Startup cryptocurrency was originated in 1972. Financial protests began against the laws that overtaxed metals like stocks. Security was finally provided in 1976 in the form of Dual Sig Confirmation, created by Whit Difee and Martin Hellman. This is a process that requires signatures, to both send and receives money and messages. A website with a black, brown, yellow, and white theme was created by The Bitcoin Co. ltd. of Thailand to sell loyalty tokens for websites, which overthrew the "cash cow" which was only a gambling chip for rich tech people.

Then came the "Bitcoin", which replicated the regulatory layer of finance. Since the users are not autonomous nations such as Germany, Seminole Creek, etc. this fact makes cryptocurrency a derivative or security. Satoshi Nakamoto viewed the benefits of Bitcoin that can be traded publicly but could not distinguish between Bitcoin and cryptocurrency.

The people who plagiarize stuff on the internet, gaining control of all the networks and tools, put forward on their own the minor details of the problem that are included in the website that they plunder. Even though their viewpoint assures more but creates the following of a growing number of opponents. As people were made aware of Nakamoto's plans, splinter groups resembling an anemone were laid by Nakamoto, which resulted in the mass spread of cryptocurrencies & blockchains everywhere. It would have been an impeccable camouflage (the 2014 ICO Boom) for the attempt of the group at a coup on the United States, but failed when the boon of the industry was doubted as treachery by the US and Cicada stayed legally latent.

Even though I am not aware of the true initiative of Cicada but what I do know is that Cicada and Henrici are inclined to question in contradiction the ways of peace established. Similarly, Nakamoto questioned against the established ways of finance. With Nakamoto's paper began the Decentralized myth in cryptocurrency which meant that the government controlling the worth of value wouldn't be good. Like stocks, the governmental regulations do not determine the value of Bitcoin but instead, it gets its value from the values of its enterprise.

Nakamoto, whose identity nobody knows, through his name into the woodworks of an enterprise. Hypothetically an enterprise talking to a government. In order to control law enforcement high crime subsidies, in 2005 the United States was on the outlook for financial services. President Bush was counseled by his advisors to take notice of the usefulness of the storage of the value Bitcoin possessed, but it was a small-scale company and hence it didn't fit the desires of the American public.

The Homeland Security Act's Byrne Justice Assistance Grant was the winner of the competition for law enforcement. Robert Byrne of VA who was an ambulance chaser started this and it has been the hole in the bowl leaking America's funding. The first payment was made by the grant in 2006 with $6 billion being paid to the 17 states with peaking crime rates. The following year our Treasury secretary and a few of his pals start price-fixing credit ratings for promissory notes.

His action is conceivable only if the Nakamoto paper belittles governments and the funding of high crime states for having high crime are all about money, which they were. This action ended up collapsing three industries i.e., Banking, Housing, and Automobiles.

Successively, there was a scarcity of jobs in not only America but the world too.

Satoshi Nakamoto went underground and was never heard from again. Further calamity was caused in America as the money used to subsidize law enforcement high-crime grants could not be used to fortify banks, so naturally, America had to ask for money. The promoting businesses, who were held accountable for this catastrophe received money, which resulted in businesses coming up and discovering new ways to fund the catastrophe (Oil Surplus) to accept bailout similar to the promoting businesses. All those who actually contributed to this catastrophe would come across a calamity from their own business plans but Bitcoin would prove to be a savior for a few.

2008 has Bitcoin catch traction with the introduction of Reddit and 4Chan. This turned Bitcoin into a cryptocurrency used to gamble, buy chat room game collectibles, buy NFTs, which was soon followed with it being assumed "real-world" value with the initial "transaction" when for 10,000 Bitcoin, two large Pizzas were bought from Papa Johns. Which was followed by the big leagues as the designer NFTs and the Pizza story turned into a bizarre art and costly electronics out of China. The Casinos of the Chinese Islands were told that they needed to be a part of the act, so they built an online casino that only accepted Bitcoin

At present, Decentralized Autonomous Organization (DAO) has the ownership of numerous cryptocurrencies of their own, not Bitcoin. Even though loyalty is centralized, Bitcoin is still used at the Casinos for loyalty tokens. Their point is that they are their own business and it didn't take long to understand that, nor did it matter.

The significant concept of the decentralized myth is Loyalty. Initially sold as a loyalty token Bitcoin became the target of attempted plagiarism which ended up stealing a 99% share of the market awareness. It was sheer luck that the remaining 1% turned into such a strong network of finance which was equivalent in wealth to the economy of Venezuela, the 6th largest economy in the world. The aggressive attempt certainly had a windfall, and market analysis anticipates regulation to end the oppression and create a strategy for mass adoption.

Bitcoin is not Satoshi Nakamoto as a BX in Thailand, as proved by regulatory issues. Policies like AML/KYC, introduced by governments to capture Satoshi Nakamoto were utilized Bitcoin's home exchange. Additionally, determining projects such as Civic by Roger, Ver, or Pavo by IBM, within cryptocurrency seek to do business with governments. Laws of all the top 10 nations with well-developed economies permit the fair trade of cryptocurrency under-regulated measures which is the description of regulated by a central bank.

The dominant philosophy of the decentralized myth that started with the publishing of the Satoshi Nakamoto paper was to upkeep misconduct by derestricting currency. The weakness was that the governments have money as well.

Though the decentralized myth did give us some positive outcomes. Firstly, the elucidation of how transaction processing was crowdsourced by Bitcoin through publicly outsourcing mining algorithms procreated the concept of crowdsourcing. Crowd-funding was acclaimed as a harmless method of finance while the Initial Coin Offerings (ICOs) were thought of as evil.

$200 million was gathered by the ICO market in the year 2017, which was its peak time. But unfortunately, it also brought a lot of fraud and scams. Out of all the ICOs that collected the money barely half of them started doing business. Since it was free money, there were no accountabilities if you didn't raise enough. It wasn't expected for the cryptocurrency to go any farther than video games and the internet unless it had a blockchain.

2018 was the revolutionary year because this was the time when every project was unexpectedly in need of a real-world application. Cryptocurrency and Bitcoin was no longer just a token for video games but instead, it was an entire financial instrument. The products related to agriculture presently had validation of freshness and were followed by augmented reality games and artificial intelligence.

2019 witnessed the dirty business of manipulation and deregulation. Manipulation is all about setting up others just so your chances are better. In cryptocurrency, manipulation was all about the fights regarding the decentralized myth with the biggest question being about mass adoption. "Bitcoin Purists" were in favor of upholding the instability of the currency to keep the hedging long, while finance-minded organizations were in favor of stabilizing the currency. The gamers and coders and had the power to diverge the steadiness and ensure volatility. The BCC fork was more of an inspiration to Congress for needing a diverse structure for the tax for a few businesses. So, we can say that deregulation of the cryptocurrency created more users in a way. This is something that would flame the arguments that shaped the modern cryptocurrency exchange.

Now according to the AML/KYC policies, the US has to tax structures for Bitcoin businesses who envisioned the 'deregulation' as the position the industry would stand on going into the next decade, and over 34,000 crypto exchanges. To the public eye, the word decentralized has developed into an occurrence that is greater than cryptocurrency... crowdsourcing.

But crowdsourcing is only one of the concepts of decentralization. The deleterious aspect that was discovered by the myth has both good and bad consequences. On one hand, crime is being lured into the industry. Cryptocurrency is seen by many as a way out of an undesirable lifecycle, while according to those in finance who are wise, the myth is drafting criminals for an overthrow plot, which is similar to the chance taken by Pro-Trump demonstrators when attacking the capital.

The only real danger posed by the myth was that it was supposed to target governments so that companies like General Motors could protest against the government until being given a bailout. All in all, decentralization took on more significance than the threat posed on the world by Lee Iacocca. Lee Iacocca wanted to build every car driven and own every business. And he would go to any limits to achieve his aim and nothing would stop him to accomplish what he wished for and wanted, not even a forged racial identity.

Blockchain is not a threat:

Media and pundits alike are inspired by cryptocurrencies and their fundamental technology – the blockchain.

Since the technological setup of the blockchain is complex and would confuse not only the average reader but the crypto-lovers too, they might not be acquainted with the financial terminology and payment infrastructure.

Due to this unfamiliarity, many persistent myths have been born that have reinforced most blockchain discussions. Most of these myths are either wrong or too one-dimensional and, thus they cloud the aptitude of decision-makers to make judgments and ability to reach conclusions.

There are three tangled assumptions that jointly fuel the argument regarding blockchain technology breaking banks.

Myth 1: "Open blockchains rather than closed will power tomorrow's economy"

The main reason for the spread of blockchain technology was the excitement and enthusiasm of people about getting rid of banks. When Bitcoin was created in 2008, due to the financial crisis the following of blockchain technology grew rapidly. A solution to the financial system run by big financers was presented in the form of the technical arrangement of Bitcoin and its decentralized nature it has. Although it was later seen that decentralization was not mandatory for a blockchain.

There are two general major blockchain setups:

- Centralized or "closed"
- Decentralized or "open"

Every blockchain system has a system of multiple nodes to upkeep a ledger instead of having a middleman. This shows that the blockchain system is distributed. In decentralized ("open") no node is advantaged over the others by the algorithm. On the contrary, in centralized ("closed") chains some nodes are given more weightage than others.

In a decentralized blockchain- like Bitcoin, where everybody can participate in verifying transactions and each node carries the same weight.

Though, there is not always a precise discrepancy. In Ripple, one out of the three major crypto coins, the degree of centralization is still debated and disputed upon within the industry. The case with it as a blockchain is similar, the transactions that are recorded are not piled up as blocks, instead, they look like a large ledger. So the question arises, why does this distinction matter?

There are many limitations to the original, decentralized model. Some of these include the unmaintainable energy-consumption, the unapproachable necessary scale, the usability a pain, and regulation a thing to be circumvented by design, financial transactions taking far too long, moreover the currency problems faced by crypto-coins and this can lead us to understand the cynicism of many officials. All these weaknesses and limitations could have been eliminated in the centralized blockchains as the majority of the financial institutions regard it as the model of choice.

Despite all this why is the hype around the open blockchain? This technological disagreement is indicative of a deep ideological split at the center of the blockchain debate. On one side, there are officials of the banking and payments world, whereas on the other side what we see is an unusual coalition of crypto-evangelists, anarcho-libertarians, entrepreneurs, and fraudsters who are set for the commotion. The concluding group characterizes the founders and early adopters of the blockchain and still carries substantial weight in determining public debate about it. What they see in the blockchain is the means to bring down any kind of trusted institution which according to them is only possible with truly decentralized applications.

Myth 2: "With the success of the blockchain comes the downfall of banks"

Bearing in mind the background of primary investors of crypto, it is possibly conventional that banks are announced to be the first targets of the blockchain.

As stated, however, the model with at least some kind of centralization will be the winning model. This already cries out for a dealer of trust, implying that banks will be part of the equation. And even if the algorithm is completely decentralized there will still be some institutions that would need to handle data and rights to access pre or post a transaction. Bitcoins also have such institutions which are exchanges, you can trade, buy or sell bitcoin on these exchanges. Even bitcoins need institutions such as exchanges where you can buy and sell them.

Just a small part of the banks' value chain is comprised of payments. Even if cryptocurrencies succeeded to displace banks from moving value, what they wouldn't be able to do is replace them in providing everlasting and steady storage of value. Neither could the supplying of finances work devoid of financial institutions. Blockchains do not break into the banks, but the banks can break into markets so they can accept the digital standard.

Myth 3: "FinTechs are the banks' main challenge"

This third myth impeccably merges in with the first two. Decentralization, as opposed to the very nature of banks, lays the foundation for their fall and therefore, there also needs to be an immaculate challenger to push them from their throne.

The young and nimble FinTechs are responsible for this role. They start anew and can dedicate their entire energy to new products. Dynamic FinTechs can easily follow along any direction that the market takes. It has already happened to retail and hardware-manufacturing, and now it is also happening to finance?

The real reason why these examples are so noticeable is that they are the exclusion rather than the rule. Studies show that an industry structure is missed up not only due to greenfield competition, but the majority of the time it is due to incumbents or by market recruits prevailing in other industries. As a rule, new applicants lack the scale, financial muscle, and brand awareness. Typically, it takes longer to build those up than to guide mandatory supertankers into the winning direction.

Paypal is an example that is frequently mentioned when showing that banking is not immune to modernization. Dissimilar from Visa or Mastercard, it is not a result of banking collaboration, nevertheless, it has hitherto become the chief online payment system in North America. It comprises over 354 billion USD in payment volume internationally. The amount of active user accounts on Paypal has surpassed 200 million. But Paypal surrounds itself around the currently existing system. It does not succeed in credit cards or bank accounts but instead supplements them. Blockchain start-ups are an entirely different tale. Banks have realized long ago that the technology will aid them in saving a lot of money in the back-end. Innumerable initiatives, attainments, and blockchain labs are evidence of this. They will not be caught slumbering again.

And finally, one critical question rests: Do FinTechs really want to relocate the existing incumbents? Most mission statements definitely read as if this is the goal, yet in a study, 75.5% of all FinTechs announce that partnering with a recognized firm is their main goal. An intention might be that now the majority of the start-up blockchains are driven by obligatory investment like Veem took $25 million from cooperation run by Goldman Sachs.

The perseverance of these three myths definitely has sustained the interest in blockchain technology. These myths are unpretentious, speak to an engaged target group, and can be supported with carefully selected attention-grabbing examples. Believing them gullibly might end up costing you actual money – regardless of the fact if you are bearing in mind buying a crypto-coin or as a corporate decision-maker you anticipate financing original infrastructure.

Due to its mass of mechanisms and the resulting fuzziness, even more, fallacies surround blockchain technology. To devise a longstanding plan for blockchain that will not be directed by the latest news items, it is obligatory to clear those up.

6

CHAPTER

WHAT DOES A DEFI DEVELOPER NEED TO DO NOW?

Before getting involved in this field is very important that you know and understand all the layers that make up this new field. Below we shall discuss all the layers that constitute the DeFi network. It will help you clear up your mind and you will be able to understand better.

Body of Knowledge #1

We know that bitcoin was the first crypto currency generated and even today bitcoin stands out amongst all the other digital currencies. So the first thing that you do is to understand bitcoin. Understanding bitcoin would enable you to know and comprehend the primary concepts upon which these digital currencies work, not just that but it would also help you in understanding the basic concept of blockchain. Try not to miss this step no matter what, that is because it helps you in understanding the basic concepts and you are supposed to build up on them. You would face confusion if you move deeper into DeFi.

You should know and understand and explain the following concepts well:

Your digital wallet is not a physical entity. It can either be a private key or a seed phrase that you can use in order to make transactions on the bitcoin network. If after all the explanation that has been provided previously, you think of a wallet as a thing that you can keep on your phone. Well, then you get to go back and start from the beginning.

What is a transaction and what makes a valid one versus an invalid one?

You need to have complete information regarding the nonces, and UTXOs which are the inputs and outputs.

What is a block and how are the blocks constructed and then mined to become valid on the network? How do miners avoid mining the same transactions?

How is it made sure that the history is not re-written and no one cheats in a bitcoin network?

Understanding and knowing that hacking bitcoin would not increase its value, rather doing so would depreciate the value of a bitcoin.

What are hard-forks and soft-forks?

Understanding of Segwit2x and its controversial nature.

Body of Knowledge #2

By this time, you know that how the Proof of Work (PoW) blockchain actually works, the UTXO model, and why Bitcoin is groundbreaking and innovative. Now we will move forward and understand what are the features that make ethereum special. As well as what are the benefits of an Account-based blockchain in comparison to a UTXO one. Ethereum was created so that all this is taken to an advanced level. Blockchains were introduced later.

Ethereum is primarily a state machine. Every transaction that happens over the Ethereum network is basically requesting an update of the global state of this meta-machine. This meta-machine is powered by lots of physical machines.

It is important to know how accounts in Ethereum work and the difference between an EOA and Contract. The majority of the people consider the smart contract to be a "digital paper contract". These contracts are used to automate the execution of transactions.

To better understand the Ethereum Virtual Machine and the working of storage on the Ethereum network, you should go and revisit all that you have studied about it. This is a great way to learn the concepts.

The majority of the people find it hard to understand the role of gas cost, gas limits, and the gas price in the construction of Ethereum.

Getting a feel for how Solidity looks like and understanding the flow of Solidity -> ABIs -> Bytecode. Try your best to look into all the concepts so you are able to understand them better. Diligently study the ABIs as they are your best friend while working with smart contracts.

Understanding all the characteristic differences between the working of sending a token and sending Ether to another account. It is critical to understand that tokens are not currency whereas Ether is a currency that can be used on the network.

Dig deeper into the working of transactions, logs, events, and filters. This is especially important if you want to build an application that reads data off-chain.

Having a better understanding of the restrictions limitations of full nodes, light nodes and archive nodes are + how to connect to them via Infura + Ethers.js/Web3.js.

You should also try to read and gather as much information as you can on the subject of the security of smart contracts. It will provide a better overview of smart contracts and why is the making of smart contracts a hard thing to do.

Body of Knowledge #3

At this time, you are now well aware of all the things about Ethereum from designing to using it. The next step in all this is to get yourself equipped with information that is necessary for the DeFi. To better understand DeFi you need to know everything about the working of finance and its building blocks. The topic below is somewhat beyond the scope of the domain we have been discussing so you may find it difficult.

It is important for you as a DeFi developer to know these concepts on finger tips. As a DeFi developer, you are basically a finance engineer and if you don't understand these very basic concepts you would not be able to do your job well. You may end up losing lots of money because the framework that you would come up with lack of knowledge is not sufficient. Not only will you be creating security bugs, but you'll also probably have a twisted understanding regarding the working of DeFi and what products are in demand of your users. It's about time we dig into it. Well if you are a finance engineer you need to know and understand the following concepts. Not just that you should also be able to explain them to others.

What is Liquidity and why does it matter so much in this field? What are fixed and variable interest rates? What are the boon and bane of fixed and variable in the conventional monetary world? What is debt? What are the different types of debts? What is the use of debt in the finance industry? You may know what credit card debt is. But do you understand why these companies and organizations take debt worth billions even when they do have enough cash?

What is leverage and what is the use of leverage? You would know half of the DeFi concepts if you are able to understand what are the consequences of having more money than you hold? What is margin Trading and what are its uses? What are the famous locations for margin trading in crypto currencies?

What are Order and what are depth/volume/bids/asks/limit orders etc.?

What are the options?

If you know all these topics and understand all the concepts well, you can move forward. If not, try going back and revisiting all these concepts so you know them well. If you are not well-versed in options, try to clear your concepts because they are sprouting section in DeFi.

Some of the resources that you may find helpful are as follows, however, there are abundant resources that you can find over the internet.

Body of Knowledge #4

You are now getting closer to the end. In this last stage, we will let you know how you can learn regarding the prevalent DeFi applications. These resources will help you with it. Reading whitepapers and blogs that provide deeper knowledge about DeFi and what are they trying to achieve with DeFi? Using DeFi applications to understand them better. In order to know everything in detail, go through their codes that are easily available on Github. Using the DeFi applications will give you insights that nothing else would. If you use the DeFi applications, you will be able to develop them as well. What you can do is to purchase $1,000 worth of ETH. Consider it as tuition money with high chances to lose.

Here is what you can do.

Developing in DeFi

All the primary concepts from conventional finance have been brought into decentralized finance. The next leg in DeFi will be new things and involve a combination of:

New novel financial instruments that do not exist. (merging primitives)

The integration of more novel assets with unique features. (time decay assets)

Reckoning how to map DeFi to NFTs.

Developing on new emerging chains (Ethereum is where all the DeFi activity happens but opportunities on other blockchains are unchartered territory)

Creating interfaces to help understand the complex activity of on-chain data.

You also need to understand the reasons for all the DeFi setbacks and exploits that happened in the years 2020 and 2021.

There are some areas where the competition is high. Money markets, exchanges, and asset management are highly competitive spaces and you need to have a lot of information and a better understanding of everything. If you feel that you are not there yet, below are a few other areas that you can explore:

Become a part of a prevalent DeFi project. Give your 100% and try to learn as much as you can.

You can also launch your own DeFi project if you don't want to get involved with an already existing one. You would polish your technical skills with this.

Work on an idea and continue hacking on it. It can take longer but eventually, you will get there. A few of the top projects began their journey like this. You can go through some ETH global hackathons as well.

Become a part of the community by offering whatever skills you have. Help people with your knowledge, this is a great way to polish your skills even more. You can help in the crypto community and polish your developer skills.

The ways that have been provided above can be utilized to gain as many insights about the DeFi network as possible. Every engineer that is a part of the community will have something on which he can work.

7

CHAPTER

DESCRIBING DEFI PROJECTS

Dapps and infrastructure such as asset management tools, DeFi infrastructure & Dev Tooling, decentralized exchanges (DEX), and others are known as the DeFi projects.

These DeFi projects are relatively new so investing in them at this point in time is pretty risky. But with time they are highly likely to become more optimized and in the future launch better tokenomics.

1. CHAINLINK (LINK)

Oracles are needed by the dapps in order to work together with various kinds of data in a crypto environment.

Chainlink uses the decentralized data set via oracles and smart contracts. These provide neutral territory for real-world data and blockchain applications.

Ever since 2019, Chainlink has been recording exponential growth. It is able to dispense over 75 price feeds to 300 smart contracts and decentralized applications.

Chainlink after development was evolved enough that it can now be funding crypto initiatives that are of use to the system.

Chainlink plays an important role in the DeFi network by helping other projects with the oracles. It makes sure that the system functions.

A few examples of prominent projects using Chainlink oracles are Synthetic, AAVE, KyberSwap.

Supply

- Max Supply: 1,000,000,000 LINK
- Total Supply: 1,000,000,000 LINK
- Circulating Supply: 432,509,554 LINK

Market Cap

The market cap of LINK token is around $7.9 billion presently.

Allocation & Distribution

LINK tokens are pre-minted. This makes the Max Supply and the total supply similar.

As per Etherscan, the total supply of LINK is distributed as follows:

- 35% locked in smart contracts
- 41% In circulation
- 24% allocated to node operators

Vesting & Inflation

LINK does not have any vesting or lock-up schedule.

However, by monitoring the past data on CoinMarketCap with WayBackMachine, it shows that Chainlink is responsible for surging the circulating supply by 4-5% each year.

Utility

Use cases of the LINK token are mentioned below:

- smart contracts
- fees network
- staking

2. SYNTHETIX (SNX)

One of the fastest-growing DeFi is Synthetix. It is a decentralized asset insurance protocol that is built on Ethereum.

Synthetic versions of the real-world assets are minted as tokens using the Synthetix. It pegs the worth of the asset that they represent.

The synthetic assets uphold their peg via no-arbitrage principle arbitrage that allows the stakers to burn any extra synths and the open market liquidity for synths on added decentralized exchanges.

Supply

- Maximum Supply: 219,252,220 SNX
- Overall Supply: 215,258,834 SNX
- Circulating Supply: 114,841,533 SNX

Market Cap

Presently, the market cap of the SNX token is $753 million.

Allocation & Distribution

The SNX tokens are pre-minted. As per the research of Binance. The overall supply of the SNX will be distributed as follows:

- 0.87% Pre-Sale
- 19.20% Private Sale
- 3.05% Public Sale
- 18.49% Team
- 0.77% Advisors
- 4.62% Foundation
- 1.93% Partnership Incentives
- 1.16% Bounties/Airdrops
- 49.92% Staking

Vesting & Inflation

The inflationary money supply schedule of the Synthetix tokens was presented in March of 2019. It displayed a 1.25 inflation rate decreased every week.

Period of time	Increase in SNX Supply	Total SNX Supply after inflation	SNX inflation rate
2018.	0	100,000,000	0%
2019	75,000,000	175,000,000	75%
2020	37,500,000	212,500,000	21%
2021	18,750,000	231,250,000	9%
2022	9,375,000	240,625,000	4%
2023	4,687,500	245,312,500	2%

Utility

The SNX' use cases are mentioned below:

- The principal use of the SNX token is staking and collateralizing synthetic assets
- Yield Farming
- Trading Fees
- Governance

3. DODO (DODO)

Dodo was developed using the ERC20 on Ethereum. Dodo is said to be an on-chain liquidity provider. Dodo offers constancy via an active market maker. Dodo was later stretched out on Binance Smart Chain.

Dodo ensures management of the provision of sufficient liquidity in comparison to some of the best-centralized exchanges (CEX). It enables it to be used by smart contracts for on-chain transactions like liquidation and public sales.

Supply

- Maximum Supply: 1,000,000,000 DODO
- Over-all Supply: 1,000,000,000 DODO

- Circulating Supply: 110,551,965 DODO

Market Cap

Presently, the market cap of the DODO token is $99 million.

Allocation & Distribution

The DODO tokens are pre-minted. As per the Binance research, the overall supply is distributed as follows:

- 6% Seed Sale
- 10% Private Sale
- 15% Team & Advisors
- 8% Operations & Marketing
- 1% IDO Liquidity
- 60% Reserved for the community

Vesting & Inflation

Release schedule of the Dodo's tokens, there are chances of the circulating supply to increase progressively to up to 100% of the complete supply by the end of 2025.

1. By the end of 2021, the Circulating Supply will reach 40% of the Total Supply.
2. By the end of 2022, the Circulating Supply will reach 60% of the Total Supply.
3. By the end of 2023, the Circulating Supply will reach 80% of the Total Supply.
4. By the end of 2024, the Circulating Supply will reach 90% of the Total Supply.
5. By the end of 2025, the Circulating Supply will reach 100% of the Total Supply.

Utility

A few of the use cases of Dodo are mentioned below:

- Governance
- Crowdpooling & IDO Allocation

- Staking
- Trading Fee Discounts
- Minting vDODO

4. PANCAKESWAP (SWAP)

An Automated Market Maker for the Decentralized Exchange that is designed on the Binance Smart Chain is PancakeSwap. PancakeSwap does not need any KYC. PancakeSwap got grants from the Binance. They got the funds by being a part of the DeFi acceleration program of the company on a Binance Smart Chain.

PancakeSwap is an exact replica of UniSwap with a few added features. They are mentioned below:

- Lottery tickets
- There is an auction market for numerous NFTs
- A primary farm offering
- Gamification via using community teams, leaderboards, various tasks, and achievements

Supply

- Maximum Supply: No Limit
- Over-all Supply: 185,651,569 CAKE
- Circulating Supply: 185,651,569 CAKE

Market Cap

Presently the market cap of the CAKE is said to be $2.5 billion

Allocation & Distribution

The BEP20 CAKE token is pre-minted. As per the BscScan, the distribution goes as follows:

- 38.35% of it is locked in the main staking contract
- 38.41% of it is for wallet used for burning tokens
- 23.24% of it is allocated to various smart contracts and holders

Vesting & Inflation

The inflation rate at which CAKE functions is 750,000 CAKE each day. Nevertheless, 60% of the tokens that are freshly emitted are distributed amongst the Yield farmers and 40% amongst Syrup Pools.

If tokenomics is concerned, it is deemed that CAKE has a calamitous inflation rate. But the developers are looking to make it deflationary. They want to do so they work on the burning parameters at all times.

Utility

Staking is the basic use of the CAKE token is staking. But this token has other uses as well, they are mentioned below:

- Crowdpooling
- NFTs Auctions
- Chipping in several features of the PANCAKESWAP environment.

5. REN (REN)

REN can be used for transfers of the tokens in different blockchains. It is basically a decentralized interoperability protocol. It is a cross-chain value transfer key that does not create synthetic tokens or wrapped tokens rather transfers liquidity from one system to another with prevailing smart contracts.

RenBTC and Wbtc function on a similar concept. Both of them have one difference only. Bitcoin retains on the network of decentralized nodes which are also known as the Dark Nodes. These dark nodes are authorized by a code. In bitcoin it is different.

REN protocol functions like a machine. The users are allowed to make as many requests as they can with no time limit.

The Ren Virtual Machine can be united into many DeFis. It makes the liquidity available without KYC.

Nodes receive fees in the cryptocurrency that is exchanged through the RenVM.

100,000 REN is required for a node to operate.

Supply

- Max Supply: 1,000,000,000 REN
- Total Supply: 999,999,633 REN
- Circulating Supply: 997,163,051 REN

Market Cap

Presently, REN has a market cap of $339 million.

Allocation & Distribution

Ren was pre-minted as an ERC20 token. As per the Binance Research, the token is distributed as follows:

- 18.67% Bonded in the Dark nodes
- 19.9% Reserve funds
- 10% partnerships, development, and other related activities.
- 56.6% investors and lending pools.
- 13.5% other holders

Vesting & Inflation

The majority of the Ren tokens are circulating. However, those tokens used to bond are taken off the market. More tokens will be bonded upon demand for operating nodes.

Utility

The main use case of the token is to be used as a Bond for a dark node to operate.

6. UNISWAP (UNI)

Uniswap is currently leading the decentralized exchange space. It is a decentralized exchange that is built on the Ethereum network. Hayden Adams was the founder of Uniswap.

An on-chain automated market maker (AMM) was what provided the basis for this trading protocol.

Uniswap lets its users' exchange and trade several of the available DeFi tokens. Not just that but it also acts as Liquidity Provider tokens. If you are unable to look for an ERC20 token in the list, you will be able to create a pair and then exchange it in return for crypto. You can do so if you find the address of the smart contract.

Uniswap makes it possible for the users to exchange and provide liquidity in existing pools or create new pools as well.

Supply

- Max Supply: 1,000,000,000 UNI
- Total Supply: 100,000,000 UNI
- Circulating Supply: 575,202,575 UNI

Market Cap

Presently, the market cap of the UNI token is around $9.8 billion.

Allocation & Distribution

The UNI tokens are pre-minted originally as ERC20 tokens. As per the Uniswap, distribution of the tokens mentioned below:

- 60% goes to the Uniswap community
- 21.266% is allocated to the members of the team and employees who would join in the near future
- 18.044% is allocated to investors
- 0.69% is allocated to advisors

Vesting & Inflation

The vesting period of the UNI tokens is 4 years, among which 40% of it is distributed amongst the team, employees, investors, and advisors. UNI is to function with an uninterrupted inflation rate of 2% after that.

Utility

Use cases of the UNI token are mentioned below:
- On-chain governance
- Staking in pools
- The reward for staking in pools

7. MAKER (MKR)

Maker is a decentralized organization MakerDAO and software platform Maker Protocol that assists in the issuance and management of DAI.

MKR uses the Ethereum blockchain as an underlying technology. It is a decentralized institution, the software platform of which is authorized by the ERC20 token, MKR.

The MKR protocol works as voting rights in the environment.

Maker is said to be the first project that tried designing and building the products that are related to decentralized finance. It also worked on making smart-contract-enabled blockchains.

MKR provides the users with direct participation in the DAI authorization.

The people who have the MKR are eligible to vote or any changes that may be suggested to be incorporated into the protocol. The voting of the holders of MKR is dependent upon the number of staked Maker tokens.

Supply

- Max Supply: 1,005,577 MKR
- Total Supply: 994,654 MKR
- Circulating Supply: 991,423 MKR

Market Cap

Presently, the market cap of the MKR token is around $2.1 billion.

Allocation & Distribution

The MKR tokens are pre-minted. As per the Etherscan, the number of tokens is circulated as follows:

- 21.35% Maker: Governance Contract
- 8.42% Maker: MCD Pause Proxy
- 55% Liquidity providers, exchanges, and investors
- 15.23% Other accounts

Vesting & Inflation

MKR is hard-capped at 1,005,577. This means that the tokens would always remain fixed and won't surpass this figure. The Marker system works on the buyback-and-burn system, this helps in maintaining the price and tokens that are being circulated.

Utility

Use cases of the MKR tokens are mentioned below:

- Governance
- Paying Fees
- Staking
- Recapitalization system

8. FANTOM (FTM)

The main objective of Fantom is to grow into a DAG-based smart-contract platform that uses aBFT principles to attain a consensus. Lanchesis protocol will make the smart contracts Lanchesis protocol will help in enabling the smart contracts in a directed acyclic graph-based system.

Fantom uses a unique consensus mechanism in the DeFi environment that enables the services that DeFi and the smart contracts have to offer. It is said to be a unique feature of Fantom.

The Lanchesis mechanism is assured to offer two-second transaction finalization as well as a secure proof-of-stake algorithm.

Supply

- Max Supply: 3,175,000,000 FTM
- Total Supply: 2,545,006,273 FTM
- Circulating Supply: 2,545,006,273 FTM

Market Cap

Presently, the market cap of the FTM token is around $620 million.

Allocation & Distribution

The FTM token is pre-minted. As per the Binance Research, the distribution is as follows:

- 3.15% Seed Sale
- 37.04% Private Token Sale
- 1.57% Public Sale
- 7.49% Team
- 12% Advisors
- 6% Token Reserve
- 32.75% Block rewards

Vesting & Inflation

There is a steady rate of increase of about 1.1 % every month in the release schedule for the FTM tokens. This steady rate will continue till the August of 2023.

Utility

Use cases of the FTM token are:

- Staking
- Paying network fees
- Granting user rewards

9. POLKASTARTER (POLS)

The pools and auctions in order to raise money are supported by a protocol called Polkastarter. It is a cross-chain protocol. It can be used for those projects that center around Polkadot.

In the Polkadot network, the fixed swap pools and cross-chains swaps are made possible by the Polkastarter. This results in the less costs of transactions and maximizing the output within the Ethereum Network and other blockchains in order to keep liquidity rolling.

Supply

- Max Supply: UNKNOWN
- Total Supply: 100,000,000 POLS
- Circulating Supply: 70,133,982 POLS

Market Cap

Presently, the market cap of POLS tokens is $71 million.

Allocation & Distribution

As per the documentation of the Polkastarter's, the token is distributed as follows:

- 10% Foundational reserve
- 15% Seed Sale
- 10% Team & Advisors
- 27.5% Private sale
- 15% Marketing Fund
- 22.5% Liquidity Fund

Vesting & Inflation

The supply of tokens is to be unlocked at around 7% per month for almost 2 years.

Utility

Use cases of the POLS token are:

- Governance
- Transaction Fees
- Staking

- Liquidity mining

10. UMA (UMA)

UMA is the abbreviation for Universal Market Access. UMA is a protocol that is used for the creation of synthetic derivatives.

Trustless smart contracts are used in order to carry out a trade between the two parties, this trade is made possible by the UMA protocol. The smart contract is programmed in a way that it does not need any third party to be a part of the trade. The automatic smart contract regulates margins for both sides and makes sure that the trades are collateralized.

UMA is becoming more notable and recognized because it has minimized usage of off-chain oracle price feeds. This is done to eradicate the risk of oracle manipulation.

Supply

- Max Supply: 101,172,570 UMA
- Total Supply: 102,816,269 UMA
- Circulating Supply: 60,883,617 UMA

Market Cap

Presently, the market cap of the UMA tokens is around $537 million.

Allocation & Distribution

The distribution of the UMA tokens is as follows:

- 2% Initial Uniswap Listing
- 14.5% Future Token Sales
- 35% Developers and Users
- 48.5% Founders, Early Contributors, and Investors

Vesting & Inflation

UMA token has no unlocking schedule. but considering tokenomics, it has an inflation rate of 0.05%. This helps in increasing the supply every time a vote is held. Tokens are burned in order to avoid any profits that may be made due to the oracle corruption.

Utility

UMA token has the following utility:

- Governing the UMA ecosystem
- Disputes
- Fees

11. 1INCH (1INCH)

1Inch is growing and expanding at a very fast pace. It is a decentralized exchange aggregator that is used to associate several DEXes into a single platform. It arranges for the users with the capability to exchange tokens efficiently.

The 1Inch system is authorized via 1INCH token.

1INCH is an ERC20 token, it is however non-custodial. All the trades are made possible with a single transaction. This connects the user wallet to the supported network. Currently, you can combine the protocol with Ethereum, Uniswap, Kyber Network, Oasis, 0x Relays.

Supply

- Max Supply: UNKNOWN
- Total Supply: 1,500,000,000 1INCH
- Circulating Supply: 172,778,256.50 1INCH

Market Cap

Presently, the market cap of the 1INCH token is $451 Million.

Allocation & Distribution

The Inch tokens are pre-minted. As per the Binance Research, the total supply is distributed as follows:

- 53.3% Core Backers and Contributors
- 30% Community Incentives
- 14.4% Protocol Growth and Development
- 2.3% Advisors

Vesting & Inflation

About 6% of the overall supply of the 1INCH token supply was released by the end of the year 2020. It was received through airdrop to all the cryptocurrency wallets it worked with. After that around 0.5%, more tokens were released in a two weeks' time span. The rest of it is to be released in the coming 4 years.

Utility

Use cases of the 1INCH tokens are mentioned below:

- Instant Governance
- Staking

12. AVALANCHE (AVAX)

Avalanche is a smart contract platform. It is interoperable and is used to launch DeFi applications, financial assets, and various other services. Ethereum virtual machine, application-specific sharding, network-level programmability, and NFTs are supported by the platform.

Avalanche practices a proof-of-stake consensus protocol to bargain a network where the trade of decentralized assets takes place.

Supply

- Max Supply: 720,000,000 AVAX
- Total Supply: 385,922,102 AVAX
- Circulating Supply: 172,418,164 AVAX

Market Cap

Presently, the market cap of the AVAX token is around $1.9 million.

Allocation & Distribution

The token supply is 720M. These tokens are distributed as follows:

- 50% Staking rewards
- 9.26% Foundation
- 10% Public sale
- 3.46% Private Sale
- 2.5% Seed Sale
- 7% Community & Developer Endowment
- 5% Strategic Partners
- 10% Team
- 2.5% Airdrop
- 0.28% Testnet Incentive Program

Vesting & Inflation

There was a time period of 1 year for the Seed Sale and Private Sale and Public Sale of the tokens previously. Presently, the tokens have a minting rate of 7-12% as staking rewards.

AVAX has introduced a new mechanism for burning that eliminates the network fee. This helps in balancing the supply that is brought into the market.

Utility

Use cases of the AVAX tokens are mentioned below:

- An incentive for securing the network
- Paying Fees
- Staking
- The base unit of account amongst multiple blockchains positioned on Avalanche

13. WRAPPED BITCOIN (WBTC)

The tokenized version of bitcoin is known as WBTC. It is found on the Ethereum network as an ERC20 token. It is authorized via a DAO.

The holders of BTC can act together in the environment with the dapps inside the Ethereum network. They have the complete right to use the services provided by DeFi. They are able to do so after they wrap their bitcoins.

The Wrapped Bitcoin and the bitcoin will uphold a similar value because they are pegged 1:1.

The Bitcoins are swapped for Wrapped Bitcoin. A custodian keeps them safe till the WBTC is redeemed.

A wrapped bitcoin is minted after a bitcoin is deposited. AWTBC is burned after a BTC is redeemed.

Supply

- Max Supply: NO MAX SUPPLY
- Total Supply: 191,025 WBTC
- Circulating Supply: 191,025 WBTC

Market Cap

Presently, the market cap of the WBTC token is $6.5billion.

Allocation & Distribution

The WBTC tokens are minted on demand. They are also minted by observing the Etherscan. Though, the supply and allocation of the are dynamic with the evolution in demand.

Vesting & Inflation

There is no scheduled vesting or inflation of the WBTC token. The price of this token is always close to that of BTC. Each of the exchanged WBTC is burned so that the pegging is maintained as 1:1.

Utility

Use cases of the WBTC token are mentioned below

- Interaction with Ethereum dapps and DeFi projects
- Provision of liquidity to several protocols
- Used as collateral in DeFi ecosystems

14. DAI (DAI)

DAI is a stablecoin. It is based on Ethereum and is authorized via a Maker Platform and MakerDAO.

DAI is completely decentralized. Not just that but it is also combined with a lot of dapps and DeFi projects. This is the main difference between the DAI and other stablecoins.

The DAI stablecoin was collateralized only with Ethereum. Presently that is not the case, it can be multi collateralized.

Unlike the majority of the stablecoins, DAI has achieved fame and popularity by maintaining its permanent price of close to 1 USD. In order to keep the pegging stable, stablecoin is collateralized excessively by the Decentralized Autonomous Organization.

Any person that can store collateral has the ability to mint the DAI tokens, that is why there is no centralized organization that manages the process of minting the tokens.

Supply

- Max Supply: NO MAX SUPPLY
- Total Supply: 5,192,006,295 DAI
- Circulating Supply: 5,192,006,295 DAI

Market Cap

Presently, the market cap of the DAI token is $5.2 billion.

Allocation & Distribution

DAI tokens are minted by its users. They are minted so they can be stored in the collateral. This results in dynamic supply and distribution.

Vesting & Inflation

There is no type of vesting and inflation on the DAI token. The price of this token is permanently around 1 USD. The DAI tokens are minted and burned with the evolution of the market.

Utility

Use cases of the DAI token are mentioned below:

- Interaction with Ethereum dapps and DeFi projects
- Providing liquidity to countless protocols
- Collateral in DeFi ecosystems

15. THORCHAIN (RUNE)

Thorchain is said to be a decentralized liquidity protocol. This protocol lets the exchange of cryptocurrency between blockchains promptly.

The developers of the protocol did not disclose their identity and chose to remain anonymous. This protocol is highly decentralized and transparent.

RUNE is the token used by the Thorchain protocol. It is available on both its own blockchain and the Ethereum blockchain. On Ethereum blockchain it is available as an ERC20 token. On the Binance Smart Chain, it is available as a BEP20 token.

It is not a profit-oriented platform. This makes all the fees directed to its users.

Supply

- Max Supply: 500,000,000 RUNE

- Total Supply: 461,668,422 RUNE
- Circulating Supply: 233,836,800 RUNE

Market Cap

Presently, the market cap of the RUNE token is around $1.4 billion.

Allocation & Distribution

The RUNE tokens are minted beforehand. The entire supply is distributed as follows:

- 44% Service nodes & liquidity incentives
- 13% Operational reserves
- 12% Community reserves
- 10% Team & Advisors
- 6% Seed investors
- 14% Presale Investors
- 1% Initial DEX Offering

Vesting & Inflation

One-quarter of the RUNE token is programmed to vest every month for the next three years. This would result in locking 22% of the total supply. This will be locked till the mainnet is achieved.

44% of the distributed service nodes and liquidity is soon to be progressively released. This will be released as rewards for the validators and provision of incentives and rewards for the liquidity pool.

Utility

Use cases of RUNE tokens are:

- Bootstrapping of novel chains to thorchains
- Paying Fees
- Staking

In the year 2021, multiple projects were launched that had great takenomics. These projects had the ability that could help evolve the whole crypto industry.

You need to keep a close eye in order to avail the opportunities that come your way. Also, you need to keep doing your research, this would numerous new doors for you. Cryptocurrencies have a lot of potentials and it is going to go big in the future. In fact, if we say that cryptocurrency and blockchain are the future, it won't be wrong.

8

CHAPTER

SMART CONTRACTS

Smart contracts became extremely popular due to the CryptoKitties in the year 2017. In the year 2018, its popularity reached a peak after they were able to sell a CryptoKitty for $140,000. Smart contracts are still popular, unlike the CryptoKitties.

Smart contracts have a lot of uses and the utilities that come with them are also becoming popular with every passing day. Smart contracts are not restrained to the CryptoKitties only, in fact, there are a lot of uses of the smart contracts. Here are a few examples to show that smart contracts are more than CryptoKitties.

Smart contracts have enabled Decentralized Finance services. Smart contracts played a major role in making DeFi the next big thing.

Through DeFi, the borrowers and the lenders can communicate and interact with each other as well as use all the services that the blockchain provides.

But, how are smart contracts of use to you?

If you're looking to borrow

There may have been some emergency comes up. It could be due to anything.

In order to deal with the emergency, you would require to loan some money. Loaning money using the traditional way would have been such a hassle. A credit score check, salary/earnings report, etc. would be required in order to allow you to loan them money. Then after you were approved for it, you will have to wait a few days for receiving your funds. Now if you look at this process this is pretty hectic. However, using the DeFi methods this process has become really simple.

DeFi can benefit you in this regard by the following advantages.

- No credit check.
- Fund dispensing in 30 minutes if you choose stablecoins.
- Lending in various fiat currencies too.

How is that possible?

If you plan to borrow money, the process would work the following way:

- Look for a DeFi platform that matches your needs.
- Select the amount that you want to loan and the rate of interest.
- Pledge BTC, ETH, or other coins as collateral.

After you refund the loan that was issued to you, you will get the coins that you used as collateral back. This results in there being no credit checks and fast distribution of loan funds. Your bad credit does not matter in the smart contracts; you receive the funds either way.

The smart contracts release your funds automatically after it has checked that you were able to deposit the amount that you agreed upon as collateral.

There are advantages of the DeFi industry that you can benefit from, but there are cons too that need to be addressed. They are stated below:

- As it is a relatively new industry so the loopholes can be negatively exploited.
- Instable price of Crypto may end up liquidating your collateral.

- Keep a track of all your personal information and your public and private addresses.
- DeFi is a brand new industry. It is flourishing presently but it comes with growing pains.

The platforms that lend the DeFi can be hacked, there have been several cases where the users have been scammed and got their money stolen. In such cases, the coins that you have used as collateral might drop all of a sudden. Its value would decrease so much that it would decrease from the amount that you have loaned. When that happens, the coins that you have collateralized would be sold in order to cover your loan. Make sure that the address that you have provided so you are able to receive your collateral back is all correct. If they are not correct, they would be sent to some other address and you would not be able to retrieve them back.

Using DeFi services may be risky but it is still considered to be the best option.

If you're looking to lend

If someone is interested in hoarding HODL no matter what may happen to the price of bitcoin they are still holding on to it.

This is great but why should you let your crypto bags just lie around like that?

DeFi platforms allow all those people who HODL to keep doing just that, this helps them with earning a profit on the side as well.

But how do they do it? Well, the process is quite simple. Here is how you can do it:

- Go to a DeFi platform that you trust and want to use.
- Go through all the interest rates for lenders.
- Credit the amount of BTC, ETH, or any other coins that you would like to earn some interest on.

- Whatever platform you choose, you can use that and keep earning a handsome amount of interest for all that time when your crypto is on the platform.

Know that the cryptocurrencies that you have deposited on the platform will remain protected by default from the person who is going to borrow. The borrower will have to use some of his coins as collateral if in case the borrower is not able to return the amount he loaned. The coins that are used as collateral by the borrower will be sold if he is not able to pay back the loan or the price of crypto drops by a huge number. This is a way to compensate the lender.

There may be different risks that can be faced in these DeFi services. The DeFi platforms that are newly created and still have not resolved their bugs are more prone to attacks by hackers and scammers. In order to keep yourself safe from such events, you should double-check the addresses of your wallet. Check them every time you send and receive cryptocurrencies.

2. eSports gaming + smart contracts

Games like basketball and football that were played with baseball are now referred to as traditional or conventional sports. A game item such as a baseball can be used to play a lot of games. It can become a collectible that's worth money if it is signed by some famous player.

Now a majority of these games have been replaced by e-gaming and e-sports. Presently, in eSports and other online games, any items that the player bought belong to him. The items that the player bought can only be used in a single game.

Now, let's talk about the Multiverse.

The players can sell the collectible to someone else in a multiverse. That collectible can then be utilized by the player who bought in a game that is totally different.

All this is possible due to the innovations and enhancements that Enjin bought into the Ethereum smart contracts called ERC-1155.

Games like CryptoKitties and others run on the ERC-721 smart contracts. This concept gave birth to the concept of non-fungible tokens.

Now, what is non-fungible? It is a representation of an item claiming that it is unique and cannot be exchanged with some other entity. Cryptocurrencies can be exchanged with other cryptocurrencies of the same worth but these tokens are unique and thus not interchangeable. ERC-720 smart contracts are used by the CryptoKitties as the crypto kitty is said to be non-fungible.

ERC-1155 is a whole new standard.

ERC-20 and ERC-270 standards are merged to form ERC-1155. This lets one contract create fungible and tokens that can be used as an in-game currency. Non-fungible tokens are created as well that can be used as unique legendary swords.

"ERC-1155 Crypto Items improve on this by combining the benefits of both. You may create thousands of different types of items for your game, and depending on the use case, each unit may have a unique index or be fully fungible with the others."

The list of benefits is long enough. ERC-1155 tokens can be exchanged automatically, help you save the gas fee by multi-transfer abilities, and a lot more.

It's a whole new world of gaming.

3. Smart Contracts on the Supply Chain

Smart contracts are a great way to work the B2B applications. Not just that but also used in eSports and DeFi.

Smart contracts are a way to make the whole task automatic. These tasks usually involve people but due to smart contracts, all the process is automated. Smart contracts make the whole transparent by increasing visibility.

How?

Smart contracts are immutable.

The data of the products are recorded in the blockchain. The data that is recorded on the blockchain cannot be changed, this is a way to make sure that the product is unique and authentic. Smart contracts are a great way for companies and industries to know where have the parts been sourced from and what companies have been involved in the process of making the whole product.

This can help in cultivating the relationship between companies who are working and providing parts for it. All these are recorded on a blockchain that can be tracked at all times.

The Future of Smart Contracts

We say that smart contracts are the future but why is that so? Well, there is a reason. It has incredible momentum.

Lots of people are constantly working on resolving the bugs that are found in blockchain technology. The developments in smart contracts are pretty interesting to see. Nike came up with an entire line of sneakers that were authenticated by the smart contracts. The health sector has become more secure and accessible due to smart contracts. These smart contracts have brought great advancements in our lives, ranging from digital ownership to health care.

All this information that is stated above shows that smart contracts are way beyond the CryptoKitties.

CHAPTER

ICOS AND DEFI

In the section below, we will match and distinguish the gains amongst decentralized finance (DeFi) tokens and the initial coin offering (ICO).

In 2017, when the ICOs were most popular, the majority of the businesses launched assets like it on the Ethereum blockchain. In the same year, 435 ICOs "listed" with each project raised an average of USD 12.7 million, for a total of USD 5.6 billion. The total amount that was accumulated through the ICOs was more than the "...early-stage venture capital funding for internet companies...." by the end of August. This was reported by CNBC. A number of warnings were issued so in February 2019 SEC formalized its first enforcement against an ICO for securities law violations.

Investors of DeFi earn interest by the appreciation of assets and by using DeFi. COMP governance tokens of Compound and Yield farming are the two ways through which they seek profits. The overall money that has been raised by a number of DeFi platforms has reached 4.2 billion in one month. The COMP token also increased its worth and attained gains 5 times over in just a few days after it was launched. Currently, it has a market capitalization of $337 million. LEND token of Aave has also increased its value 6 folds. This rise increased the market cap of LEND tokens and brought them back into the game. SNX token of Synthetix has also seen an over 5x increase from May end. The market cap has risen to $410 million.

This efflux of DeFi has been a contributing influence to Ethereum. It has seen a 70% increase. This increase brought Ethereum from $225 on June 30 to almost 400.

The transaction count of Ethereum has shown continuous growth and almost reached its all-time high in January of 2018.

No doubt that DeFi will attract managers and regulators. But if you look back in the past you will realize that the action that SEC took against the ICOs happened after much long. This means that the regulatory risks that are associated with DeFi may take a while to be caught by the eye of the concerned authorities. But one of the SEC Having said that, once SEC prosecution when arrived ended the ICOs. This example should be enough for the investors to make sure they are not doing anything that they shouldn't be doing.

Similarities

1. This results in the reduction of the supply of ETH that is in circulation. ICOs and Defi motivate the buying and locking up ETH and its tokens. This shows a decrease in the supply of crypto assets that are in circulation. This reduction leads to its appreciation in price. ETH is accepted as an investment by ICOs. It also provides its investors with a new token as well as holds huge percentages of ETH as capital. Newly created tokens are distributed in return for staking ETH and its tokens.

2. The basic objective of both the ICOs and DeFi is to decentralize the previous models but they are also working on the token speculation. This token speculation would result in increased usage and the creation of new communities. DeFi is a way to supply decentralized versions of exchanges and lending platforms but has principally grown liquidity by speculation on newly minted tokens.

3. ICOs and DeFi both resulted in very high fees and crowding on the ethereum blockchain, incentivizing research and investment into scalability solutions. In the year a long account of "ethereum killers", which focused on scalability,

plasma chains, sidechains, and another layer 2 scalability resolutions.

4. The protocols that were launched supported ICOs and DeFi activities like Ethereum. These protocols did provide support but none of them did as much as the Ethereum in regards to ICOs and other DeFi activities. As far as ICOs are concerned, the "composability" assistances of launching ERC20s comprised of a comprehensive base for supporting infrastructure as well as wallet support. It also provided an extra benefit for the simple addition of the wallets to exchanges. As for DeFi, the composability benefits may go beyond these. That is because the protocols used by the DeFi projects have vast interaction and cross-chain solutions remain promising.

Differences

1. New tokens were sold in return for ETH. DeFi hands off new tokens for free in exchange for staking ETH and other projects that are based on Ethereum. If you look at it from the regulatory point of view you would see that most of the ICOs were the security sales. On the other hand, the majority of the DeFi tokens were those that were received in exchange for work. This means that some of the tokens were discharged from the security regulations as non-securities. This may be less optimistic for the ETH in comparison to ICOs. ETH is recycled immediately between different projects in order to mint new tokens by the same stockholders.

2. In ICOs, the person that uses the product or user is different from the investor base in a token. But on the other hand, if you look at the DeFi services you will see that the lending and distribution of the tokens to the same people allow the investors to become users at any time. This will optimize the growth in the communities.

3. The majority of the activities that take place in the DeFi community are "circular". It is possible due to the temporary token incentives that exist because of temporary token incentives. This is a great way to provide crypto traders with liquidity immediately. However, countless projects that were launched via ICO did not come up with any usable product.

10
CHAPTER

DEFI AND ETHEREUM

Five Years In, DeFi Now Defines Ethereum

In order to show its actual capabilities and true definition to everyone out there, Ethereum has faced a lot of challenges. With the emergence of DeFi, not only Ethereum developed but also was able to let the world know what it is truly capable of.

DeFi Dad is a DeFi super user who shares his experiments related to money and other tutorials on Twitter and YouTube. He is an organizing member of the Ethereal Summit and Sessions, host of The Ethereal Podcast, and contributes weekly to The Defiant and Bankless.

To tell the world about what Ethereum has always been a difficult subject. The founders have also struggled with letting the world know what Ethereum is. Ethereum has always been difficult to explain to a layman. They used metaphors to let the world know about it. "World commuter" and "gas" are a few of the metaphors used in order to explain Ethereum to the people. But now it has become more clear and we know and understand what Ethereum is and what is it truly capable of.

In 2017, there was a huge ICO craze, due to that Ethereum came out as a distributed technology platform that could compete with the Initial Coin Offering (ICO). There was no example of a financial use case that could be talked about. During those times, a lot of white papers were published. Some of the teams made assurances and some of the teams did progress. These projects are now considered as the leading DeFi projects like ChainLink, Kyber, and Set. But again, the majority of the benefits had yet to be delivered.

Speakers of the time from the Ethereum community spoke very well about Ethereum and made people think that Ethereum was something that could bring a significant change in the world. All it took was a newcomer who was both enthusiastic and ready to stride through innovative ideas, intricate foreign concepts and inundate on novel information every day.

Joe Lubin at the Ethereal SF 2017 spoke very well regarding Ethereum and the changes it could bring to the world. He gave away an inspiring and motivating message from his talk. It would have made anyone think about investing in Ethereum technology and how it could change the world for good.

ConsenSys and other companies that worked with Ethereum in its early days kept educating the enterprise software companies and other institutions regarding the benefits of Ethereum and explained the use cases of blockchain on Ethereum. Partnerships with Microsoft, IBM, and Hyperledger helped solidify the credibility of Ethereum in the enterprise blockchain race.

In July of 2018, while people were still recovering from the aftermath of the incidents in 2017, it was realized that Ethereum needs to find a group of people who can use it with dedication. Every startup in order to grow and develop needs to have a bunch of users who finds it useful and that can't substitute with something else.

DeFi days

The ethereal summit is a series of events that are arranged in honor of the founders and creators of the decentralized network on Ethereum. It was during that time when a change in the narrative of Ethereum was seen and observed.

Decentralized finance was associated to be all that was happening during that time, it is also known as DeFi. It was in 2018 when the terminology DeFi was invented. This invention was made by the 0x team members. At this point, the industry kept getting bigger and better.

Thorough research of every project that was hosted at the Ethereal was made. Projects such as PoolTogether, Kyber Argent, and Zerion. While all this continued to happen, products were tested and used, this was considered to be something more far-reaching and deep-seated. was done.

The testing and use of these applications were to see that the investment that had been made earned profit or not. This was also done in order to realize the potential of these DeFi applications. Dai was lent on Compound with more than 10% APY. This was something that helped a lot. Dai was lent and was borrowed by other people without the interference of any third party. This was something great as the lender was able to lend them money and earn interest while the borrower paid a minimal fee. Not just that but these transactions were facilitated without any knowing your customer (KYC) or permission of someone else.

Better explanation of what Ethereum is and more of the visual representation were a few of the things that hindered the way of more people using Ethereum.

In order for more and more people to adopt the Ethereum and the DeFi applications, it is very important to have a good user interface. You need to keep the design as minimal and as user-friendly as possible. This is something that most people talked about. But it was seen that those people who were advocating such denunciations had no experience regarding the DeFi applications. Most people thought that this narrative was something that lingered around all this for long enough that people thought it was true.

In comparison to today, the DeFi community has become huge. In the late months of 2019, the DeFi community was a small bunch of people. It was only a few hundred or maybe a thousand users at the time but it created excitement and encouragement among people. DeFi was defined as the simplest way to do any peer-to-peer transactions. It was built around Ethereum. You just need to have a Web 3 wallet, such as MetaMask. If you call ETH your money, then DeFi can be your bank.

DeFi was a concept at first but now that concept has been implemented and that has become an economy. This economy is basically applications that are linked to one another. DeFi industry has a worth of $4 billion. Not just that but DeFi was able to transform the views of people regarding Ethereum and the DeFi system.

A meme is born

All this gained motion in the late months of 2019. Another concept that really started getting popular during that time. The concept introduced was Total Value Locked (TLV). TLV was invested by DeFi pulse.

Total Value Locked is basically the sum of all the TVL refers to the sum of all the value that is credited in the smart contracts of a DeFi application. It does not matter if the value is in dollars or in ETH. TVL mirrored this innovative benchmark to be accepted. This will help in seeing that what is the level of trust that the users put in a DeFi application. There are defects in this but still, those flaws and defects are no worse than the price reduction of bitcoin.

DeFi played a major role in DeFi in coagulating the meme, "ETH is money". As per David Hoffman, ETH is an asset that is triple-point, that is because it acts as a store-of-value, a capital asset, and an asset that can be consumed. In order to let the people, know and understand how ETH works and how it is used on Ethereum "ETH is money" was used in order to distract the world from "ETH is gas".

Plain and simple: ETH is money. ETH was money and to say that it wasn't was considered as a product marketing mistake in the initial years of Ethereum.

Yield farming has become viral and is based on Ethereum. DeFi is an all-inclusive category of the peer-to-peer service, self-custody, KYC-less, finance apps that are based on Ethereum, but yield farming labels popular enticements program where liquidity is provided in return for a DeFi application.

Universal appeal

A few years back there were only theoretical concepts of Ethereum. There was little to no practical implementation. Even if you look back 3 years ago, you would see stationary adoption of the concepts.

But now, times have changed. Ethereum has become more of a practical thing. There are assets of almost $4B that have been deposited on the DeFi network. Presently, there is an increase of 227% year-on-year in ETH locked in DeFi, and a 20X increase in tokenized BTC on Ethereum.

The DeFi apps help in the validation of value and utility, it is something that you cannot find you cannot find anywhere else. Learn all the basic concepts if you have missed them in case. Ethereum and DeFi concepts are just about to become the talk of the town.

CHAPTER

WHAT ARE THE DEFI DIGITAL WALLET

Understanding Decentralized Finance Wallet

Bbefore you get involved in decentralized finance, it is important for you to understand and know possibly everything about the DeFi digital wallets. You need to know what the right tools are and how to use them in an appropriate way. Before we get into the tools, let's understand what the DeFi digital wallets basically are. In order to take part in any DeFi activity, you will require a DeFi digital wallet. You would not be able to process any transaction if you do not have one. They also help you in keeping your assets safe and secure.

The two main things in digital wallets are to ensure the security and protection of your assets and to keep the interface for the user as simple as possible. You can use the DeFi digital wallets to keep your assets secure, you can do so without any internet connection. But in order to interact and work with the DeFi protocols, you would require an online wallet. In addition, that online wallet will help you in exchanging crypto-assets compliantly.

After this, you need to know about the traits of a DeFi digital wallet. Below are some of the key traits that can help you in distinguishing a decentralized finance wallet:

Key-based

The crucial trait of the DeFi digital wallet is the unique key pair. This key pair helps in differentiating between decentralized wallets and centralized wallets. It is very important for you to keep your keys protected. Keys are protected by using a seed phrase. This seed phrase is 12 words long.

Non-custodial

Non-custodial wallets are used in order to make sure that the sender and the receiver are the only ones that can have access to the funds in the wallet. It helps the users in sending and receiving funds.

Accessibility

If you look at it from the virtual point of view, you will see that the non-custodial wallets could easily manage a complete suite of assets.

The wallets that are based on Ethereum can help the users to credit ETH, stablecoins, ERC721 tokens, and ERC20 tokens into their wallets as well.

Compatibility

You need to make sure that you opt for a digital wallet that is compatible with the DeFi services. You can access all decentralized wallets if you connect a web3 wallet alongside. Mobile wallets are also a common practice nowadays, you can use the mobile wallets and get yourself integrated with the dApps browsers, this will ensure that you establish a connection with the DeFi applications without leaving the app.

Lately, DeFi has become the talk of the town and has made some noise. In order to make the financial services more simple and easy, they have launched a new product. But before getting into that, it is important to know what are the best DeFi wallets that you can use for your transactions.

In order to take part in any activity in the DeFi network, it is important that you have access to a DeFi digital wallet. DeFi wallets come with a variety of features like usability, and security. Your DeFi wallets help you store your assets in a safe and secure way.

Let's get started and discuss some of the best options of digital wallets that are available for you to choose from:

Best DeFi Wallets to use in 2021

1. MetaMask

MetaMask is said to be the most popular digital wallet. MetaMask is both a wallet and a browser. You will be able to spend, buy, sell, and interchange your digital assets with ease by using the app.

Through this wallet, you can log into websites safely and trade assets, buy or spend money, lend, borrow, publish content, play games, etc. all with ease and have your wallet protected.

MetaMask also assists you in providing access to web3 applications by using browsers like Google Chrome.

You can send and receive Ethereum transactions in a few minutes.

You can ETH, ERC20 tokens, ERC721 tokens in your digital wallet as well. It is backed by two exchanges. You can use these exchanges to purchase cryptocurrency.

You can use MetaMask on a lot of devices. MetaMask supports three browsers including Google Chrome, Brave, and Firefox. You can use it on the IOS and android devices using an app.

2. Coinbase Wallet

The other wallet that you can use is the Coinbase wallet. Like MetaMask, Coinbase is also considered to be one of the best wallets out there to store your assets. The app is not exclusive and customized for your DeFi assets only.

Cryptocurrencies and NFTs can all be stored in a single place by using a digital wallet. It enables people to trade 500 assets on DEXes. Not just that but also permits you to get interested in your holdings. It is not mandatory for you to own an account on a coin base.

More than 500 tokens are accepted on the wallet. BTC, ETH, USDT, UNI, LINK< LTC are a few tokens that are accepted.

You will also learn more about decentralized exchanges, DeFi protocols, collectibles, and crypto apps.

You can access the CoinBase wallet via an app for both android and iOS devices.

3. Eidoo

You can help manage your assets using the Eidoo wallet in a much efficient way. A lot of tokens can be accessed in an enhanced way using a DeFi exchange which comes built-in. This provides ease in buying, selling, trading, and managing your digital assets.

Your ERC-20 tokens will be stored in a single location so you are able to access them easily and not have them scattered across multiple platforms.

You can also store your BTC and other tokens that you possess on whatever device you want. Not just that but you can also access all your assets that are distributed across multiple devices.

Automatic swaps are possible due to a decentralized exchange that comes built-in with the wallet. By using the Eidoo app you can manage more than one accounts, this wallet makes it easy for you to do this. Just in case, you want separate wallet addresses, you can simply have them.

Your portfolio management becomes really easy using Eidoo. You get to try new things on the DeFi network as well.

Additionally, the Eidoo wallet can be used with OSX, Windows, and Linux. It also has Android and iOS apps.

4. Trezor

Trezor is also considered among one of the leading digital DeFi wallets that the user can use. This cold storage wallet basically has two models, namely Trezor and Trezor Model T. Improved affordability is a feature that is provided in the first model Trezor. The second model of this wallet, Trezor Model T is considered to be used in high-end pricing. Both of these wallets are great to use as well as provide the best possible security features to keep the assets of its users safe and protected.

In order to access the wallet, the users would require a pin. The order of the keypad changes continuously with every usage. Using the Trezor Model T's touch screen can make the input of a pin easy.

5. Argent

If you talk about the finest DeFi wallet that is available, well, then that's Argent. Like every other wallet, Argent helps you store your Ethereum and other DeFi tokens safely and securely. It has a very simple and easy-to-use user interface. Additionally, you can also trade, buy, sell and exchange your assets using this wallet in a few minutes. Not just that but you can also earn interest from these assets.

Secondly, this wallet helps you in keeping your assets secure by multi-signature security. With the multi-signature security, you will not require a seed phrase. You can lock and unlock your wallet with ease and no seed phrase is needed.

You can also access the DeFi and Ethereum, Compound, Uniswap, Lido, Yearn, Aave, WalletConnect, all with a single click.

Using Argent will allow you to exchange at the best price using decentralized exchanges like Uniswap, Balancer, Curve, and others.

This digital DeFi wallet can help you in providing a simple interface and even simpler process of displaying, sending, and storing your NFTs securely. Purchasing crypto is also very easy, you can do so by using a credit card or bank transfer.

6. MyEtherWallet

Another great wallet that you can use is the MyEtherWallet, also known as MEW. This wallet can be used for free. It allows the users to interact with the Ethereum blockchain by using a client-side interface.

Using this wallet, you can also interact with smart contracts. This is basically an open-source project. However, you can use this wallet on IOS and android devices only.

Not just that but by using the MyEtherWallet, you can exchange your cryptocurrencies with fiat currencies, BTC and ERC-20.

Above was a list of a few DeFi digital wallets that are at the top of their game. Each one has its own features and characteristics. Do your research and see which one of them is going to work best for you.

12

CHAPTER

UNDERSTANDING DECENTRALIZED INSURANCE

Much appreciation and praise have been gathered by every of the service that is associated with the Decentralized Finance sector such as Crypto loans, Crypto Derivatives, Futures Trading, etc., although Decentralized Insurance is the one area holding significance that is not frequently discussed. The riskiness of the finance sector demands that there be a mechanism to protect against risks and threats. One such concept that has the potential to act as a protection against threats is the Decentralized Finance Sector.

The immoral and illegal functioning of the Decentralized Insurance industry can be disturbed by the transparency and trustless feature of the blockchain forming the foundation of DeFi. Demonstration of protocols of decentralized insurance are protective measures that can act as the safeguards of the crypto industry, this is analogous to blockchain acting as the safety net of the industry.

In this blog, we will understand how Blockchain technology can influence Decentralized Insurance to protect crypto assets and cover risks.

Use-Cases of Decentralized Insurance

Over the past few years, huge losses of investor funds have occurred due to innumerable cases of hacking smart contracts, cyber-attacks on exchange platforms, etc. A malware attack could not even be prevented by the platform's benevolent DAO, which can cause a loss of billions. Such results could be prevented by quite a few use-cases of Decentralized Insurance.

Crypto Wallet Insurance

In order to cover the danger of robbery of crypto wallets during an attack, solutions have been developed by companies like Etherisc. In the survey conducted by Etherisc to comprehend the requirement for decentralized insurance, it was agreed by the majority of users that wallets should be insured but rarer options available in the market for the same. Crypto wallet insurance covering a large sum was started being provided by Etherisc once the need for crypto wallet insurance was understood. This is considered to be the best use case of DeFi.

Protection for Loans That Use Crypto as a Collateral

The insurance policy pays off a crypto loan if the collateral provided by a borrower is destroyed or stolen. Another remarkable application of decentralized insurance is the creation of a consortium for protecting and securing crypto-backed loans, this was carried out by Etherisc, along with several other companies including Sweetbridge, Celsius, Nexo, Libra Credit. Mac McGary, who is the President of the Sweetbridge Alliance, said that nowadays the collateral insurance provides both the borrowers and the lenders with some security from the crypto lending networks in an unstable market.

Smart Contract Cover

Smart Contract Cover, which is an amazing result of decentralized insurance, this insurance makes up for the damage caused in case the address of a chosen smart contract is hacked by a hacker and then the hacker uses it for exploiting the investor's account which may lead to losing funds or transferring the funds to another address. In the case when the funds are lost permanently and are not recoverable, that loss is also covered by Smart Contract Insurance. This results in easy and smooth loaning of crypto loans from the investors, without caring much about repayment or losses. The Smart Contract cover has been developed by the company Nexus Mutual.

Benefits of Decentralized Insurance

Complete protection of DeFi deposits, safeguarding risk against crypto instability and flash crash as well as defense against the threat of theft and attack on crypto wallets are some of the facilities offered by Decentralized Insurance. Users are protected against any imaginable DeFi risk which covers both technical and financial risks, which builds a feeling of safety among investors. Apart from this the platforms also make it certain the complete process of submitting, claiming and processing and payouts occur in an exceptionally safe, reliable, and transparent environment.

1)Safeguarding the DeFi deposits.

2) Protecting against the instability of crypto and flash crash.
3) Instant improvement of tokenized crypto
4) Protection against the peril of theft and attack on crypto wallets
5) Protection of funds on exchange platforms from hacks
6) Covers technical and financial risks
7) Immediate claim payouts
8) Trustless claim and risk assessment

Decentralized Insurance Platforms

There are some renowned decentralized insurance providers in the market present nowadays including Nexus
Mutual, Etherisc, CDx, Opyn, VouchForMe, etc.

The smart contract cover was innovated by Nexus Mutual, which is a decentralized insurance platform built on the Ethereum network. Insurance policy can be chosen by users who have loaned money on exchanges like Compound or Dharma.

As stated already, some remarkable products have been built by Etherisc for the purpose of crypto wallet insurance and covering collateralized crypto loans. Loss of funds caused due to exchange hacks is covered by a platform CDx.

Decentralized Insurance — A favorable area for DeFi

Due to the transparency and protection offered to investors by Decentralized insurance, it is considered to be a promising sector Only a few products are offered as of now but it surely has the potential to become bigger and vaster in the upcoming. For many years to come the market will be ruled by DeFi and its applications like Decentralized Finance.

13

CHAPTER

FUTURE OF DEFI

During the summer of 2020, what is also said to be the decentralized finance summer, Ethereum finally escaped from the shadows of Bitcoin and took hold of the market. DeFI which was designed to reconstruct customary financial systems with fewer traders is now being widely used for lending, borrowing, and the buying and selling of tokens. Ethereum runs a large part of these decentralized applications (DApps), and a lot of traffic was seen on the network in 2020. This activity also trended upwards due to yield farming, which is also known as liquidity mining, this allows holders to produce rewards with their crypto capital.

But with the rise in activity, Ethereum's transaction fees also increased. May came with the news of Ethereum's gas fee skyrocketing. It's instinctive that dealing in DeFi is only meaningful when managing capital exceeding any network fees. Consequently, the users understood that the blockchain was nearing being unusable.

No doubt Ethereum is a dynamic and populous blockchain, but alternatives are being provided by other potential buyers. For example, billions in assets are attracted by Binance Smart Chain (BSC) and Solana (SOL) which are layer one protocols, whereas layer two solutions such as Polygon (MATIC) are seizing the attention of Ethereum's dissatisfied users as they are not only compatible but Ethereum based products but are also delivering low gas and rapid speed of transactions. Even though Ethereum's gas fees have reached a high over the past year and the faster networks are growing rapidly, these other chains are yet to beat Ethereum.

As the end of 2021 is approaching, the narrative of "Ethereum vs. the rest" is finally changing. Developers are now realizing the worth of a cross-chain future instead of having to pick one blockchain to build on. We are no longer creating a solitary chain with a competitive edge, but instead, we are concerned with making certain that all chains can operate synonymously to develop the industry.

More blockchains, more value

It's unavoidable that projects will ultimately connect manifold blockchains, thus making the transfer of information from one chain to another smooth. Actually, the cryptocurrency market and adopting multichain is not as much of a zero-sum game as is often mentioned. And, as we understand the multichain future better, the capabilities, usability, and expandability it could potentially bring to the new users will become more distinct.

Instead of doubting the actuality of the multichain feature, it should be viewed positively. Numerous smart contract platforms impact the accessibility, economic feasibility, and innovation of blockchain. Even though blockchains are disjointed right now, they will eventually come together and create a compatible and fast protocol network that will accomplish our demands. Because of this, we won't have to worry about how we're transacting or what we're transacting on since it won't be important.

If we look at the interoperability at this point, we still haven't reached there yet. This problem can eventually improve when it is adopted by the masses. And once it is done, then there would be nothing that would stop this industry from going even bigger. A lot of projects are planning to move to the multichain future in order to stay relevant.

Rapid growth has been seen in Decentralized Finance (DeFi) since mid-2020. Even though this is still the beginning of DeFi we have realized that decentralizing financial services at scale is possible. Here are a few important insights that need to be addressed in order to make this industry go bigger and better.

Back in 2008, the world was going through a global financial crisis, the people who were interested in bitcoin and understood its true potential saw it as an independent and innovative network of digital money. Audacious claims were made by them and they stated how bitcoin will open doors to a new and improved financial system. They also stated that bitcoin will influence the ideas and data privacy that was implemented previously.

In the year 2013, Ethereum was launched and it took bitcoin a step further. A lot of changes and enhancements were made in the bitcoin system that was presented originally. Not just that but during the same time, the concept of smart contracts emerged. Bitcoin is an interchangeable and easily transmitted store of values that are recorded on a digital ledger. recorded on a decentralized, shared ledger. Smart contracts allow the users to carry out a transaction by executing a certain line of code without any intermediary. Smart contracts are electronic in nature. Not just that but it makes sure that the payments are all released at the same time the goods are delivered. Smart contracts have become a very important use case of these electronic financial services.

Ever since DeFi came into play, it had foreshadowed Ethereum. DeFi provides a platform on which instructions can be executed as they are written. It can be associated with the control of assets digitally and can lead to designing of the financial products. This is the method that is adopted by those who provide these financial services. Previously it was the intermediaries and other third-party applications that we're trusted to make sure that the products are all operating the way they should. However, in the DeFi systems, it's the code that has to be trusted.

What makes DeFi unique?

The motivation as to why it is so tempting to use blockchain technology to remake the finance space lies in how the market can become accessible to anyone. Another reason that makes this concept so enticing is the fact that anyone can rearrange a DeFi that is present already contributing to constructing a new one. The composability of a network successfully constituted of blocks of interconnecting components, also means that newer inventions and wants in the finance space can be effortlessly constructed on top of the network and plugged together, where everything is being overseen by smart contracts.

Programs that spontaneously accomplish an action when after the occurrence of a certain event is called Smart contracts which enable users to define rules overseen by technology. In order for the smart contracts to work how they are intended to, there are conditions. These conditions are defined and written into smart contracts. These conditions when are fulfilled will result in the triggering of either sending or receiving funds as per the instructions that are written into the code in the smart contracts. Other smart contracts also work in a similar way. This is a way to automate the distribution of standing financial services over the blockchain network. Not just that but new services can be created and run where the network makes sure that the conditions for the execution of smart contracts.

Smart contracts are essential for DeFi applications and projects. The majority of the smart contracts are created on Ethereum. That is because of the extensive accessibility of developers and the capability to work with the programming language of Ethereum, the language is known as Solidity. The creation of smart contracts is backed by Solidity. The majority of the blockchain networks now agree to DeFi applications as well.

The DeFi landscape

DeFi projects continue to be profitable ventures. In the majority of the projects a large portion of the token supply, or the electronic shares that control and protect the operation of the main net. are reserved by the development teams. According to this not only can the teams earn profit from the assumption of costs but the firm is also enabled to be a member of the correct operation of the protocol, which earns it rewards for effectively securing the proper operation of the network.

14

CHAPTER

TIPS FOR INVESTMENT IN DEFI

As it is evident from the name, DeFi that it is a term that refers to decentralized finance. It is a network that is based on blockchain and consists of tools used by digital financial that comprise all digital securities and cryptocurrency to NFTs (Non-Fungible Tokens) and CBDCs (Central Bank Digital Currency). DeFi is a peer-to-peer financial service that licenses you to trade crypto and other relevant services. DeFi is dependent upon the Ethereum blockchain and cryptocurrencies. The DeFi market grew bigger in the year 2020. Statistics recorded raised from $700 million to $13 billion. Presently, this figure has gone up to $40 billion.

The global financial systems are evolving and transforming digitally. This displays that the DeFi financial system has a lot of potentials and can become even stronger and draw the attention of the world. But it is important that you know and understand the asset first and then how to invest in the market.

DeFi Assets

Trading DeFi assets, which are tokens representing DeFi networks, applications, or protocols, is one of the ways to invest in DeFi, this usually involves buying low and selling high. Not everyone can do this because there is a high risk involved and is extremely volatile. Nonetheless, the prospects thrive. A few examples are Uniswap (UNI), Terra (LUNA), Wrapped Bitcoin (WBTC), and Chainlink (LINK).

DeFi Staking

Another option for achieving passive income based on DeFi is staking. In staking funds are locked by users in a crypto wallet and they participate in maintaining the operations of a PoS blockchain system, which results in users getting a rate of interest that is already defined. When everyone is offering negative rates of interest, receiving a reasonable interest rate on your holdings, especially if you intend on selling them anyways is worthwhile. Assets worth a total of around $21 to $23 billion are staked on DeFi platforms, as of January 2021.

DeFi Yield Farming

Yield farming has become viral and is based on Ethereum. DeFi is an all-inclusive category of the peer-to-peer service, self-custody, KYC-less, finance apps that are based on Ethereum, but yield farming labels popular enticements program where liquidity is provided in return for a DeFi application.

DeFi Lending & Lending Protocol

Users are allowed to give away their crypto to someone else and in return earn interest on the loan on DeFi Lending platforms. Defi lending benefits lenders as well as borrowers. Not only does it offer options for margin trading, but it also enables long-term investors to lend assets and earn higher interest rates. Moreover, it also allows users to access fiat currency credit to borrow loans at lower rates than DEX. Furthermore, it can be sold by the users on a centralized exchange for a cryptocurrency and then lend to a DEX.

DeFi Funds

Trusts and Funds are another way to invest in the DeFi network. This is the most welcoming way for beginners to get acquainted with DeFi. Bitwise's DeFi Index Fund, Grayscale's Diversified DeFi fund, and Galaxy Digital's DeFi index tracker fund are some examples of DeFi funds.

Risk vs. Reward with DeFi

What makes DeFi an eye-catching and possibly profitable investment is the multiplicity of investment prospects, as well as the sustained progression of the market. However, just like with any investment, this also has risks that market investors should be made familiar with before they dive in. Not only is there a risk of the impact the crypto volatility may have but there are also security and scam risks with DeFi, that can be attributed to the DeFi protocols relying on smart contracts having weak spots that can be exploited.

The weaknesses can be decreased by the DeFi market, the technology running it, as well as the required regulations that will unavoidably be achieved, and the appeal of this digital finance system will increase. So all one has to do is be patient, be smart, and never miss a good opportunity.

Decentralized Finance (DeFi) has gathered a lot of courtesy recently. The innovation has been led by Uniswap and Compound.

Some distinguished developments include:

- DeFi market capitalization has surpassed $10 Bn
- Uniswap has outdone Coinbase

Yearn Finance has gone beyond the worth of Bitcoin for a solitary unit, it's all-time high touching the $43,000 mark.

Nonetheless, the DeFi landscape has a dark spot that is deeply hidden. The market has been tainted by rug pulls and hacks. Some people went through huge losses of money. It is significant to know the risk areas and stay safe.

Some tips to help you to take better Yield Farming decisions are given below:

1. High APY does not always guarantee high returns:

The very first thing that deceives people is high APY. For numerous projects, the opening APY is more than 10,000%. It is a great way to upsurge your money. Two questions arise:

The first one is will the High Yield be maintainable? Assess the timeline of the high yield. The supply in the early days is devaluated which results in high yields. It is halved in rapid progressions. However, this falls significantly over a short period.

The second question is will you be able to sell at a profit? Most of the time if you are able to earn a considerable amount in the early days of devaluation, you will be unable to sell the token as a majority of them will be locked. Assess the number of earned tokens you'd be able to sell.

For instance, three-quarters of Token in Luaswap is locked for initial 16 months.

2. Invest in Those Tokens That Have Authentic Use Cases:

Question yourself about why do you need the token given by the project. For many projects governance is highly overvalued. Can the token be used in any other way apart from Governance?

Are you aware of the fact that UNI can be used as collateral to get loans on other platforms? That is an actual convenience that gives UNI worth. Many other DeFi tokens are acquisitive and greedy without proper usefulness and are intended to fall.

3. Only invest in Audited Projects:

Invest in a project only and only if it is audited by a renowned organization. It is mandatory for the code of the project to be audited.

Many people invested in the yet "in production" project Eminence, when Andre Cronje revealed his connection with it due to his good reputation. But since the project was still not completed and was not audited, it was unavoidably hacked and the hacker stole $15M.

4. Inclusion of Gas Fees in your profit calculations:

It should be noted that in the present days of high gas fees the actual investment consists of the fees for buying Pair of tokens in Uniswap, accepting Liquidity Pool Pair in Uniswap, approving LP Staking in the Yield Farming Protocol, Actual Staking in Yield Farming Protocol, Unstake in Yield Farming Protocol, sell yield token in Uniswap, Removing Liquidity in Uniswap.

All these things add up to be the total fee that cannot be neglected and should always be a part of the profit calculations.

5. When Do You Plan to Enter Yield Farming project?

The time you enter a project is also very crucial because after the first few days the market inclines to fall. So it should be carefully decided when you want to enter the project. If you plan to enter a project after some time, which can be as early as a day. You cannot say that there is a selling pressure created which is from the first day's profit.

6. Take Impermanent Loss into consideration:

The amount of tokens that you have combined in the liquidity pools is adjusted by Uniswap as the worth of yield farming tokens falls. What will happen is that the amount of your yield farming token will raise and your second token (for instance ETH) will fall.

This will fall in the ratio of your unique pool submission. Your whole worth will be lower than what you would have got if you would have just held these two tokens. However, it should be noted that temporary loss is not sustained till the time the liquidity is removed. This problem can be solved by a long-time liquidity supply in the pool.

7. Don't Forget to Calculate the Price on Over-all Supply:

In the beginning, the token price is pretty high due to the low circulation but as more and more tokens are in circulation in the upcoming days. the price of the token will fall. Ascertain the position where you want your invested project to land in the CoinMarketCap ranking and try to conclude its unit price on the basis of another project with a similar supply in that CMC ranking. You will be surprised to find how low the unit price could reach!

There are high risks involved when investing in DeFi. You should only invest the amount if you are prepared for losses. Invest only in trustworthy projects. Do not invest only because of the fear of missing out. Spend some money on the cost of learning.

15
CHAPTER

WHAT IS DEFI MARKETPLACE

TThe terms 'cryptocurrency', 'blockchain', and 'Bitcoin' have revolutionized the world entirely. Since the time when these terms were introduced tons of modernization has been witnessed in this space. DeFi is one such trend that has taken over the world of crypto over the past year, especially after BTC reached a new all-time high. Just in a short amount of time these decentralized marketplaces have made great progress, and have resulted in a very substantial modification in the world of crypto. If you are uncertain as to which DeFi marketplace is best suited for you this piece will help you figure it all out.

What are DeFi Marketplaces?

DeFi marketplaces are decentralized marketplaces which means that there is no middleman involved. The fundamental idea of DeFi marketplaces is very comparable to blockchain, in which the software can be downloaded by a user who can get directly linked to everyone else using the software at that instant of time.

This is how an extraordinary level of transparency is guaranteed by the platform, around the rules and working of the marketplace. Another characteristic of blockchain, which is also followed by the DeFi marketplaces is its permanence, meaning that data cannot be deleted or withdrawn by any means once it is logged into the secured system of a blockchain.

What makes DeFi marketplaces important is that centralized exchanges like Binance and Coinbase would not be used for trading if the idea of decentralization brought into view by digital currencies was better received and loved by the audiences.

Top 5 Defi Marketplaces based on Transaction Volume:

Below is a list of the top 5 decentralized marketplaces based on total trading volume concerning data from the last 30 days.

PancakeSwap

PancakeSwap is a digital exchange that was developed for the exchange of BEP20 Binance Smart Chain tokens. PancakeSwap uses the Automated market maker (AMM) model and has a market value of somewhat $16 billion.

This is how trading could be done against a liquidity pool by the users of the platform. The platform permits users to credit an amount of money into the pool, getting LP or liquidity provider tokens, which are traded for the money. The other name for the Liquidity Provider (LP) tokens is FLIP tokens.

UniSwap

UniSwap is another protocol for Ethereum's automated market maker, UniSwap also has a market value of $16 billion, just like PancakeSwap. It was launched in the year 2018, the platform is termed as a comparatively simple and smart border for swapping ERC20 tokens.

Analogous to PancakeSwap, a model has been formalized for the creation of a liquidity pool of reserves. The platform is used by liquidity providers and traders as one open-source frontend. UniSwap could be considered as a pioneer in this arena, in order to continue its leadership, it launched UniSwap v3 just recently.

MDEX

The smartest exchange innovation of recent times, MDEX is an automatic market-making decentralized exchange that functions around the fundamentals of fund pools for its users. The market volume of MDEX is well over $15 billion and it operates around Ethereum and Heco Chain.

It runs as a single hybrid platform and is a combination of the low transaction fees from the Heco chain and the vast ecosystem of Ethereum.

SushiSwap

An exchange platform based on the Ethereum blockchain network, SushiSwap is a rapidly developing DeFi marketplace. This platform has a market value of over $77 million, and it strives to encourage users to trade in crypto.

In order for it to achieve the trade goals, SushiSwap functions over the liquidity pool.

BurgerSwap

BurgerSwap is known to be the very first democratized decentralized American Metal Market (AMM), it operates on the binance smart chain. The market volume of BurgerSwap is around $51 million. BurgerSwap is one of the most noticeable and trustworthy platforms and enables any user to create proposals that let them review the transaction fees, block rewards, and make complete use of other such exchange parameters.

DeFi and blockchain function in the same way in terms of not needing any traders and the storage of transaction data on different decentralized systems. DeFi currencies serve a multitude of motives, such as easy transactions which are comparable to the functions of a virtual currency like Bitcoin. Unlike currencies like bitcoin, Defi currencies can also be used for intricate financial operations. Not only this but using DeFi marketplaces enable you to stay true to the original vision of cryptocurrencies and blockchain tech.

16

CHAPTER

INVEST IN DEFI PLATFORMS

TThe banking system functioning today has been working the same as it has been for the past so many years. This process has become more and more convenient for the users through the use of the internet. The Internet has greatly transformed the way global transactions are now handled. But this current banking system is centralized. This means that if any fault occurs at a point that would mean the crashing of the whole system. All those people who have their money deposited in the bank would be lost as a result.

Now if you look at the concept of decentralized finance, you would see that it is more of a blessing to the whole banking sector as well as the finance sector. With cryptocurrencies and blockchain technologies becoming common, the practices in the conventional banking system are diminishing.

Decentralized finance comes with a new realm of possibilities for its users. It is gaining popularity with each passing day. But it is still regarded as a new industry and it is still struggling with people commonly accepting it for use. There are a number of decentralization finance protocols developed by people who are really trying to change the DeFi game for good.

Commonly used DeFi protocols are explained in detail below.

Aave

Aave was created back in 2017. Aave is considered to be one of the best platforms for DeFi. It has all the features and characteristics that are enough to swap the conventional finance and banking practices with decentralized platforms. This decentralized platform has made the whole transaction process easy for its users. The users can borrow and lend digital currencies without a hassle. Now we know that the basic function of banking is to lend and borrow money. This protocol enables you to do so, which means that this protocol can change the whole game of conventional banking for good. It also allows the borrowers and the lenders to feel satisfied as the system will work the way it should. This is made sure by the smart contracts.

Compound

Most of the De-Fi projects are based and run on the Ethereum blockchain. Similarly, Compound also runs on an Ethereum blockchain. The compound was developed in the year 2017. Using this protocol, the user can both borrow and lend money contradicting the collateral that is often used in such borrowing and lending services. The lenders credit all their coins and money into a liquidity pool for a trade. The best possible rates for the trade are structured as per the demand and supply of the user. Smart contracts are used in order to automate this process. This is a great way for users to earn profit from the Compound liquidity pool.

Curve Finance

Curve Finance allows the users to exchange and trade Ethereum. Curve finance is basically a decentralized cryptocurrency exchange. It is also responsible to maintain and deliver liquidity in the DeFi market.

Curve Finance has some very interesting features, such as it can let you exchange your stablecoins with a very reduced mining fee. The majority of the DeFi platforms use cryptocurrencies as a source of liquidity. This liquidity is powered by the instability of cryptocurrencies.

Uniswap

If you are discussing the DeFi protocols and not talking about Uniswap, that would not be fair. Uniswap is a renowned protocol of the DeFi network. Uniswap allows the users to be in complete control of their funds. This is the key characteristic that provides an edge to Uniswap over any other centralized exchange. Plus, a listing of coins can be done without any cost.

Uniswap majorly has two smart contracts that it is composed of. The exchange smart contract and factory smart contract. Both of these have their own features and purposes. Both of these smart contracts are independent of each other and thus both of them can perform the functions that are assigned to them without any interference. Exchange smart contract is responsible for trading and token exchange whereas the factory smart contract is responsible for adding new tokens to the platform.

MakerDAO

Maker is a decentralized organization MakerDAO and software platform Maker Protocol that assists in the issuance and management of DAI.

Maker is said to be the first project that tried designing and building products that are related to decentralized finance. It also worked on making smart-contract-enabled blockchains. MKR provides the users with direct participation in the DAI authorization.

The people who have the MKR are eligible to vote or any changes that may be suggested to be incorporated into the protocol. The voting of the holders of MKR is dependent upon the number of staked Maker tokens. In Maker when the transaction is completed and approved by both parties, the tokens are then burnt so there is no left.

Synthetix

Synthetix uses the Ethereum network and its inherent standard smart contract. One of the fastest-growing DeFi is Synthetix. It is a decentralized asset insurance protocol that is built on Ethereum. Synthetic versions of the real-world assets are minted as tokens using the Synthetix. It pegs the worth of the asset that they represent.

The synthetic assets uphold their peg via no-arbitrage principle arbitrage that lets the stakers burn additional synths and the open market liquidity for synths on other decentralized exchanges. This protocol has proved to be helpful in improving the manifestation of investors towards cryptocurrencies.

Yearn. Finance

Yearn. Finance is another important and one of the major protocols of the DeFi.

Andre Cronje developed Yearn. Finance in the year 2020. It is a protocol that deals with the optimization of the yield and increasing the abilities of DeFi by automatically switching between different lending protocols. In order to decentralize Yearn Finance more, Andre handed out a governance token in July of 2020. The token that was created was handed out through liquidity mining. It gave away no VCs, no funder rewards, no dev rewards. This model was very famous among the DeFi community as money was being collected in the incentivized liquidity pools topping $600M. There are several independent products that Yearn. Finance provides for users.

Pancakeswap

Pancakeswap may sound like a very delicious breakfast but it actually is a DeFi application. This DeFi application provides a way for blockchain developers to present crypto projects of their own. Not just that but also allows them to exchange crypto coins and do crypto farming. Pancakeswap is built on the Binance Smart Chain. This blockchain has all the abilities to replace the Ethereum blockchain which is one of the most famous blockchains. It can then become a go-to blockchain for the DeFi platforms.

Sushiswap

SushiSwap was launched in the latter half of 2020. It was developed by a team that did not disclose its identity and chose to remain anonymous. A new concept was presented in SushiSwap. It was named a Vampire attack. It works on tapping the liquidity out of Uniswap. SushiSwap was able to gather liquidity of $1B. This was so because the people who provided liquidity were given Sushi tokens in return. SushiSwap backs 14 distinctive blockchains as well as 20 wallets, all being different from the others. It joined hands with a number of DeFi platforms like Aave and Yearn. Finance.

Falconswap

FalconSwap is a second layer protocol for DeFi on Ethereum. Falconswap comes with a variety of pros. Apart from a reduced gas fee, improved privacy, etc., there are two of the most key advantages that Falconswap has over the other protocols. Falcon pool and Falcon exchange are two great offerings of Falconswap. It can be associated with different protocols, exchanges, and wallets. It has improved decentralization in finance up to a great extent. You can do immediate and permission-less transactions using Falconswap. The liquidity it has gathered and the numbers that they present are indeed not a hoax.

After the introduction of DeFi, the finance sector has improved a lot. The innovations that are being brought about in this field are a great way for it to grow and make it big. Although, it is relatively new right now, with time and evolution of technology it will be soon enough that it would replace traditional finance and banking. Well, right now is a good time for any investor or stakeholder to invest in this field and for a developer to develop DeFi applications that can be run on these platforms. You can reach out to the blockchain development companies that know and understand DeFi, they shall be able to guide you in the best possible way so you launch into this field with numerous opportunities for you to avail yourself.

CHAPTER

WHAT ARE DIFFERENT DEFI DERIVATIVES

It is assumed that the DeFi derivate market will expand a lot in the year 2021. This expansion and development in the market would allow a number of investors and traders to earn a lot of money in the form of interest. To know and understand it better, it is important that we look back at the history of derivatives in the DeFi market. It would also get clear that what is going on right now and what will the future look like.

Before moving forward, let us understand what a derivate is?

For all those people who never heard of derivatives before. Financial securities that originate their worth from something else, such as an asset or collection of assets are known as derivatives. In conventional finance, derivatives are very popular and commonly used. These derivatives let people invest in things that are financed by something else such as a stock, bond, commodity, or currency. Basically, derivatives are contracts where people agree to trade certain assets at specific pre-established prices.

A brief history of DeFi derivatives

In order to understand the DeFi derivatives better, let's take a look at the past and see how they came into being. DeFi markets initially used the Synthetix in order to achieve some grip. Synthetix is a project that was launched back in 2017. Synthetix allows its users to create synthetic versions of real-world assets as tokens. These assets are called synths. There are a number of other platforms for DeFi derivatives as well such as Hegic, Pulse, and Mirror.

What's so good about DeFi derivatives?

If you compare the DeFi derivatives and the centralized finance derivatives, you will see that DeFi derivatives are more advantageous and provide a wide range of benefits. Primarily, DeFi derivatives are easily accessible. You do not have to give away all your personal information such as proof of ID, previous bank statements, national insurance, or social security numbers. Just because they are not centralized, it is not mandatory for your identity to be proven. The majority of the people can access DeFi derivatives than they can CeFi, as CeFi projects require this information to be given away. Because of this, DeFi derivatives have the latent to grow considerably higher than CeFi.

You are able to create synthetic contracts that are attached to your assets using the DeFi derivatives. On the other hand, this is something that you cannot do in the CeFi derivatives as they are all created by a central authority that controls everything. As anyone can create derivatives means that many more derivatives can be made because the number of people who are making them is higher. Transparency is ensured as they are created on a blockchain network.

The current state of DeFi derivatives

There are a number of reasons to monitor the DeFi derivatives market. But here a question arises and that is that what is the reason people think that in the year 2021 DeFi derivatives will go big? Well, that is because as per the statistical data recorded in the year 2020 estimates that the market is at this point worth 15.5 trillion in gross market value. There was an increase of 34% in the market even after the pandemic. Now, that the pandemic is almost over it is highly likely for this number to increase even more. This market would expand more if the DeFi markets permit people to develop their own derivatives.

Ethereum 2.0 was launched back in 2020. This is also a plus point in regards to the DeFi derivatives. This will make Ethereum further scalable. Scalable means that Ethereum will be able to deal with and manage more users, transactions, lower transaction fees, blockchain activity and speed up transaction times than it is now. If you look at the scope and extent of the derivate market you would see that it would greatly help Ethereum and the DeFi network grow.

DeFi has been the talk of the town and caught a lot of attention from the media in the past months. This would further aware people of what they are and what is potential they possess. This means that a lot of investors and traders would be drawn towards this field.

Now you know about all these features and influences, so you know why is everyone in the market keeping track of what occurs with the DeFi derivatives. This brings us to conclude that yes, 2021is a big year for this industry, and the day is not far when the traders and investors opt for DeFi over CeFi when talking about derivatives.

Some Of The Most Important Derivatives Protocols In Defi.

At this point, you have gathered a little information about the derivatives and what they are. So let's move forward and discuss a few salient protocols in DeFi.

Synthetix

Synthetix has to be the first protocol that comes to our minds when talking about derivatives in DeFi.

Synthetix uses the Ethereum network and its inherent standard smart contract. One of the fastest-growing DeFi is Synthetix. It is a decentralized asset insurance protocol that is built on Ethereum. Synthetic versions of the real-world assets are minted as tokens using the Synthetix. It pegs the worth of the asset that they represent. You can also use this protocol and trade fiat currencies and commodities as well. You can use platforms such as Kwenta, DHedge, and Paraswap. You are supposed to provide collateral in order to supply a token that represents a synthetic asset. The token that is issued is the SNX token.

Synthetix is now moving to layer 2 of Ethereum. This transition of Synthetix will lead to the gas fee reduction as well as make the protocol further scalable. Not just that but it is considered to be the very first protocol that is transitioning to layer 2.

Presently the worth that is locked in the Synthetix protocol is $1.8B. If you compare this number with any of the other DeFi derivative protocols, it is the highest.

UMA

In order to create synthetic assets, you can use the UMA protocol as well.

Synthetix was an over-collateralizing protocol whereas UMA is not. You can create derivatives that are free of price as this protocol does not depend upon the price oracles. This provides a way to add a lot of assets. These priceless derivatives make this possible in UMA whereas, in Synthetix, it would not have been possible due to the price feed.

Presently, the worth that is locked in the protocol is $63M.

Hegic:

Hegic is also a new protocol that has been launched in the DeFi network which permits the users to conduct a non-custodial and permission-less trade.

Users have the power to purchase put and call options on ETH and WBTC. Not just that but the users can provide liquidity and sell ETH calls and put options.

The total worth locked in the protocol was $100M, 3 months after it was launched. A total cumulative options trading volume of ~$168M and generated over $3.5M in fees.

The hedge was developed by one person only. This displays that it only takes one person or a small team that could develop a product so useful for DeFi space.

Opyn

You can trade options through Opyn as well. Opyn was launched at the beginning of 2020. It allowed protection to ETH downside and upside.

It also permitted its users to hedge against ETH price movements, flash crashes, and volatility.

The protocol that they launched recently offers European, cash-settled options that exercise on their own when expired.

European and American are the two options styles in Opyn.

European options can only be exercised at the time of expiration on the other hand the American options can be exercised until expired.

Hegic uses the American style options and Opyn uses the European style options.

Ever since opyn launched, it has gathered $100M volume from trade.

Perp

The perp is considered a new addition to the DeFi derivatives protocols.

Using this protocol, you would be allowed to trade perpetual contracts. Now, what is a perpetual contract? Let's understand it. Centralized platforms like Bitmex, Binance, and Bybit use a popular product for their trade-in cryptocurrency network, which is known as a perpetual contract. You can trade and hold a perpetual contract for as long as you want because of no date of expiry.

This contract lets you trade ETH, BTC, YFI, DOT, and SNX. USDC, a stablecoin used in the DeFi system enables trades.

xDai Chain which is a solution of layer 2 scaling is used for processing the trades on this protocol. The gas fee that has to be paid is reduced a lot.

You don't have to pay any gas fee right now on trading perp protocol. You are required to pay for the gas fee only while you are crediting the USDC onto the platform.

Presently, the perp has achieved to attain $500M in volume and $500k in trading fees.

dYdX

dYdX is a protocol that was launched as an exchange of decentralized derivatives that allows you to spot, margin, and perpetual trading.

The dYdX design merges together the non-custodial and on-chain settlement with an off-chain low-latency matching engine with order books.

The volume of its trade covering all its products is $2.5 billion in the year 2020. This is a 40x increase if you compare it to the trade volume of the past year.

Just some time ago, dYdX was able to raise $10M in a Series B round managed by Three Arrows Capital as well as DeFiance Capital.

BarnBridge

Price instability and hedging yield productivity can be done by using the BarnBridge protocol. BarnBridge is basically a protocol for risk tokenizing.

Two products are of the BarnBridge are very much in use.

Smart Yield Bonds: Smart Yield Bonds help in reducing the rate of interest instability. Debt-based protocols are used to achieve this.

Smart Alpha Bonds: Smart Alpha Bonds help in the reduction of market price exposure risk. Distributed volatility derivatives are used to achieve this.

Presently, the worth that is locked in this protocol has surpassed the figure of $350M.

A program that mines liquidity is being run by BarnBridge. Through this program, it gives over its token to all the users that stake stablecoins, BOND-USDC LP tokens, or BOND tokens on the BarnBridge protocol. BOND is the token that is distributed.

18

CHAPTER

DEFI BENEFITS AND CHALLENGES

Before we discuss the boon and bane of DeFi, let's look back and discuss the history of traditional finance. We would also discuss how was the need for a new system felt that did not include any third party.

The finance methods that were used previously are diminishing now and it has come a long way. This historical overview will help us comprehend that why do we need decentralized finance and how we can introduce this concept to different areas.

During the beginning of human history, there was no concept of finance as the humans at that time were only concerned with food and finding a place to live. They would hunt in order to have something to eat. With the passage of time, humans increased and this led to their communication and interaction with each other.

Slowly and gradually, the concept of trade was born.

Trading started with the direct exchange of goods, people would exchange one good with another. You can exchange something you own for something somebody else owns.

The ratio would look something like this, 1:1, 2:1. But this was something that was not so clear.

This was not the only problem that was faced but another one was that majority of the people were not willing to exchange the product back or it might take long for this exchange to happen, which would make the goods become worthless.

With time the need for an index for the valuation of goods grew. This gave birth to money systems and finance systems. The first money was in the form of coins. These coins were made of electrum came around in 600 B.C.

A new way to trade

Now the way people are exchanging goods with money.

As the industry evolved, a lot of assets and money became known widespread. This led to the development of finance, banks, and third-party applications in order to manage these transactions and trading.

A few questions came up at this point:

- Did it resolve the problems that were faced?
- Who has the power and authority over money? Is it people or the governments?
- Was this money distribution fair and justified?
- Is money solving peoples' problems?
- Are the money transfers and transactions secure and protected even with the use of third-party applications and middlemen?

When there is an authorizing power that controls this money, it may give birth to a number of issues.

Unrestricted Printing of Money

Initially, the governments took it upon themselves and were thus granted the right to print money. They played the role of intermediaries in these transactions by creating central banks.

This is a fact that the more money you print, the higher the prices of goods become. If the costliness persists, it would do you no good even if you have a rise in your salary.

On the other hand, gold is a sparse asset, rare art, plus the bitcoin have also become of great value.

The value of money has been reduced due to monetary policy and high inflation.

The conventional financial systems have led people to lose confidence in finance. People have now discovered the benefits and advantages of decentralized finance.

Bitcoin creation led to attaining this aim.

The invention of bitcoin and other cryptocurrencies has opened new doors of opportunities for people who are interested in DeFi systems. The changes that have been made are momentous but they are still not considered as DeFi. The majority of the financial transactions are facilitated by the centralized exchange.

What's the dissimilarity between a bank and a centralized crypto exchange?

If you look at the two on a broader level, you would see that there does exist a difference between the two. Decentralization can lose its essence if a third party intervenes a lot in this system.

Let's consider a system that is entirely decentralized. But does this system is enough to meet our needs?

DeFi is flourishing and its popularity is increasing with every passing day. There are countless projects of DeFi on a number of blockchains. The majority of the conventional finance systems can be eased and simplified via DeFi. This is made possible without the intervention of any third-party applications. This is one of the most key features of the decentralized finance system.

This is said to be the new generation of financing.

A lot of people are of the view that DeFi is the future of finance and it can allow them to have considerable returns. Do these investments and transactions have any risks or are they risk-free?

In order to help the people who are new to this field to know and understand the pros and cons of the decentralized finance system.

Where DeFi shines

1. Decentralized exchanges (DEX)

Online trading services based on smart contracts. DEXes allow users to complete token exchanges as well trading that too without any third-party interference.

2. Automated Market Maker (AMM)

AMMs are similar to DEXes but with one major difference. Order books are used by the DEX platforms, pricing is done through this. AMM on the other hand practices a mathematical formula for pricing the assets. Tokens are earned from the liquidity that comes from liquidity providers.

3. Lending

Crypto loan is a very interesting feature that attracts a number of people. In this process, people who lend money earn interest on the payments whereas the borrowers can get the money they need.

4. Staking

A few of the blockchains are built on proof-of-work (PoW) such as Bitcoin while others are based on proof of stake(PoS). In a network based on PoS you get returns by locking your assets, staking helps with that in exchange for the provision of security and approving blockchain transactions.

5. Non-Fungible Token (NFT)

Non-fungible tokens have a lot of uses in the crypto network such as identification, arts (digital ownership), gaming, collectibles, sports, media & entertainment, real estate, etc.

6. No-Loss Games and Lotteries:

Another interesting feature that the DeFi has is that of Games and Lotteries. 'No-loss' lotteries may appear to be of zero risk. This leads the participants of the lottery to get the money back and the profit that has been generated is given to a lucky winner. All this is done without any third-party intervention by using smart contracts.

Where does DeFi have an Advantage?

1. Bye-Bye to human error and mismanagement

The majority of the issues that arise in the finance sector are due to the interference of the third-party applications and mishandling of the Central Banks. Due to smart contracts, these human errors gets eliminated. In case, they are written poorly, then this risk would persist.

2. Quick and permanent access

In traditional finance, if you ever required a loan then you would have to go through a huge hassle. This process is pretty time-consuming. But with DeFi you can loan whatever amount of money you want with just a click. The process would take a couple of minutes to process and get the loan immediately. The market can be accessed whatever any time you want from wherever you want. All you need is a stable internet connection.

3. A Healthier System

Global shocks like the pandemics can be really hard on the Centralized systems. Covid-19 had been an example that showed the vulnerability of these systems. The reason for this vulnerability is that these systems are based on the direct interaction of people. However, in decentralized systems, you don't really have to come in direct contact with each other. Prices of cryptocurrencies and companies have been doing better in this prevailing crisis.

4. Permission-less Operations:

Intermediary grants permission for any trade and transactions to be carried out in the traditional finance system. If you have to withdraw some money from the bank, you will have to wait for its approval, and once approved you will receive it only then. However, in the case of DeFi, all the financial activities are carried out permissionless. This is a pretty long list and not limited to these only. You can do some research from the internet and discover more of the benefits of the DeFi projects.

But does that mean that are all the DeFi services and platforms free of any risk? Well, of course, they are not risk-free. There may be risks and challenges that can be faced in the DeFi space.

What are the challenges facing DeFi projects?

There may be pros of DeFi projects but there are some cons as well. The majority of the DeFi projects are built on the Ethereum blockchain network and the problems that are faced by these projects are also faced due to it. Below is a list of risks that are faced by a majority of the DeFi projects:

1. Uncertainty

There may be instability and uncertainty in the blockchain network and these instabilities and uncertainties are succeeded into the DeFi project that the blockchain hosts. There are still a lot of changes that are being made to the Ethereum blockchain. There is an Ethereum 2.0 that has been introduced as well. A significant amount of mistakes were made when the system was moved from PoW to novel Eth 2.0 PoS system might acquaint it with new risks to DeFi projects.

2. Scalability

Scalability is an additional problem that is faced with the DeFi projects.

Scalability further gives rise to other problems.

a) Confirmation of the projects takes longer b) Transactions can be pretty costly when the traffic is high

If Ethereum is functioning at its maximum capacity has the ability to process 13 transactions every second. If you compare this to the centralized system, it has the ability to process thousands of transactions.

3. Smart Contract Problems

Smart contracts can be pretty vulnerable. This may result in huge problems in DeFi projects. Even the smallest mistake may lead to losing lots of funds.

4. Low Liquidity

Liquidity is a major issue for DeFi token-based projects and blockchain protocols. In October of 2020, the total worth that was locked in DeFi was recorded to be $12.5 billion. If you compare this value to the traditional finance systems, it is very minimal.

5. Over-collateralization

The crypto loaning service may be of a lot of interest to people, but it is a reason for businesses to suffer from over-collateralization. Over-collateralization happens when the value of the staked asset is excessively high if you compare it to the loan. DeFi projects have high collateralization so that the elimination of hindrances can be countered.

6. Low Interoperability

There are a number of blockchains available and operating. Bitcoin, Ethereum, Binance Smart Chain, etc. to name a few. Each of these blockchains has its own DeFi space. Interoperability allows these DeFi platforms, tools, DApps, and smart contracts on different blockchains to interact with each other. However, this is very low.

7. Lack of Insurance

Insurance is a kind of protection against hacks and other scamming activities. It is a good practice but is almost absent in the DeFi projects.

8. Centralization

DeFi is basically decentralized finance and has its own features but sometimes there may be a case where the system does not work as it should be working. "Sushiswap" was one of the DeFi projects. SushiSwap was able to gather liquidity of $1B. This was so because the people who provided liquidity were given Sushi tokens in return. Later, the ChefNomi who is said to be the main developer of SushiSwap sold all the Sushi tokens. Due to this, the protocol was able to take the majority of the liquidity of Uniswap to a new platform. The price of the SUSHI token climbed high in value to $10 after forked from the Uniswap protocol and dropped to 0.6$ This is a great example of how failure at one point can be a case in DeFi as well.

9. Your Responsibility

There may be little to no risks and challenges in the DeFi space but still, mistakes occur and if those mistakes are from your side, then it is you who is going to be responsible for it. As there is no intermediary to facilitate the transaction, all the responsibility falls on your shoulders. So you have to be very careful so you don't make any mistakes and end up losing your funds. You are free to do all you can do but you have to show responsibility as well. It is high time that tools are created so the users don't end up losing their funds due to small minor mistakes. As DeFi is a relatively new field, there still exist issues that need addressing. In terms of security, there are a lot of vulnerabilities. The people who are enthusiastic regarding this field are looking forward that these issues being addressed and resolved.

CONCLUSION

Decentralized finance is a system that allows the availability of financial products on a public decentralized blockchain network. The concept of decentralized finance is now becoming popular. More and more people are transitioning towards DeFi from the conventional finance models. DeFi refers is a software system that allows the buyers and sellers, lenders, and borrowers to interact peer to peer. The only intermediary that may be involved in the transaction is software and not a company or a person. These software systems are based on blockchains. In order to attain decentralization a number of technologies and protocols are activated. For instance, a decentralized system is said to be a combination of open-source technologies, blockchain, and proprietary software. All these products are made available via smart contracts.

Smart contracts are a great way to automate DeFi transactions. Specific lines of code that are intended to trigger some function after pre-determined conditions are met are written into the smart contracts. The smart contract can be tricky, if you end up making a mistake or write the smart contracts poorly that can result in messing up your whole transaction.

What makes decentralized finance from the traditional financing methods is that those methods were under the authority of a centralized system. However, decentralized as the name suggests are not controlled by any authority and users have all the freedom they want. Centralized models were very commonly used in the past. Now slowly and gradually these models are being replaced by decentralized models. The models that are responsible for decentralized finance use the technology that eliminates any middlemen that may be a part of the transactions. This allows them to let anyone use the financial services anywhere no matter what the age, ethnicity, and cultural identity of a person is. DeFi services and apps are created on public blockchains, and they either duplicate the offerings that currently exist or they offer innovative services custom-designed for the DeFi ecosystem. This lets the users have more power and authority over their money. This power is given to them by the usage of personal wallets and trading services that overtly cater to individual users instead of institutions.

Like any other system, there are pros and cons of the DeFi network as well. It makes the transactions more convenient but the scalability of the Ethereum blockchain network may be an issue. Similarly, there may not be any middlemen or intermediaries involved in the trade and transactions but this means that all the responsibility falls onto the users and they have to be very careful. Even a small mistake could lead them to lose their funds.

As the technology evolves, it will result in the evolution of the DeFi system as well. Not just that but the developers are constantly working on making the DeFi applications as simple and easy to use for people as possible. Before jumping into the bandwagon and getting yourself involved in the DeFi world, it is highly advised to do all your relevant research, see what you want and what works best for you, only then jump into the DeFi space.

It is a relatively new field but it is growing and getting better. The developers are working on the weak points and loopholes in order to make this system even improved and enhanced.

NFT INVESTING FOR BEGINNERS

Non-Fungible Tokens (NFT) Art & Collectibles Money Guide. Invest in Crypto Art, Blockchain, Trade Stocks, Digital Assets. Earn Passive Income with Market Analysis, Art Tokens & Royalty Shares

By

Satoshy Nakamoto

Table of contents

INTRODUCTION

UNDERSTANDING BLOCKCHAIN

A distributed software network that is used as a digital ledger, as well as a secure way of transferring assets, is known as a blockchain. It is a mechanism that helps in transferring the assets in a fast and secure way without the need for an intermediary. The flow of information digitally is said to be internet technology similarly, the technology that is responsible for the digital exchange of units of value is said to be blockchain technology. The Blockchain network works on tokenized entities. All the tokenized entities ranging from currencies to land titles to votes etc. can be stored and exchanged in a blockchain network.

Blockchain technology initially emerged in the year 2009. The bitcoin blockchain first appeared as a bitcoin blockchain. The bitcoin blockchain is considered to be one of the most secure and resistant to censorship electronic cash systems. This electronic cash system is a peer to peer technology. Bitcoin is easily available and accessible to everyone; thus it is an example of an open blockchain. Open blockchain is basically a blockchain that doesn't require any permissions.

Nowadays, there are a number of blockchain technologies. The forms of blockchain technology in today's world are many. There are blockchains designed for a group with a few participants with limited access to the network. Private blockchains or the blockchains that require permissions fall under this category.

A permanent record of the transactions that have been taking place over the network is provided in real-time to all the people that are involved in the transaction. These records are forensic and transparent. These records are maintained in order to benefit all the participants involved.

Irrespective of whatever type of blockchain protocol is installed, the importance of blockchain technologies is increasing ever since. Blockchain is a promising technology that is being used to change the business models that are centuries old. It paves the way for lawfulness in the government. This results in the coming up of great opportunities for the common public.

CHAPTER NO 1

WHAT IS A NON-FUNGIBLE TOKEN?

N
on-fungible token is a new concept the popularity of which is increasing with every passing day. Saturday Night Live recently did a skit on this concept which clearly shows that this concept has now gone mainstream. The majority of the people have responded to the notion of the Non-fungible tokens by SNL. Some people feel confused and still skeptical regarding as far as this concept is concerned but we know one thing for sure and that is that these non-fungible tokens are going nowhere and are here to stay. Not just that but these tokens will prove their worth in the digital economy. Now, let's move forward and discuss what these non-fungible tokens are and how is the blockchain ecosystem effected by these?

As discussed above, blockchain is a software network that works as both a digital ledger and a way to transfer assets in a secure manner. This ledger is distributed over a number of nodes in a network. The difference between blockchain technology and online databases or trading platforms is its stability. The digital assets are traded peer-to-peer. That is so no one is able to change or alter any transactions that have been happening over the network. Another advantage it has over the internet is that these transactions cannot be reversed by the majority of the people that are on the same network.

Bitcoins are digital assets that are nowadays used to make payments over the blockchain networks. Bitcoins are digital or cryptocurrencies and are fungible in nature. If the value of bitcoin is compared to the value or function of another bitcoin, it is the same. We can say that the value and function of every bitcoin are the same. Suppose, you are trading in bitcoins, you can easily swap one bitcoin with another one. You can do so without having to violate any of the terms of clause of your trading agreement.

Non-fungible tokens are a representation of a singular value item. Suppose in a trading agreement, you cannot swap Andrew Wyeth's painting with a Mike Winkelmann art and then think that no one would have noticed the difference. There are a number of different types of NFTs. NFTs are a set of assets that are unique. NFTs are not just something that you can collect over a period of time but also include birth certificates, death certificates, property papers/deeds, and the distinctiveness of objects on the internet of things.

NFTs possess are great potential. There has been some noise over the work of the auction of Beeple's work which clearly shows the prospective of NFTs although the bubble around the CryptoKitties-the original NFT Phenom has collapsed. The value creation of the NFTs is confined only by our imagination, creation ability, marketing gimmicks, accounting, and the legal support for it. Otherwise, there is great potential in this field.

In today's modern world, we can say that the NFTs are present-day collectibles. You can sell and buy these collectibles online and then display proof which is going to be digital as well for its ownership. The technology that is used in cryptocurrencies and NFTs is alike. It is the blockchain technology that records NFTs securely. Blockchain technology is used so that the asset that is involved is of a unique nature. This technology also makes it difficult for anyone to make any changes and alterations to these NFTs.

In order to know more and have better insights regarding the NFTs, it is advised for you to be well acquainted with this economic concept of fungibility.

What are Fungible items?

Those items can be easily switched or swapped with each other. These items can be swapped with each other easily because their value is not associated with their distinctiveness. An example of a fungible item can be that you can easily interchange a dollar bill with another. This process can be done with ease although the serial numbers on both bills are different.

What are non-fungible items?

Unlike fungible items, non-fungible items are cannot be exchanged. In the non-fungible tokens, you can exchange one token with another one. That is because each token has its own properties and value that distinguishes it from another. The worth of each NFT is different from the other one, even if the tokens are similar.

Here, the question arises that why are people spending so much on the NFTs? That is because, when a creator creates an NFT, he is able to corroborate the authenticity of anything digital. This is said by the co-founder and COO of Calaxy, Solo Ceesay. He also says that if you compare this concept with the traditional selling of the art you would find a number of fake copies of the famous MonaLisa painting but in reality, there is only one original painting. The NFT technology basically helps with assigning the owner ownership of the original and authentic piece.

Here are a few examples of selling NFTs in the art world.

- "Everyday — the First 5000 Days" was sold by Beeple for $69.3 million via a Christie's auction.
- A video clip of 20 seconds of LeBron James "Cosmic Dunk #29" was sold for $208,000.

- A CryptoPunk NFT sold for $1.8 million at Sotheby's first curated NFT sale.
- CEO of Twitter, Jack Dorsey put up the NFT of his first tweet for auction, which was sold for $2.9 million.

There may be a number of copies of the original item you may own NFT of, but no fake copy is worth the original item you own. People may come up with fake copies of an image, video, or any other digital item that you may own but again, what you have is of more value than the ones who own the copies.

Difference between an NFT and Cryptocurrency:

Basically, cryptocurrencies and the NFTs may work on the same blockchain technology but if you look at its uses and purposes, you will come to a conclusion that they are completely different from one another. Although the marketplaces where you can buy and sell the NFTs may accept payment in the cryptocurrencies. But creation and uses of the two are completely different from one another.

Cryptocurrencies, as the name suggests are digital currencies that work as currencies that you can use to buy or sell anything. Cryptocurrencies are similar to fiat currencies in nature. For example, a dollar. Whereas on the other hand, NFTs are completely different. NFTs allow you to have rights of ownership over any digital goods. NFTs are not currencies but unique tokens that display your ownership over something.

CHAPTER NO 2

HISTORY OF NFTs?

Now, let's discuss the history of NFTs. The term CryptoArt is often associated with the NFTs. Bringing up the term CryptoArt means bringing along all the blend of emotions that comes with it. CryptoArt and NFTs merge together the era of time-based art. This is based on blockchain technology which is decentralized and authentic. CryptoArt was discussed in an article published by Artnome in the January of 2019. The article was focused on what CryptoArt was at the time the article was published. You can check out the article in more detail if it is something that interests you, however here we will provide a short background of it.

Non-Fungible Tokens and Its Importance:

If we are discussing the reasons that why are the Non0Fungible tokens important, so let me tell you the reasons are many. As discussed earlier, a non-fungible token or an NFT is a display of the ownership rights over a digital asset on an Ethereum blockchain. This makes it unique and something that is of great value. The creation of NFTs has led to the formation of a new medium for those artists and creators who wish to exhibit their collections and creations. This is a way for the artists and the creators to monetize and generate revenue from their work. This will make their work more genuine and transparent.

The assets that come under the NFTs may be digital art, collectibles, an extension to music, or something which may seem like a combined effort of the three. It can also be something that is entirely new which no one has explored and created yet. To introduce something innovative and revolutionary, NFTs can be used. This will help the artists push their creative boundaries.

Here may come up a question that what would happen if someone screen-grabs an NFT and does not purchase it. Well, you can but that would be different from the original NFT and you would not be able to sell at the same worth as that of the original. Let's again take the example of the Mona Lisa painting there may be a million copies but you would find it so hard for it to find a collector, that is because that is something that is not original. In an NFT market, whenever a buyer purchases an NFT, the price that the collector pays and the asset for which the NFT is purchased is recorded. Now that's the beauty of blockchain technology, everyone can see but no one can make any changes to it. These certificates of ownership are available for everyone to view over the internet. These NFTs can actually guarantee the emergence of the assets to which they may be in connection.

Donna Redel who happens to be a teacher of crypto-digital assets courses at the Fordham Law School says that what you do not buy the asset such as any digital image or a video but what you actually buy are the fundamental rights to the image or any other digital asset. The code that you purchase manifests as images. This is actually you buying art in a different form. The tools that these artists use that differentiate their work and authenticate it from others are NFTs. NFTs allow people to know about the origin of that particular digital asset which makes it scarce. This also allows the artists and creators to set a rate of their work. They are in control of the revenue that is generated from their creation. Given that, they are also able to have a grip and control over their secondary market.

Who was the Creator of the First NFT?

By now, we know what an NFT is and how it works, so now let's discuss how did all this originate? Who was the first person who created these NFTs and how has this technology gained such a fast pace? Kevin McCoy is known to be the very first person who created NFTs. He created them in the May of 2014. He brought the Non-fungible tokens into the market long before the CryptoArt market made waves. He named these non-fungible tokens Quantum.

Now, what is quantum? Quantum is said to be a whimsical depiction of an octagon, that octagon is then further filled with denoting circles, arcs, and other shapes. All these shapes share a common center. The large shapes surround the smaller ones and hypnotically pulses in fluorescent hues. A Quantum art piece is a majestic piece of art that is put up for sale for seven million dollars.

Kevin McCoy and his wife Jennifer are rated as top-class digital artists. Both of them are exceptional and creative at what they do. McCoy says, "The NFT phenomenon is deeply a part of the art world." The work that they present is remarkable and outstanding and is bought by wholehearted and passionate art collectors. McCoy believes more in buying and selling at galleries every once in a while. Metropolitan Museum of Art has its work "Every Shot, Every Episode" on display.

Who is Eligible to Create NFTs?

Here a question might arise in your mind that who is eligible to create these NFTs? So everyone can create an NFT. Anyone from an artist to an entrepreneur, author, art advocate, social media influencers, and personalities. Everyone can create these NFTs. It does not require having any prior experience. What you need is to be able to prove that the work that you are creating an NFT for is your original. You have to own the content legally. If you can do so, you are eligible to mint an NFT.

The History of Non-Fungible Tokens:

CryptoPunks, Rare Pepe, and CryptoKitties were the firsts to initiate the CryptoArt category. The reason these pieces of art brought infamy and dishonor was the effects that the viral network conveyed and their desire for collecting huge sums of money for it.

2012-2013: Colored Coins

A lot of artists, people, and projects are a part of this journey. To understand it better, let's get into it and find out.

On a Bitcoin Blockchain, the initial coins that were issued were the colored coins. These colored coins gave birth to the idea of the NFTs. What are colored coins? Colored coins are kind of tokens that are used to symbolize the everyday assets on a blockchain network. These colored coins were used to attest evidence of the ownership of an asset or entity. The assets could be anything from real estate to equities or bonds. This gave birth to the raw possibilities for the future prospects of utilization.

2014: Counterparty

In the year 2014, Robert Dermody, Adam Krellenstein, and Evan Wagner established CounterParty. CounterParty was an open-source internet protocol that was created on the Bitcoin Blockchain. It was a peer-to-peer financial platform and had a distributed nature. Due to its distributed nature, it made the decentralized creation of assets possible. This helped a lot of users to come up with and create currencies that they could trade. It also provided a way for meme trading that too with no counterfeit issues. Not just that but it helped in creating numerous opportunities for people.

2015: Spells of Genesis on Counterparty

In the April of the year 2015, CounterParty and Spells of Genesis became partners. Founders of the Spells of Genesis created digital in-game assets on blockchain technology. They made it possible via CounterParty. They also launched ICO. Another in-game currency by the name of BitCrystals was issued to provide funding for the development of CounterParty.

2016: Trading Cards on Counterparty

In the August of 2016, other trends were seen. One of the most widespread and prevalent trading card games Force of Will partnered with CounterParty. Force of Will launched their cards on the platform of CounterParty. The success of Force of Will was immense and stood at the fourth spot after Pokemon, Yu-Gi-Oh, and Magic in ranking in North America. It was able to earn this spot as per the sales volume of these cards. These assets were never seen on the blockchain network before, which means that they were newly introduced to the ecosystem. This clearly showed the worth of putting up such assets on a blockchain network.

2016: Rare Pepes on Counterparty

Memes were introduced to the blockchain in the year 2016. CounterParty platform paved way for the memes in October of 2016. Assets were added by the people to a meme called "Rare Pepes". The meme Rare Pepes garnered a huge fan base over time. It is a meme that features an interesting frog character. Before it became a viral internet meme it was a character from a comic named Pepe the Frog. Ethereum became popular in early 2017 and by the same time, trade for the Rare Pepes also started. The first auction for the Rare Pepe was held live by its founders Jason Rosenstein and Louis Parker. Rare Pepe wallet gave birth to CryptoArt. It was during that time, people started showing interest and started to sell their artworks from all over the world. It was also considered to be the first time where digital art displayed fundamental value.

2017: Cryptopunks

After the popularity of the Rare Pepes on the Ethereum blockchain network, John Watkinson and Matt Hall created some other unique characters on the Ethereum blockchain. Cryptopunks is the name of the project and it was cited from an experiment with Bitcoin back in the 1990s and can be labeled as an ERC721 and ERC20 hybrid.

The ERC20 is a standard for a token that is pretty widely used. This permits the tokens to interact with one another. Although it is not considered to be a good way for generating tokens that are unique.

ERC721 helps in tracing down the rights of ownership and movements of the tokens that are individual and have come up from a single smart contract.

CryptoKitties NFTs used the ERC721 NFTs. They hit the ground using the same tokens too. CryptoKtties is a virtual game that is based on the blockchain network. Ethereum is used by the players to adopt, breed, or trade the virtual entities which in this case are cats. This became very famous in no time and got featured on major news stations. CryptoKitties was able to raise funds in a pretty short span of time after going viral and increase in their users. Axiom Zen developed the game. The company turned CryptoKitties into Dapper Labs.

2018-2021: The NFT Explosion

NFTs recorded a slow growth between the years 2018-2021. In the year 2021, a drastic growth was noticed in the NFTs.

This movement which was not so popular before has now taken mainstream art by storm. The slow transition from an underground and not-so-popular movement reached enunciation on Valentine's Day of 2018. An artist by the name of Kevin Abosch teamed up with GIFTO. They teamed up for an auction, the money of which would go to charity. A majestic piece of CryptoArt that goes by the name The Forever Rose was sold for a million dollars. It should be of notice that Kevin Abosch is not the only artist who is involved in this form of expression, there are a number of other artists who are doing the same.

If you look closely, you would realize that the NFT market is pretty proficient and well-organized. There are more platforms online that host a number of creators and collectors trading their artworks. Auction houses and traditional brokers end up collecting 40 percent of the fee. One of the most popular and largest marketplace for art, music, domain names, collectibles, and trading of cards is Opensea. Other platforms like Mintables are busy making the whole process of minting more convenient for the creators whereas Portion is working in making itself an NFT platform that acts as a bridge for the NFTs, DeFi, and DAOs. Here the holders of the governance token are in charge.

CHAPTER NO 3

WHAT WILL YOU NEED TO GET STARTED WITH NFTS?

Now let's understand what do we need to have in order to get started with the NFTs. If you find yourself at this point, you are either a digital creator or an entrepreneur. If you are a digital creator, you are most probably trying to use the NFTs to help you push your creative boundaries and if you are an entrepreneur you are trying to use the NFTs to make money.

At this point in time, it is too early to judge the NFTs but below is a few cool and interesting uses and applications of the NFTs, let's have a look at those.

Digital Artists & Photographers:

If you generate your monthly income from digital art, you are among the lucky ones. NFTs enable you to showcase your art digitally anywhere in the world, not just that but also allow you to trade or sell it to anyone with no fear of it getting plagiarized. You do not need to have any person to handle your dealings, because in blockchain technology each time you are able to trade your art, you get a commission for each sale.

Musicians:

NFT technology can now be used as a platform to release music albums. Kings of Leon was the first band to do so. It is more like a limited edition vinyl release with other perks and benefits.

NFTs allow the music artists to release a few of their music albums or tracks digitally, that too not fearing any piracy or plagiarism issues. It will allow the artists to have a hold over the copyrights of their music tracks. They can also be sold in an open market as a limited edition.

Physical Items:

Digital items are not the only things that you can trade using NFTs. NFTs have other uses too. Blockchain technology keeps a track of all your transactions as well as has all your history and encrypted information too.

- NFTs can be used to authenticate art and antiques and tell them apart from any copy.
- NFTs are a great way to track down vehicle histories
- The sales that happen in real estate can also be achieved and managed using the NFTs.

Licensing & Record Keeping:

Record keeping is another great application of the NFTs. There are high chances that the NFTs will be sued in the future to maintain sensitive information and records. NFTs can also be used to issue patents and licenses.

You can begin with NFTs using the following platforms. If you are an artist or a collector, these three platforms are great for you to get started with.

- OpenSea
- Rarible
- Foundation

OpenSea has to e one of the most commonly used as well as the cheapest platform, to begin with. You are supposed to pay the gas fee whenever you put up something on the Ethereum blockchain. Ethereum blockchain on this platform has a gas feel of The gas fee of $40–$60.

If you want a platform that you can use for longer series of artworks, OpenSea is a great option. You are only supposed to pay once that too on your first transaction after the creation of your digital art store. OpenSea is not completely exclusive and complicates everything due to the volume. If you compare Rarible and Foundation to OpenSea, you will come to the conclusion that these two are more exclusive in terms of art and pieces that you can trade indivisibly. But you are supposed to pay for every piece that is being put up. You either need to have an invite from an already existing artist member there or you have to make your way into it through the community upvotes in the case of Foundation.

At this point, choose OpenSea as it is more convenient for you. This will allow you to begin and then you can move up to the other two platforms and experiment.

A short guide to collecting NFTs:

Firstly, you have to determine what you need to do. You will have to see what you need to do the most. These are completely different categories. If you feel like you are interested in the art pieces or digital collectibles. If you feel like you are more into artworks, you need to choose those artists whose work you can clutch for long.

Digital collectibles on the other hand are those that are the talk of the town. If you find yourself interested in digital collectibles opt for OpenSea whereas if you are more interested in the art-focused go for Rarible and Foundation. You will for sure end up finding interesting pieces due to CryptoPunks, CryptoKitties, etc.

You need to do all the relevant research before you purchase. Your research should be focused on the long-term plans of the authors. It is hard to predict anything regarding the values of pieces changing with time, thus research is crucial.

Community is the key and you need to know that you need to focus on both sides, i.e. creators and collectors.

CHAPTER NO 4

WHO SHOULD USE NFTS?

There are risks that are important for you to consider before purchasing.

The recent crypto hype has given birth to another façade known as the NFTs or the non-fungible tokens. Their popularity has increased ever since. There had been trading of more than $250 Million worth of NFTs in the year 2020 alone. If you look at this number, you will see that this number has drastically increased up to 299% in comparison to the year 2019. NFTs are tokens that represent the ownership of rights over an asset or entity. The entity or an asset could either be digital like art, music, sports, in-game collectibles, etc. but you can also have these non-fungible tokens for the items in real life. However, this practice is not no widespread.

Fungible means you can exchange that asset with an asset of the same type. If you consider money, you can exchange a dollar bill with another dollar bill because it is fungible. But if you look at an original piece of art or a signed edition of some book, you cannot exchange or interchange that. Why so? Because it is not fungible. It is unique in its entirety.

Considerations when buying NFTs:

This is still a relatively new market and still highly unpredictable. A huge risk that you may end up facing if you are looking to buy NFTs is the same. This is not the only risk but several others as well. High consumption of energy is another risk involved with this. Below are a few things that you need to keep in mind before you choose to purchase the NFTs.

THE ASCENT'S CHOICES FOR THE BEST ONLINE STOCK BROKERS

Find the broker that is best for you among these top preferences. As long as you're eyeing a special sign-up offer, amazing customer support, $0 commissions, spontaneous mobile apps, or more, you'll find a stock broker that fits your needs.

1. It's a very new market

NFT market is relatively new and we still can't say anything certain if it is going to develop in a few years or a few decades. Let's consider Beeple's digital art as an example. Beeple's art was recently sold for almost $69 million but we still can't determine if it may appreciate or depreciate in the coming years. Many experts have come up with the conclusion that NFTs are here to stay and they will become even popular.

The Crypto market is doing great at this moment. The value of bitcoin has been increasing like anything. Only this year it has increased multiple folds. People are spending huge amounts of money on crypto without paying attention to the substance it holds. If you do not have much knowledge regarding the art, you will find this whole process to be pretty perplexing.

2. Fraud and theft:

NFTs are sold so that the artists who work digitally can have copyrights over their work, they should be able to claim ownership over what they have created. It is one of the main reasons why it is so common among digital artists. Before this, there had been numerous instances of their work getting plagiarized. However, the risk of their work being plagiarized may have been reduced but still, we can't say that NFTs are completely immune to the frauds and thefts that happen over the internet.

Even on the Ethereum blockchain network where everything is being recorded, there have been complaints from multiple artists of their work being plagiarized and tokenized. All this has been done without bringing it into their knowledge. The issue of reclaiming the ownership of the intellectual property of an artist after it has been illegally entered into the blockchain network is yet unresolved.

You deal with the cryptocurrencies using the crypto exchange, similarly dealing with NFTs would require you to check the NFT exchange. You are supposed to be vigilant while you are dealing in an NFT exchange. Look out for the security credentials of the artists.

There have been cases of NFT theft too. These are similar in nature to cryptocurrencies theft. This issue has still not been resolved.

Whenever you purchase NFT over any NFT exchange platform, make sure you use a strong password to keep them protected from any unauthorized access. Enable your two-factor authentication security so nobody illegally steals your NFT tokens. If you have NFT tokens that are of high worth, it is advised not to store them online where they can be easily hacked, rather try storing them in an offline location where nobody is able to access them.

PURCHASING YOUR INITIAL STOCKS: DO IT THE IN THE BEST WAY:

Make sure you buy from the right brokers and right stocks. If you are new to this all, make sure you do all your relevant research beforehand. You can start with Stock Advisor. You'll get two new stock choices monthly, you will get 10 starter stocks and best buys now. Over the past 17 years. The average stock pick of Stock Advisor average stock pick has perceived a 618% profit; this profit is 4.5x.

3. Copyright:

You need to clear all your concepts regarding the NFTs and copyrights. If you purchase an NFT, you will most probably not own rights to that art. That is because it is highly possible that the artist may have withheld the copyright. The artist will then be allowed to claim royalties in this case. The majority of the people who purchase NFTs fail to understand these technicalities.

Let us consider an example to better understand this concept, If you purchase a signed or autographed copy of some favorite book of yours, you cannot say that you now own the copyrights for that book. Similarly, in the case of NFTs, every token has a smart contract. That smart contract determines the rights that a particular NFT owner possesses.

That is why make sure you understand the whole concept in thorough detail before you get yourself involved.

4. Storage

We have already discussed how there have been instances of NFTs being stolen. Well, that is not the only case. You are not allowed to stockpile assets that you own individually on a blockchain ledger. A token is stored on the ledger rather than the original file.

Your NFT token does not contain the original file, it contains a link to the assets that you have purchased.

This means that the asset that you have purchased will actually be stockpiled someplace else. Have you considered what if the file stops working or gets corrupted? When you buy, it is highly important that you know all these things. You should know where your asset file is stored and what steps have you taken to make sure that it is safe and well-maintained.

Should I buy an NFT?

Well, the issues that we have discussed above are not something that cannot be solved. All these issues have their own solutions but we are still uncertain about one thing and that is that we still don't know which way will the wind blow and what will the market look like in the future. At this point, predicting the future of the market is too early. We don't know what the future of the NFT holders will look like?

If you end up buying NFTs now, you are taking too much of a risk. The market is highly volatile. The market for cryptocurrencies is volatile too at the moment.

If you are looking to invest in the NFTs, you have to see if you check any of these boxes?

- You have a better understanding of the art market
- You have been involved in the trading of such assets prior to this
- You are looking for something long-term

If you feel you don't check any of these boxes, it would not be a great time for you to invest in NFTs at the moment.

If you still want to take the plunge and invest in this market, make sure that you have enough savings. Invest only if you have your emergency funds available. There are chances that these NFTs will increase in worth but you have to make sure that you remain cautious for any worst-case scenario too.

Using the wrong broker could cost you serious money

If you are getting yourself involved with a broker who is not right for you, you are exposing yourself to a lot of risks. Investing in the stock market may end up increasing your wealth in long term but working with the wrong broker means reversing any of the profit that you may make. Make sure you find yourself brokers that are credible and have great reviews.

CHAPTER NO 5

CRYPTO CURRENCY AND THE FUTURE OF NFTS?

Non-fungible tokens are a great way for the artists and other creators to dispense their creations but here the question arises, how do these NFTs work?

Elon Musk has announced that his company Tesla would invest half a billion dollars in cryptocurrency and bitcoins. Many people started to discuss the effects this could possibly have on the market. Not just that but if other companies are going to do the same. A $1 billion was grown from the investment that tesla made in a time span of ten weeks.

These non-fungible tokens are also a great and exciting way for artists and entrepreneurs to make money. You can sell anything on an NFT and generate huge sums of money. The revenue generated is in millions of dollars.

Now, let's discuss what is an NFT and how can you mint and sell one?

Cryptocurrencies and NFTs have the same basics. In order to know what NFTs are, you need to be aware of cryptocurrencies and their basics. One of the first and leading cryptocurrencies is bitcoin. The worth of a bitcoin is $55,000 USD. Bitcoin theory was presented by Satoshi Nakamoto in the year 2009. The limit of supply that he set for Bitcoin was 21 million. This number is still not completely public to the market. Mining is the process through which bitcoins are created. Advanced algorithms are solved so that more Bitcoins are able to enter the market. As the demand for bitcoins increases the supply increases. The supply of Bitcoins is said to be limited.

After Bitcoin, the second popular and commonly used cryptocurrency is Ethereum. Ethereum is used to run decentralized apps on the blockchain. It records all the transactions, making the whole ledger safe and secure.

Ethereum blockchain is used to run the non-fungible tokens. NFTs are a code that helps you purchase the copyrights to a piece of art. NFTs allow you to have access to the copyrights of the digital art that is sold. It is kept together in a file that has all your information and that information is stored on the Ethereum blockchain.

The owner sets the value and worth of the NFTs purchased. This process is different from Bitcoins and Ethereum. NFTs are used to purchase artworks of any form, they are mostly digital art. They can be purchased using Ether. Ether is the mode of currency that is used to purchase the NFTs.

In order to deal with the NFTs, it is important for you to have information on the cryptocurrencies and crypto exchange markets. The Ethereum blockchain minting market is currently responsible for dealing with the NFTs minting market. Whenever you choose the blockchain, you will have to top up your wallet with $50 - $100 in ether (ETH). You will have to use the ERC-721 which is the NFT standard. From there, one would use online NFT marketplaces, such as OpenSea, Superfarm, or Rarible to upload their artwork and mint their NFT to distribute amongst the masses.

The cryptocurrency and NFTs market is pretty volatile and this volatility of the market is important to discuss because it is used to determine the longevity of the market. NFTs are mostly sold by artists. They use this medium to increase their assets because it allows them to generate revenue directly.

Tesla has invested huge amounts in the NFT market which has put a lot of other large corporations in confusion. Popularity of this market is increasing with every passing day Due to this reason, artists and creators have started to push their creative boundaries. This new technology is inspiring more and more artists to release their work independently and then gather funding from these large corporations. As this is a new technology, people are still reluctant in investing their money, time, and energy. As this technology works on peer-to-peer dealings and trade, many people are most likely going to come towards it if they want to distribute their art independently.

Here are some thoughts about what the immediate future holds for cryptocurrency, NFTs, and blockchain:

The popularity of cryptocurrency is going to be one of the main reasons why cryptocurrencies will grow. A number of investors have started to invest in the cryptocurrency market.

Bitcoin is one of the most popular cryptocurrencies that will be used in trading in the future. Bitcoin is an expensive perception and its value is growing ever since.

When it gets big and popular, regulators that are encouraged by bankers will respond in a more hostile way. Regulation of crypto will unavoidably diminish to playing Whack-a-Mole where valuations, transactions, and exchanges will continue to be examined as moving targets. There exists a skulking main risk here when cryptocurrencies become widespread. This may result in the investors becoming more violent. The same is true of NFTs, though here too "regulation" is inaccurate. The usage of the NFTs will keep growing.

NFTs are mostly used in digital assets in comparison to physical ones because digital assets can be created fast. This is another substantial method for the artists and creators to generate revenues easily and fast. With that being said, there is absolutely nothing that would stop those people who priceless assets by monetization.

There are many new areas in which this technology can be put to use. Blockchain is finding areas where to find other areas of application. Healthcare looks like a promising area of application. The voting is highly likely to grow much faster outside the US (though, incredibly perhaps, "over the past two years, West Virginia, Denver and Utah County, Utah have all used blockchain-based mobile apps to allow military members and their families living overseas to cast absentee ballots using an iPhone."

The Enterprise Play

What is it that is needed to be done by these companies regarding these trends? Bitcoins are now widely accepted in the markets, if they aim to go big they need to think about this aspect too. They need to start doing their trading in Bitcoins too. Even as debauched followers, the risk is abridged, and if it all crashes and burns then companies can stop at that point. Investing in Cryptocurrency might sound tricky and complicated at this point. The hypothetical nature of crypto is a serious danger to its investment appeal. Everybody is well aware of the money that has been made in crypto in the last ten years.

Secondly, they should assess their collections and portfolios for the monetization of their digital assets. Patents and unique creations of art are created by smart algorithms. What other digital assets might they have? What physical assets might be monetized?

Visit the NFT marketplaces and get answers to your unanswered questions.

There are various technologies developing that are related to the technology-enabled business models, so the companies should consider NFTs, cryptocurrencies, and blockchains. Begin with creating a digital wallet and fill it with some Ether, the cryptocurrency that many NFT marketplaces use. That is because this is the technology that is used by the Ethereum blockchain. There are several sites through which cryptocurrencies can be sold, Ether included. A few of the popular ones are Coinbase and presently PayPal. After a company buys Ether, they can proceed to OpenSea (or other NFT marketplaces such as Rarible or SuperRare). There are a lot of digital items on sale. Companies can purchase some items on OpenSea and then sell them. This will help them understand the working of all this. They can then browse their own portfolios for something to sell, or consider creating something they can sell.

All this might look like something which is very complicated. But it is not in reality. Well, it is not a difficult task like developing your first AI application by programming or a machine learning algorithm, training a complex image recognition system, or designing your first neural network. If you look closely at an AI application, you will observe what the difficult part here is? Basically, it is the blunt scrutiny of what the issue may look like considering NFTs. What a company may be planning to create or to sell and the value of both. Will there be any increase in the worth of an art piece that I am purchasing today and may sell sometime in the future? How is all this different from investing the money in the stock markets. You never know how will your investments be affected in the next few months or years. Looking at all these things, it would be a wise step if the companies start taking some risks and exploring cryptocurrencies, NFTs, and blockchain technologies. All these of which are trying to stay as per the experts.

CHAPTER NO 6

ETHEREUM AND NFTS

How is Ethereum Helping in Leading the Way for the NFTs in The Future?

If you feel like you need to venture into this market, you know all the basics. Do you know what cryptocurrency is and what Bitcoin is? Here, in this case, we will be discussing and talking about Ethereum in order to divert the focus of the readers towards this technology. Ethereum is important to understand if you are looking to invest n the NFTs. Ethereum blockchain is one of the most important parts affecting the cryptocurrency markets today. It is something that you need to know at all costs because it is the future.

What is Ethereum?

Ethereum originated in July 2015 as open-source blockchain technology. This technology came as a support to the decentralized applications and the functionality of the smart contracts. Ethereum came into existence so as to inflate and develop the abilities of Bitcoin by introducing the practice of smart contracts. It is a system of decentralized apps that are independent of each other. NFTs are influenced and controlled by the blockchain that uses the standard of ERC-271 non-fungible Ethereum token.

What is an NFT?

NFTs are non-fungible tokens that are in common use nowadays. They are used to display the copyrights of digital assets by any digital artist. This is a great practice for these artists to trade their work digitally all over the world without the fear of their work being plagiarized. NFT is a token that is based on the Ethereum blockchain technology. All the transactions that take place among the artists and the collectors are stored on a digital ledger over the blockchain network.

How does Ethereum play a role?

Ethereum blockchain is used to distribute the ownership of these tokens. Using the Ethereum smart contracts the man in the middle of all the transactions has been eliminated and all the transactions are exclusive between the creator and the collector. The Ethereum blockchain technology that is used in these NFTs also enables people to see and track down the owners who owned these NFTs previously. Ethereum blockchain networks make it easy to store this information on the digital ledger securely and record all the information by using smart contracts.

Why is this intriguing?

What makes these NFTs special is their uniqueness. This uniqueness helps them in providing solutions to all the problems that may come up as a result of the selling of fake and counterfeit products and goods. These tokens are legit and legal. They ensure the authenticity of the product. You cannot trade one token for another, that is because they are non-fungible. Every token is unique in nature from one other. Gaming and art industries have greatly utilized the NFTs.

Many gaming companies have tokenized avatars and add-ons that come built-in with the game for generating profit. For instance, a $270,000 digital cat was sold as an NFT by CryptoKitties' Dragon. The worth of certain digital assets such as Twitter handles domain names, merchandise, art, music, and more impel gigantic fiscal assistances that people often oversee. This is accredited to the scarce quantity of these assets and their failure to be copied. This lacks in such industries. That is because people have access to all the information. The information that they have access to are basically not owners. Presently, they choose some people who agree to pay and are able to do so.

What does this mean for the future?

The market has been growing consistently ever since the first NFT was launched back in 2017. Currently, $207 million has been spent in the market and this figure is enough for people to see the future of this technology.

With the suggestion that Ethereum 'layer 2' scaling will make its first appearance in the near future, these transactions will be both quicker and inexpensive. The majority of the creators have started to tip the iceberg into discovering the opportunities of NFTs worth in the music industry as well. Artists currently can monetize their work in the digital environment. As well as their merchandise, tickets, and much more, driving up equitable worth and mentioning to a new individuality factor and standing from digital ownership. It is highly likely to see music festivals, where the ticket would look like an NFT that is unique and based on the QR code. This would prove the ownership of the ticket and the validity of their acquisition during entry. As other creators realize the abilities that these NFTs can provide their work and help them gain profits from the work that they produce, it is highly likely that they would choose NFTs over anything else.

CHAPTER NO 7

SELLING ART AS NFTS

To better understand the NFTs let us consider the example of an artist that creates art digitally. The artist may create digital images or videos etc. That digital art is then monetized so that the artist is able to generate some revenue. That can be sold online or can also be sold in the form of merchandise. The artist can also create some digital art, modify it and then sell it online. But how would you know that the art that is being sold is original and not copied? You will never understand if the art is just a digital copy or it is original. If there is a digital copy of that art, is there any chance that there is an original digital copy?

In order to be able to find out about this, NFTs come into play. NFT enables you to see if the digital art that is being sold online is just some digital copy or an original art piece. NFT is a smart contract that is used to represent the ownership rights over digital assets. The NFTs have your digital art and the personal information stored on a digital ledger in an Ethereum blockchain network. It displays the art piece is original and you have the ownership rights over it.

You can sell the original digital assets and they will all be recorded in the digital blockchain. All the transaction history is recorded on the blockchain network It is a peer-to-peer technology that enables one-to-one transactions and trade between the two parties. You can view all your work live on the secondary market.

There are a number of reasons through which the NFTs can be used to benefit the artists and creators.

Step by step instructions for selling your artwork on NFTs

You know what NFTs are by now, but how do you create and then sell an NFT, that is a question that is still unanswered.

You may have heard about NFTs and the whole proves of their creation and selling over the news. It is a way to make money from the art that you create however, this concept is pretty debatable. In this content, we will discuss all the details regarding the NFTs and this whole process.

You may have seen that people are selling and buying the NFTs worth thousands of dollars but it is important for you to remember that these are exceptional cases. Even if you are able to sell the NFTs for such prices, the majority of the money that you would make would not go to your pocket. The reason for that is the huge prices that are charged to the NFT artists. This money is charged by the cryptocurrency markets that allow you to make transactions and trades using these platforms.

Although, you may not understand all this as of yet and there are high chances that you would lose the money rather than make money. For example, Alan Gannet says that he was able to create four NFTs, he sold one of them and in this whole process lost $1000.

How to create and sell an NFT:

All these worries aside, and if you feel like you need to take a plunge, this content would help you in taking practical steps towards exploring an NFT platform.

Here, we will explain this whole process by using the NFT platform Rarible and the cryptocurrency market MetaMask. The reason for using these platforms is not endorsing but actually an example. There are a number of platforms out there, do your research and then choose the platform that you

OpenSea, SuperRare, Nifty Gateway, Foundation, VIV3, BakerySwap, Axie Marketplace, and NFT ShowRoom, and other payment platforms include Torus, Portis, WalletConnect, Coinbase, MyEtherWallet, and Fortmatic. These are a few NFT platforms that you can use apart from Rarible.

01. You'll need some cryptocurrency
    If you are trying to involve yourself in this whole process, you need to keep in mind that you will have to pay for the platform that you intend to use. The majority of the platforms take up the payment in Ether. That is because the technology that is used by these platforms is the Ethereum blockchain technology. It is open-source and decentralized.
    Similar to Bitcoin, the value of Ether (ETH) is extremely volatile and fluctuates highly. At the beginning of writing this content, 1 ETH had a value of $2,751.61 / £1,923.66. A few hours later it got to $2,560.92 / £1,807.47. So if you're expecting to project precise figures for your costs and profit, you would be unable to do so.
    Firstly, you have to create a digital wallet for Ethereum. There are a number of wallet platforms that you can use to create the wallet. After that, you will have to link the wallet to the NFT platform that you wish to use. In this example, we will consider using MetaMask. MetaMask can be both used as a mobile app and a browser extension.
02. Create a digital wallet
    To create a digital wallet, open the website of MetaMask and click on the download button. If you

are using a PC, choose the option of installing the browser extension.

Now choose to confirm and add your seed phrase. Here a question might pop up that what is a seed phrase? The seed phrase is a list of words that stores all the information on the blockchain. Accept the terms and conditions and then create a password. Then your account will start setting up.

03. Add money to your wallet

After you set up your wallet you will have to add Ether to it. This is a pretty straightforward process, click on the "buy" button and then purchase Ether and add them to your wallet. You can purchase Ether with Apple Pay or a debit card.

04. Connect your wallet to the NFT platform

All the wallets have a similar process; you can choose whatever you want. And once you have added Ether to your wallet you will become eligible to spend it on any NFT platform that you wish to choose. Here we are using Rarible.

Go to the Rarible site. Look for an option of connecting your wallet. Choose that option, it will ask you for the wallet that you are using, here in this case we will mention MetaMask. At this point, a popup will appear on the page which will ask you to connect your wallet with the Rarible. Click on the connect option and then confirm your age.

05. Upload your file

Now, you are all set and you can create your first NFT. Click on the create option in Rarible.com. Now you will be given a few options of creating a single, one-off work or selling the same item multiple times. In this example, we'll opt for 'Single'. You are now eligible to upload the digital file you wish to turn into an NFT. On Rarible, this can be a PNG, GIF, WEBP, MP4, or MP3 file, and up to 30MB in size.

06. Set up an auction

After you are done with all these steps, you will have to opt for what way you wish to sell your artwork. Here you will see three options for selling. With the help of 'Fixed price,' you can set a price and sell it to someone directly. Through an 'Unlimited Auction', people would start bidding and keep on till you accept a bid. In 'Timed auction' there is an auction that happens for a limited time. We will opt for this option as an example.

07. Setting up the prices has to be done very carefully. Don't go for too small prices because the fee is huge and you will not be able to make any profit off it. That way you would end up losing money. We'll set our price at 1 ETH and give people seven days in which to make their bids. Now, you will see an option to 'Unlock once purchased'. This is a chance for you to offer your ultimate buyer a high-resolution version of your art, as well as any other material by means of a secret web page through any downloadable links. Further down lies an option on the form, titled 'Choose Collection'. If you consider it from the blockchain aspect, it is a pretty technical question. You can choose 'Rarible' as it is a default option and the best advice here is to just let it be the way it is.

08. Define your NFT

Then, you have to add a title and description of it, you have to do this for your listing. You need to make sure that you spend ample time in this step if you want everything perfect. It has all the information regarding the percentage of royalties in case of any resale of your art sometime in the future. This question will be asked to mention the percentage of royalties. If you enter a higher percentage that means you will make more money per every resale. But if you do that, it would make people feel put off from reselling your art. That is because they won't be able to make any profit themselves. There is a field that is optional, you are supposed to add the property files. After you get done with this, the process is almost complete.

09.   Pay the fee
Click 'Create Item'. This will lead you to connect your wallet to pay the fee for listing. If you do not have adequate funds in your wallet, you can add funds to it by clicking on the wallet icon in the right corner of the page. You will be provided with an option where you can directly add funds to your wallet that too within Rarible.

Before you do so, though: be warned. The listing fee may seem low: in this scenario, it was said to be $5.91 only. Afterward, you have to pay more in order to create your NFT. In this case, that fee is going to be $42.99. After someone purchases your NFT, there will be a commission fee that would be needed to be paid. Not just that but the transaction fee is also to be paid for transferring the money from the buyer's wallet to your own.

The volatile nature of the cryptocurrencies and blockchain technologies, no transparency guaranteed on the platforms, and the wild fluctuations of the market make this whole process pretty cumbersome. So it is advised that you wait and see the amount that would be charged from you if you end up making a sale.

CHAPTER NO 8

HOW BIG NFTS MARKETS ARE

Blockchain technology will change the world. It has become obvious and well-understood by now.

Here what is important to note is the use of the word, "world."

Take note of the usage of the word "world."

It is important to notice the emphasis on this word, here we did not state that blockchain technology would change the financial markets or currencies or banks but it is stated that blockchain technology would change the world. This is something huge.

If you are looking to make money in these markets where the dealings happen in cryptocurrencies, you need to understand everything about it. It is important to understand it well. If you look at the current situation, you would find everybody talking about blockchain technology and how it will change the finance sector. It is important to note how this technology would enable decentralized finance or DeFi.

You should not feel mistaken regarding all this, it is going to happen in the near future. The number of tokens being made for the DeFi is increasing with every passing day. And this will keep increasing.

If you wish to invest your money in crypto markets and make money, you should not invest in the DeFi sector. Look for some other sector to invest your money in. There are many sectors that will go big due to blockchain technology.

Among those sectors, one of them is the non-fungible tokens or the NFTs.

Now, what is an NFT? NFT is a token that is used in blockchain technology. It is similar in functionality to that of a physical asset but is actually a digital asset. The thing which is of importance here is its blockchain aspect.

Before this technology, people considered digital assets worth it because there was no security guaranteed. They could be easily replicated and then distributed claiming them to be the original assets even if they were replicas. These replicas ended up reducing the worth of the original ones.

But with the blockchain and its signature unassailable digital ledger, artists can now create digital assets that can be authenticated as originals. This is a reason that now the original pieces have the same worth and value as they should.

This authentication lays the base for the NFT market to flourish in the coming decade. This is not only about digital art but also about digital real estate. Digital toys. Digital trading cards. Digital assets in general.

If you look at all this, we can say that in the future the digital asset market would be as prosperous as the physical asset market. It may sound bold and gallant but if you pay attention closely you would also realize it.

An example of this could be online shopping, When the online shopping experience got as better as the physical shopping experience, a huge number transitioned to this new way of shopping. As per statistics, the number of people who are shopping online is actually getting bigger than the people who shop at physical stores and retail.

Another example of this could be digital entertainment. Digital entertainment is now something people enjoy more than physical entertainment. Online streaming websites show a great influx of people. Netflix, Disney+, HBO Max, etc. are now making great profits than any physical entertainment market has made.

Digital advertising has taken over physical advertising. People have started resorting to digital and online advertising more than ever. In the coming years, digital ad spending will comprise more than 50% of total ad budgets.

The examples have already been set!

Once digital copies of the assets from physical industries become "good," they will be replaced by digital copies.

Now you might think what would happen to the digital asset market or the NFT market? Well, the same would happen to the digital asset market too. NFT market will soon become bigger and better than the physical asset market.

The investment opportunity is that the digital asset market currently is very small in size in comparison to the physical asset market.

In the year 2020, the global NFT market made about $338 million.

The global collectibles market which comprises physical trading cards, games, toys, cars, and more – is a $370 BILLION market.

That is a pretty huge figure.

All these facts show that the global NFT market will grow by multiple folds in the next few years.

Right now is a good time to explore these markets and then invest too, if you are looking for a place to invest your money, time, and effort.

Here the question arises that how will you invest in this thriving NFT industry?

To answer this question, we will utilize the information of our ultra-exclusive investment research advisory that focuses entirely on cryptocurrencies.

Crypto Investor Network:

At Crypto Investor Network, we're talking about coins that are triple-digit and may go up to quadruple-digit which may provide benefit potential over the next few years. The average expansion in the portfolio is well over 150% which is huge if you think about it.

The world is turning its attention to these NFT and crypto markets. We are returning to naught considering chances in this space with huge positive potential and the research for this is being carried out.

All this is happening right now.

Nothing major has been missed major yet.   Rather, you're early. Now is your opportunity to take advantage of this market. On the date on which this publication was published, Luke Lango was not working on any position in the securities that are stated in this content.

Why the NFT Market Could Really Grow was a post that 1,000X appeared first on InvestorPlace.

3 Popular NFT Marketplaces

There are marketplaces for the NFTs where users are able to share their artworks and buy from others as well. Three platforms that we will discuss below are among the most popular ones. There are a number of people that use these platforms for selling their original artworks or purchasing from others.

OPENSEA

Among all the platforms, OpenSea is the easiest platform to use. You only have to pay an initial fee and after that, you would not be required to pay any additional fee. It costs around $50 to $100 depending on network traffic.

You do not need a lot of verification here, you can simply create an account and start creating and putting your NFTs on the blockchain. There are a large number of collectibles and artists that you can choose from based on their ranking.

If you are looking to submit your artwork to the platform, that is quite a hassle-free process too. Click Create and then Submit NFTs. A collection will be created where you can keep adding your artwork. There is no coding required and you can easily add your artworks or digital collectibles.

Due to its simple nature and low costs, many collections on OpenSea tend to be composed of digital collectibles rather than individual artworks.

RARIBLE

Rarible and OpenSea are somewhat similar to each other. However here you have to pay a fee for each of the artwork that you create and then put on the blockchain. This is a great platform if you are looking to mint individual pieces. Your work may not go unnoticed here but the costs are pretty high.

Minting of each work would require you to pay $40 to $80.

FOUNDATION

If you see you will find out that foundation is a marketplace that is pretty difficult and challenging to access among all the other marketplaces. In order to access the foundation marketplace, you need to have a number of community upvotes or you need an invite from a member who is already a part of the foundation marketplace. You need these things right from the beginning. You would not be able to post anything if you are unable to do so. Having a direct invitation from an already existing artist member can help you jump the queue and become a member. It may be challenging to access this marketplace but the quality of art that you will find here is going to be of better quality. This is a marketplace for the already established artists and creators with a lot of following.

CHAPTER NO 9

UNDERSTANDING THE DIFFERENT TYPES OF NFTS

one of the prominent topics gathering attention in 2021 are Non-fungible tokens or NFTs. Blockchain technology is based on unique digital assets which have gained popularity in recent times. As a result, of which the interest in understanding the different types of NFT has been growing recently.

Apart from a vision for altering predictable asset management people are fascinated by the promising economic potential associated with NFTs. The inexhaustible opportunities for NFT creators and investors can be guaranteed by the steady growth visible in the domain of NFTs. Therefore, for making better decisions in your NFT journey a vibrant impression of the different types of non-fungible tokens could help greatly.

Digital tokens are not something innovative in the world of technology. Once the digital artist Beeple auctioned off his artwork at a Christie's auction in March the NFTs started to catch the world's attention. Favorable opinions have been expressed regarding the NFTs by popular names such as Twitter chief Jack Dorsey and Elon Musk Interestingly, only six years after minting the first NFT in 2014, the NFT market cap reached almost $2 Billion, only in the first quarter of 2021. In 2020, the total value of sales reached almost $250 million. NFTs are digital or cryptographic tokens you can find on a blockchain that has the ability to preserve exclusivity. NFTs could be tokenized alternatives of practical assets or totally native digital assets.

However, one of the protruding aspects which can confuse many beginners in NFT is the association of NFTs with art. To tell the truth, NFTs are not limited only to the field of art. Different types of NFTs with exclusive traits and distinguishing use cases can be found.

The primary cataloging of types of NFTs mentions the general categories. The three common types of NFTs are,

- Original or copy of work that is accepted on a blockchain network or DLT
- Digitally inherent NFTs that own rights to an artwork that account for NFTs
- NFT metadata comprises the NFT that provides a demonstration of ownership for metadata files

The usual types of non-fungible tokens propose a comprehensive description of the standards used in NFT classification. The original NFTs are created on the blockchain network, and they remain on there. Digitally native NFTs involve issuing NFTs to numerous people with ownership rights of the asset. A significant way to classify the non-fungible tokens is the NFT metadata as it fundamentally has a link that leads to the metadata for the NFT. Consequently, you don't get ownership of the NFT and just the rights for using it.

What Are the Different Types of NFTs?

Significant topics of discussion involve the different conjectures regarding the NFT potential and the value and risks associated with them. The true origin of an asset with the functionalities of blockchain could be explained by NFTs. Holding, limiting, or rejecting access to the rights of a person could be helped by NFTs, thereby guaranteeing exclusiveness.

The applications of NFTs could be nurtured in various sectors by the development in the infrastructure and an increased opportunity for novelty in the NFTs space. Therefore, new types of NFTs can be reasonably expected to emerge. You can look at some of the notable NFT types which are popular in present times.

The protuberant records in a non-fungible tokens list would include the following,

- Collectibles
- Artwork
- Event tickets
- Music and media
- Gaming
- Virtual items
- Real-world assets
- Identity
- Memes
- Domain names

An overview of these different non-fungible tokens or NFT variants to understand their significance is given below.

Collectibles

With the development of Cryptokitties the leading example of NFTs, the collectibles emerged. As a point of fact, The first occurrence of people using NFTs are cryptokitties. As a matter of interest, Cryptokitties became popular enough in 2017 to congest the Ethereum network. One of the conspicuous accompaniments to the non-fungible tokens list in the class of digital collectibles is cryptokitties. They are fundamentally digital kittens with discrete traits that make them prevalent and promising than others.

Artwork

Another projecting contender for NFTs is the artwork. The usual non-fungible tokens in this area mention programmable art, containing an exceptional blend of creativity and technology. As of now, many limited edition artwork pieces are in circulation with the scope for programmability under certain conditions. To create images represented on blockchain networks oracles and smart contracts could be used by artists which could help greatly. Participation from the legacy arts industry has also been stimulated by NFTs.

The adoption of NFTs could be encouraged by the tokenization of real-world assets. The interesting prospects for scanning a code or sticker on assets could be offered by the possibilities of combining blockchain and IoT together. The NFT types in artwork could certify that ownership of real-world artwork on a blockchain network could be easily registered. Successively, the complete history of an artwork, such as previous ownerships and the prices for which they were sold in the past could be found by users,

Event Tickets

Event tickets are another promising addition among the types of NFTs. Attending events like music festivals and concerts are allowed to verify their identity and tickets by the use of such types of NFTs. A specific number of NFT tickets could be mined on a selected blockchain platform by the event managers. Customers could buy the tickets through an auction and those tickets could be stored in their wallets easily accessible through mobile devices.

Music and Media

The domain of music and media leads to another category of NFTs due to the experiments they are trying to carry out with NFTs. Music and media files could be possibly linked to NFTs which enables an individual with true ownership claim to access the files. The two noticeable platforms helping artists in minting their songs as NFTs include Rarible and Mintbase.

The listeners get a quality experience while the artists get the benefits of reaching out directly to their followers and new audience One of the leading reasons for infusing traits of vintage vinyl records is the intellect of uniqueness in purchasing NFT music. Consistent projections for addressing the concerns of music piracy and intermediaries could be offered by the growth of music NFTs in the non-fungible tokens list.

Gaming

In the domain of gaming, the common types of non-fungible tokens are principally fixated on in-game items. Profound levels of interest have been aroused among game developers by NFTs. The functionality of ownership records for in-game items could be offered by NFTs, thus driving the progress of in-game economies. Most importantly, NFTs in the gaming segment also focus on announcing a wide display of benefits for players.

While in-game collectibles were mutual necessities for a better gaming experience, NFTs have the prospective for changing their value Money could be easily recovered by in-game items as NFTs by selling it outside the game. On the flip side, game developers or the creators allotting NFTs could receive a royalty for every sale of items in the open marketplace.

Real-world Assets

Many NFT types could not be found serving as tokens for real-world items, it could be possible due to the progress in the NFT domain. For instance, right now many NFT projects are concentrating on the tokenization of real estate alongside luxury goods. NFTs are fundamentally deeds, that can familiarize the flexibility for buying a car or home with an NFT deed. Consequently, NFTs demonstrating real-world assets can capitalize on the prospects with cryptographic proof of ownership.

Identity

Non-fungible tokens have a critical trait and that is a rarity. Every NFT is unique and cannot be substituted with any other token. The working of identity NFTs is similar to that of event tickets NFTs. They can function as unique identifiers, hence aiding as trustworthy sustenance for the identity management systems.

The commonly used applications of identity-based NFTs are unmistakable in certifications and licensing. The identity management sector for proving and verifying records of an individual could be changed by minting certifications and licenses and NFTs. Furthermore, identity-based NFTs could also make certain that individuals could store proof of their identity without risking losing it.

Memes

The most noteworthy development in the domain of NFTs recently is the sale of memes as NFTs. While being a fragment of widespread culture and a favorite among internet users, memes have also been related to NFTs. Selling the memes as NFTS displays the prospective for unique meme creators to participate in a progressing revolutionary ecosystem.

Domain Names

Domain names are another category of NFTs which have become popular recently. The top examples of domain name NFTs are Decentralized Domain Name Services such as Unstoppable Domains and the Ethereum Name Service (ENS). ENS aids in translating long and complex user addresses to a flexible and friendly experience for users with easier onboarding.

The prevailing admittances in the non-fungible tokens list clearly portray the potential that the NFT ecosystem possesses. It is said to be a new class of digital or tokenized assets, NFTs are altering the predictable concepts of asset usage and ownership. Consequently, you can find the common types of non-fungible tokens concentrating on what you actually get with an NFT. Firstly, you can have an original NFT created and stored on the blockchain.

The second type of NFTs denotes digital natives in which numerous NFTs serve as parts of ownership rights to specific assets. The third category of NFTs only proposes access to NFT metadata, thereby permitting you to use the NFT rather than distributing ownership. The various kinds NFTs that are being distributed such as artwork, music, and media, domain names, memes, also demonstrate capable prospects for the future of NFTs.

CHAPTER NO 10

ARE NFTs A PASSIVE WAY OF INCOME?

NFTs make us able to come up with new financial applications that can then issue tokens that may represent anything from stocks and bonds to cars and real estate. Basically, it's all that you can think of.

The basis of the NFT technology is on Ethereum blockchain technology. The Ethereum blockchain is time and again termed as programmable money. Now, what is that? It means that it can let anyone come up with and create their own tokens or NFTs using the Ethereum protocol.

Essentially there are two types of NFTs:

- Restricted NFTs
- Unrestricted NFTs

NFTs that allow you to claim ownership in the buying and selling of the asset are known as unrestricted NFTs.

NFTs that do not support any such claims and transferability are termed as restricted NFTs.

If you see, you will notice that money cannot be generated from the NFTs in their basic form. What happens is that these NFTs are used to create tokens and then those tokens are made a part of the decentralized finance landscape.

NFT Vaults & Staking

If you compare mining and staking you will come to a conclusion that staking is a less resource-intensive substitute to mining. It needs maintaining funds in a bitcoin wallet to retain the security and functionality of a blockchain network. In order to earn incentives from securing your assets, the process is said to be known as staking.

The process of staking has been implemented by various cryptocurrencies, including VeChain, Tezos, Decred, Navcoin, among others. In fact, most NFT projects are to be expected to start staking as revenue of generating passive income from their platform as a result.

NFTs are the only ones that have the staking ability. In fact, in order to acquire obligatory utility out of the NFT vTokens, it has become mandatory.

NFTs can be stored in storage facilities called vaults. Issuers of vToken offer access to the token holders for their assets that are locked. Vaults are used for this purpose.

If you have an Ethereum address, you will be able to generate a vault for any of your NFT assets. Everybody has the right to credit the eligible NFTs into the vault in order to create a fungible NFT-backed cryptocurrency called a "vToken."

vTokens make use of NFTs as a security to be held in escrow during a secure, peer-to-peer lending system. This lending system is assisted by decentralized exchanges. In a nutshell, one party leaves an asset locked up as security, and the other receives a loan from that asset at a cheap rate of interest.

The person who creates the vTokens is allowed to specify the number of primary assets in a vault. He will also be able to plan the mechanism for pricing. It should be linked directly to the price of the primary asset or basket of assets. The vToken protocol has been implemented on Ethereum.

A vToken allows you to generate income from any primary asset. It is said to be a financial instrument that can be used to generate revenue from the asset which it represents. This revenue generated may be due to interest, dividends, or coupons.

VTokens allows the users to make protocol fees, trade fees as a liquidity provider, and farm as loan collateral. If you are trying to create decentralized applications, you have to keep in mind that vTokens are really crucial for that. These can compete with the rivals with centralized counterparts in speed, efficiency, and scalability.

Protocols Designed for Passive Income

A new standard for transferring and settlement of tokens has been established. That is because the skating protocols are used that allow better distribution and increased transparency in the delivery. The reach of those platforms will increase multiple folds that use these distribution protocols that may result from adoption.

New content may be rapidly used to generate liquid markets for virtual assets, which will get the most out of their utility.

If you are considering the gains of decentralization of finance, a number of skating protocols may be of use.

Lending protocols provide permissions for the formation of financial assets that can be used as security on a decentralized lending platform.

The Peer-to-Peer lending market has great potential but unfortunately, it is pretty under-serviced. The conditions that are required to progress the lending into blockchain will come from the introduction of next-generation credit scoring and asset tokenization.

Lending that is backed by assets could provide the borrowers with great liquidity, low margin rates, fast settlement timeframes, and efficient risk management protocols.

An alternative class of asset tokenization that can be used to signify the payment means and storing the value for fiat currency on the Ethereum mainnet is collateralized stablecoins.

In general, NFTs are comparatively illiquid and hard to price. Taking chances in the NFT market is a lot easier due to the skating protocols. Another gain that it provides to these platforms is to sell their NFTs faster. This also helps in providing the customers with an enhanced user experience.

Transaction costs are highly reduced and allow for near-instant transaction speeds.

If you consider the flexibility of the NFTs, you will notice that they are a really flexible class of digital assets. It has numerous applications in art, gaming, finance, and more. Decentralized applications will be controlling their own governance protocols and that is going to be made possible by this technology. Also, it will not be cutting down on its transparency and decentralization. A good way of generating revenue from the digital properties passively is to monetize NFTs.

The collateralized stablecoins that are operated on the Ethereum mainnet are found to be tremendously useful by the businesses. Stablecoin that is used as collateral can help in the protection of businesses from high fluctuations in the price as well as increase their ability to transact with customers in a quicker and well-organized way.

In order to create a standard of the next-gen decentralized finance applications or the DeFi, it is important for the next-gen protocols to set the tokenization of assets as their main objective.

NEW NFTS INVESTMENTS

You can consider NFT as a digital collectible. You might have noticed that many investors are accustomed to these collectibles. The collectibles include artwork, fine wine, trading cards, or even classic cars. These digital assets can be great investments, as their value increases with time and it tends to not draw a parallel with other investment markets. Two factors help determine the increase in their value; their creator and their scarcity. You need to know everything regarding a collectible before you invest your money into it. It is important for you to know who created it and how many did the creator create? Before you purchase any digital collectible, don't forget to authenticate it. There have been multiple cases of fraud and counterfeits items' assets being sold.

Investing in NFTs, or digital collectibles is actually the same process. Whether it's digital art, digital trading cards, or albums, investors must question that how many were created so he is able to determine the proper value of the asset. Blockchain records the history of ownership over a collectible, so it is a great way to authenticate an item. Also, such authentication is not possible in physical assets. It is a great way to speed up the whole process for the investors.

You need to know and understand well that the valuations of the collectibles are pretty hypothetical. You need to take care of this aspect in investing in both physical and digital assets. Collectors frequently procure assets for the fundamental value that lies beyond the scope of investment. This may end up as a challenge for them to evaluate an asset properly. If you really like a painter or an athlete, you may be prepared to overpay so you get to own the asset. This can make your buying process perplexing but if you are considering selling it, it might be pretty profitable.

When investing in collectibles it's best to have a long time possible, as the long-term appreciation is more likely to be safe.

Understanding today's NFT market:

NFT market is expanding with every passing day but is still a relatively new market. Like every other market, the NFT market comes with its own risks and challenges that you need to consider before you invest in it. If you pay a close eye to the market you will see that on the supply side, the creators are coming up from all over the world. They are becoming a part of this market and are minting new and unique collectibles to sell online. Similarly, on the demand side, you will notice that the investors are also investing and jumping onto the bandwagon. This is making it a mainstream market for people to invest in.

Billions to date have already been deployed into NFTs, and we're just in the early innings. The infrastructure for minting, trading, and hosting NFTs is yet to be developed completely. The marketplaces are putting an effort into bringing together the investors and the creators. The concept is relatively new to the artist and creators too. They are still getting themselves used to this process of creating goods digitally and then selling them online. But it's rising rapidly and becoming more mainstream with every passing month.

Ethereum blockchain is used to host the NFT projects and NFTs nowadays rely hugely on it, this is basically a challenge that is being faced. The increase of traffic on the Ethereum network has resulted in slow speed and a high fee of transactions. As the NFT market is growing too, the Ethereum blockchain network is coming up with ways to ease the traffic congestion problem and help the NFTs become more affordable and accessible.

Flow, Near, and Polkadot are all hastening to become the de-facto NFT blockchain. All these are competitors to the Ethereum blockchain network. These platforms have worked already on their scaled solutions. It's uncertain at this point of time to claim the winner among these blockchains or if the market is even a winner-take-all. When you are working on this and trying to find out which NFT to invest your money in, make sure which blockchain minted the item.

Another challenge is handling custody. That is because these are digital assets and they live on a blockchain. If you purchase an NFT, that means that you have invested your money in purchasing a digital asset. You need to store that digital asset in your digital wallet. Ethereum NFTs need Ethereum wallets, Flow NFTs need Flow wallets, so on and so forth. The wallets that are used by these blockchains are pretty simple to use. The security of these wallets is totally upon you. So, if you're hosting valuable assets in a wallet, be sure that you house them securely in your digital wallet by having string passwords and a private key. Know that once your wallet gets lost, you will be unable to recover it. Similarly, if your wallet gets hacked, you will not be able to retrieve it back so make sure you take the security of your wallets seriously.

Finally, as this is a new market and people are still exploring it, many investors made investments as a result. Due to these investments, the worth and valuation of a number of NFTs have skyrocketed. As discussed earlier that these valuations are speculative and when the markets are running hot that speculation can go proliferate. Here what is of importance is to keep in mind is that collectible valuations are a resultant of who and how many—not by format. A painting, painted by Picasso will have the same worth on an oil painting canvas and a simple pen and paper. You see, the medium is just a minute influence here. When you are determining which NFT to invest your money in, make sure that you don't invest in NFTs just because they are NFTs. Rather invest only if you feel that its value would increase with the passage of time. It is to be seen as a long-term approach. As NFTs become mainstream the hype around the technology will fade. Focus on the asset, not the vehicle.

CHAPTER NO 12

MONETIZING NFTs

If you are looking to monetize your digital art, pictures, videos, etc., you can turn them into NFTs and then generate revenue through that. Here is how you can do so. The popularity of NFTs is increasing with every passing day, there have been instances where the NFTs are traded for millions of dollars. Well, that may not be the case always. It is not necessary that you would generate millions of dollars every time but if you apply the right strategies you may end up making money.

Acquire skills for selling your photography, music, art, videos, and game items as NFTs for a price you decide.

How to buy NFTs

Now, let's move forward and do some NFT trading. Go to the marketplace that you wish to use. Here we are considering the OpenSea. Go to OpenSea and click on "Explore" to have an idea of what is happening. Here you may end up finding a lot of digital assets like images, videos, etc.

While browsing there are high chances that you may find what you are looking for. Let's suppose that the CryptoKitties image named Zuzu Meowfluff interests you. Check the price and you will see that it has a price of .005 ether. It is said to be $8.96 at the time this was published.

- To buy it, just:

- Tap on "Buy Now."
- Select the option "Checkout."
- Click on "Submit."

You are supposed to pay the gas fee. This is only supposed to be paid once. The gas fee on the Ethereum network costs $18.18. The entire transaction results in costing $26.68.

Now you own that Zuzu Meowfluff CryptoKitties NFT.

Now let's practice selling NFTs, this is the image that you want to sell it.

You may have heard a lot regarding this in recent years.

Mike Winkelmann, also known as Beeple became the talk of the town after he was able to sell an NFT for $69 million. Nowadays there are a lot of people who spend millions of dollars on NFT collectibles of different kinds, ranging from sports trading cards and highlight reels to digital houses, augmented reality sneakers, and music.

Ownership rights are all recorded on a digital ledger on an Ethereum blockchain network. NFTs are digital assets of a new kind. Ethereum networks underpin bitcoin and other digital currencies. An important feature of the NFTs is that they cannot be duplicated and are unique. They work as digital assets that are only owned by you and by nobody else. People may have images etc. of this digital asset that you have NFT of but they do not own the original. This feature makes the NFTs tempting. And there's the outlook that because they can be occasional. You might as well sell one later for more money. Just like you would with fine art.

Any sort of currency can be used in purchasing NFTs. NBA Top Shot allows you to purchase them with your credit card. Platforms other than this may require you to buy using some form of cryptocurrency.

Here is how you can turn your digital assets into NFTs. We will do so by using the OpenSea platform. You will learn a lot from this if you are an artist and looking to generate some revenue.

Where to buy NFTs

You may have by now started to hear how people are investing in the NFT business and how they are generating revenue from it. Here is how you can create your own collection and then sell that online to earn money. But the question that might come to your mind at this point is that how do you begin with?

One way could be shopping on online marketplaces. OpenSea is one of the most popular ones. You can go to the OpenSea marketplace and browse through different forms of digital arts and collectibles.

This is similar in functionality to an auction house. You offer bids on items and then pray to be the winner of the bid. Various listings allow you to "buy now" for a set price. Now we will discuss how we can purchase NFTs on the OpenSea. However, there are a few things that you need to get done before you begin.

How to create and sell NFTs

Let suppose you have a collection of digital art or you have a Zuzu Meowfluff that you would want to sell off as an NFT on the marketplace. Here is how you can do it. Start with making it an NFT and then list it for sale. In this example, we used Rarible, due to its reduced costs and ease of setup. It also links into OpenSea if someone comes about to search it.

Open the site Rarible.com and then tap "Create" on the top right.

Create a single or multiple collectibles, multiple collectibles can be used for a collection of, photographs or cards, etc.

Then, select "Choose File", here you will have to upload a PNG, GIF, MP3, or another file type. You can only upload a file of size 30 MB.

Set the price that you want. We will list this picture of Porto, Portugal, which we took for 0.5 ether. After a 2.5% service fee, it will become equivalent to $826.91.

Now, mention the name of your NFT and a description of your NFT.

- Set your royalties. By setting up the royalties, you will be able to receive payment for it on every resell. The price which is currently being used is the current sale price.
- Select "Connect wallet and create."
- Connect your wallet that was set up earlier. Click on "Meta Mask".
- Now pay the gas fee so your listing is processed. Here, it's $75.64, or 0.044091 ether.
- Click on "Start" to sign the sell order using your digital wallet.
- Click on "Sign" in the MetaMask pop-up.

By following these steps, you have done listing your NFT. You can see your listing on the OpenSea or Rarible if you search "Porto, Portugal." All the offers will come upon the sale page. If it is sold, the funds will be sent to your digital wallet. This can be used to buy other NFTs or cash out using an app such as Coinbase.

Creation of a digital wallet to purchase NFTs

You need to add money to your digital wallet before you start. You have to add the money so you can then spend it on the platform.

You have to buy either because it is used by OpenSea. Ether is a cryptocurrency. Consider this whole process similar to that of an arcade, when you enter the arcade you will have to buy tokens in order to play the games. Similarly, you will have to buy the tokens at OpenSea, in this case, the tokens are called ether. Don't go overboard with buying ether, you can start by buying a small amount of ether.

Let's come back to the digital wallet discussion. It is suggested by OpenSea to use the plugin for the chrome browser called MetaMask. MetaMask supports a number of digital wallets.

Plugin installation takes about 30 seconds from OpenSea. Set a password.

Click on the icon for a profile that would be on the top right of the OpenSea website.

- Click on "Get MetaMask."
- Then choose "Install MetaMask" for Chrome, or any other browser. It would install a plug-in for Chrome.
- Choose the option of "Get Started."
- Now select "Create Wallet."
- Click on "No thanks" for sharing feedback.
- Choose your password.

Try not to lose your secret phrase. Write it down with you and keep it somewhere safe. This is a kind of backup access to your account.

Click on "Next" and approve the secret phrase.

Now click "Next" to connect your OpenSea account with the MetaMask digital wallet that was just created.

Click on "Connect" again.

Now you have your digital wallet connected to the OpenSea. Purchase some ether and you are good to go.

How you can find buyers?

NFT can be sold in two ways.

- Trading an NFT that has been bought already
- Selling an NFT that you have created and then put on a blockchain

You get to pay the fee that is required for minting an NFT. In order to sell it, you have to pay the fee attached to it. This will have both the gas fees and final sale service fees that are decided by the marketplace.

How to sell an NFT you bought?

When you purchase an NFT, you actually get the right to own it. You can resell that NFT like any other asset that you own. To do so make sure that the NFT and crypto wallet is paired to the marketplace on which you wish to sell. You can sell your NFT for more than the amount you purchased. The value of NFT is not certain and can change in both the long and short run.

How to sell an NFT you Minted?

You can sell an NFT that you have created on the platform that you are using to trade your NFTs.

Set the 'Buy Now' price, or share the terms of the auction. That is the price that you have reserved for it. You can set royalties and then whenever your asset resells you will receive some incentives.

You can buy and sell the NFTs on one website. You can place the item back on the platform that you want and then collect offers. It is a good way to generate revenue because these markets are highly volatile and the values are always fluctuating. For example, if you purchase an NFT for a hundred dollars, the value of it could go up to a thousand dollars within a year. If you are looking to predict the worth of the NFTs, you can't do so because the market may drop all of a sudden and you will face a loss.

The process of making your own NFTs can be pretty complex.

You'll start by producing the art, music, video clip, or file that you wish to sell. You can take inspiration from OpenSea or Rarible. Then you will have to decide the cryptocurrencies that you would want to work with. Most people prefer Ethereum because it's well-suited with most online marketplaces, but you might prefer a different currency with a more niche following.

You can upload your NFTs to the marketplace that you are using. It can be OpenSea or Mintable. The gas fee has to be paid in order to keep the network functioning. On the majority of the platforms, you are given an option to earn through royalties whenever someone resells your NFT. You can also add some extra features and not activate them. You can activate them once you sell the NFT.

Lastly, you are supposed to pay some extra fee in order to add it to the marketplace that you are using. Then people will have an option to bid for your NFTs and purchase it. Once they purchase the NFTs, they will have options to either sell them again or store them somewhere privately or add them to their collections. Ethereum can be used to purchase NFTs.

How Much Can You Earn from Selling Original NFTs?

You may have heard that people are selling their NFTs for millions of dollars but they may not always be the case and the majority of the NFTs are sold at much less prices. It is not necessary to sell the moment you put your NFTs for sale. It might take a lot of time to sell your first NFT at all. The famous NFTs usually have some famous artists associated with them or some viral meme to them. If you are not an established seller, it might be hard for you to sell your NFTs.

It is important to know that you need to have information and you invest in Ethereum before you move to the NFT market. The marketplaces where you can trade your NFTs usually mint your work and they charge Ethereum for that purpose. After minting they are changed into NFTs. You will also be required to pay a gas fee additionally because that is the amount that is used to mint your NFTs. You may have to make huge investments worth thousands of dollars in your NFTs initially.

If your NFTs take off, you could recover your investment. But still, there is no assurance that people might purchase your artwork. It is essential that you first survey the market and see what is trending currently. Popular NFTs tend to have a specific visual that attracts buyers.

How Do You Become an NFT Broker?

NFT broker is another field that you can become a part of. You can become an NFT broker if you are not pleased with buying and selling of NFTs. An NFT broker is the owner of a marketplace where people buy and sell NFTs. With the demand for NFTs increasing rapidly, what you can do is invest in a secure website and start generating traffic to your website by attracting users. NFT brokers generate revenue by charging creators to upload their assets. A gas fee can be charged as well. This will help you in covering the network costs.

There are many reasons why you should become a broker and run a brokerage business. One of the major advantages is you would not be required to pay for any physical assets. A storefront or other utilities would not be required for you to spend money on. As NFTS are digital assets, that makes your business purely digital too. You can start your business with some money to invest in and then attracting customers and generating revenue would help you run your website. The software takes care of the main processes. It allows you to concentrate on the other things of operating your website.

You need to have an interface that is easy-to-use and attracts users in order to generate traffic on your website. The interface shall be such that it makes the whole process of trading simple and easy. On your website, you should come up with an option where people can show off their NFTs because most people enjoy doing so.

As Ethereum is an expensive currency, you need to make your customers trust you with their money. Your website needs to have an encrypted and safe website that can stop hackers from corrupting their accounts. Your website needs to have a safe way for them to connect their wallets as well.

Additionally, to the brokerage-specific features that you are providing, you will also have to finance the consistent start-up costs such as purchasing a domain name, getting a business email address, and employing a web designer for designing the entire layout of the website for you. You can reduce some costs if you know how to design a website yourself. Your website needs to be such that it attracts customers and does not turn them away.

All the above things are important but what is of more importance is that you need to have enough knowledge regarding the NFT and cryptocurrency business. You should know how the NFTs and Ethereum blockchains work. This is a risky business and you should be willing to take that risk if you are thinking of starting your business as a broker. You could still enjoy making good profits from jumping into a popular and fast-paced industry.

What Are Other Substitutes for Being a Broker?

If you want to become a part of the NFT industry but are not interested in becoming a broker or trading in the industry, there are several other ways you could become a part of this industry. Below mentioned are several ways through which you can become a part of the NFT space:

You can become a part of the NFT industry by writing eBooks and guides for people who are interested in the field.

As this is a relatively new field and people are interested in it they are most likely going to buy these instruction guides and eBooks to have a better overview of the field and what they are getting themselves into. Help people in understanding what an Ethereum blockchain is, how you can trade NFTs, minting, and cryptocurrencies, etc. These guides and eBooks can greatly help people in understanding this new concept and they can then make their moves carefully. It will help them understand cryptocurrencies more clearly. Let people know that it is not necessary to be experts in technology to use cryptocurrency like Ethereum.

In order to become associated with this technology, you can help guide others who are interested. You can build a community for them where they can have discussions and the enthusiasts guide each other. It could be anything from a Discord server, social media page, online forum, or another community-based platform. Help people through different ways so they can learn more about these concepts because they are eager to learn.

Another way in which you can associate yourself with the industry is that you can create websites for NFTs. You can create a marketplace that only the breakers can use. For example, by creating an app or software for the brokers, you will get some incentive if they end up downloading your app or becoming a part of your community. Through this, you can become a part of this community and provide a valued service.

You can also launch an NFT app. Digital wallets are a crucial and essential part of anyone is interested in selling or buying the NFTs. You can come up with an app that helps in these transactions. Your app should make it easy for them to view and manage their accounts. Extra features such as real-time market values of each type of currency can be included too.

You can become a part of a community where you can see what people are doing and what is currently trending. This will give you a head start. It will allow you to increase the knowledge that is required for you to have along the way.

CHAPTER NO 13

LEGITIMATE MARKETPLACES FOR NFTS

On Valuables which is an online marketplace for signed tweets logged and confirmed on the Ethereum blockchain that Chief Executive Officer of Tesla, Elon Musk has standing offers of $10,000 for his tweets on Twitter, as well as the classic remark: "Was super fun tbh haha."

If this surprised you or if you still feel perplexed and confused regarding the NFT market which is exploding with every passing day, know that you are not the only one.

If you want to exchange a dollar with a dollar you can do so without any problem. Similarly, in case of the cryptocurrencies, if you want to exchange a bitcoin with another you can. But the NFTs don't work that way. You cannot exchange one NFT with another because NFTs are unique in nature and that is the reason for their scarcity.

You can mint anything that you wish for as an NFT. CryptoPunks blockheads, short films, virtual cannabis farms, domain names, etc. At this point, another exciting thing has entered the NFT market and that is the digital art, sports collectibles, and video games where the users can build and govern alternate worlds also known as "metaverses."

There are a number of exchanges through which fiat currency can be exchanged into cryptocurrencies.

Coinbase, Kraken, Gemini are a few examples of the crypto exchanges where you can do these exchanges. NFTs are purchased with ether. The cryptocurrency which is used to power the Ethereum blockchain network is Ether.

Through blockchain networks such as Ethereum and Solana, users have the ability to create apps that are used to store their personal data, smart contracts that govern NFT ownership and sales. You cannot do so using bitcoins. Bitcoin is mainly used for the purpose of payments.   smart contracts that administer the ownership rights and sales on NFTs.

NFT markets are new markets for artist to sell their original work. This also helps them generate a certain percentage of money with each resells on the secondary market through royalty agreements. Those investors that are confident regarding the NFT markets see this as a great way to support these artists financially.

There are numerous statistics that show the growth of these markets over time. Fortune reported in its March issue OpenSea, which is an online marketplace saw a great increase in its sales. In comparison to the last six months, the numbers have grown momentously. The increase showed $95 million in digital objects sold in February, up from $8 million in January.

There have been a number of theft and fraud reports filed by people. The electricity that is needed to power and run the Ethereum blockchain is a reason for massive emissions of carbon. The commission fee also varies greatly as well. If anyone is interested and wants to become a part of this market, they have to make sure that they know everything that they can regarding these markets. They need to be well aware of the terms and conditions.

With all this now known to you, if you wish to start a career in this industry, here is a look at some of the most widely used marketplaces for trading.

SuperRare:

SuperRare is a peer-to-peer marketplace where the trade for single-edition digital artworks is done. The layout of the site is similar to that of Instagram tiles, where the work is showcased for the buyers to view. You will also see the prices, sale prices, and timed auctions mentioned with each artwork that is being sold. You may end up finding great artworks of the reputed and renowned artists on the site. Leading sellers like a Time Magazine cover being sold for $300,000. This site is able to generate enough traffic as well as lots of artists and bands to be selected from. The site exhibits a feature that is similar to that of an online magazine which makes it easy for the sellers and buyers to go through the artworks presented on the site. The transactions are made using ether. Ether is the cryptocurrency that powers the Ethereum blockchain network.

Foundation:

Foundation was launched in February 2021. Foundation has introduced NFT sales of the much viral internet meme Nyan Cat, Pak's Finite record, and work by creators such as Pussy Riot's Nadya Tolokonnikova, Aphex Twin, and Edward Snowden.

The layout of the site is in form of grids that display the work of artists. Trending auctions are displayed on the grids on the top of the page. The artists that are featured are displayed below. Arts that are being sold are listed at a reserve price. Extra 15 minutes are provided in case the bid is placed in the last 15 minutes. and bids can be placed for 24 hours, with a 15-minute extra time if bids are placed in the last 15 minutes. In order to purchase or mint an NFT on the Foundation site, users are supposed to set up a MetaMask wallet.

Mintable:

Mintable is a two-sided marketplace for the trading of NFTs. The website is similar to eBay. Mintable is sponsored by Marc Benioff-owned Time Ventures and billionaire investor Mark Cuban. Minatble is based on the Ethereum and Zliqa blockchains. MetaMask is automatically linked with Minatble which makes it easier for the buyers to set up and manage their crypto wallets. Creators are given an option to mint free "gasless" NFTs, short-run printable series, or traditional transaction-based items. As MetaMask is linked already, after the account set up wallet linking, the users can start buying. They can purchase listed items or bid on auctions, with winners notified by email.

OpenSea:

A team for software development by Devin Finzer and Alex Atallah founded the OpenSea marketplace back in 2017. OpenSea is said to be one of the first and largest marketplaces for users who own digital goods. It has 113,000 users, 15.5 million NFTs, and a $354 million volume of trade. The startup was able to raise $23 million in its most recent round of undertaking capital funding led by the Silicon Valley venture capital firm Andreessen Horowitz. You can find all the options from virtual real estate to music videos etc. OpenSea is a marketplace that is filtered by price and sales status. A stats tab is used for the ranking of sellers by volume, average sale price, and the number of assets sold. Buyers can purchase using their digital wallets. They can use USD Coin, DAI, or ether to purchase NFTs. Ether can also be sued to purchase NFTs on OpenSea.

NBA Top Shot:

NBA Top Shot was launched as a beta by DapperLabs in early 2020. It is licensed by NBA. It allows fans to gather and trade digital "moments" from the NBA. NBA Top Shot was released in limited editions ranging from $9 to $230. Box scores, player stats. Moments feature video highlights etc. are all available on the NBA Top Shot. Collectors can show curated collections, follow their favorite teams, and trade assets secured on the blockchain that is owned by the company itself. This platform has two million purchases and the total amount would become $300 million by March.

Axie Infinity:

Axie Infinity was designed by Vietnamese startup Sky Mavis. It is a Pokemon-inspired video game, where players collect cartoon pets, battle other players, and build farming kingdoms. Axie Infinity had more than 10,000 monthly active users in 2020. It is also said to be one of the most popular games that are available on the Ethereum network.

Sorare:

Sorare is a fantasy soccer league game that is based on cryptocurrency. Users can gather player cards as NFTs. These cards that the users collect can be used in online competitions. Sorare has 140 licensed clubs, including the teams of Major League Soccer. All the transactions that happen in this game are through Ethereum. Users are given an opportunity to become a part of this fantasy league by purchasing digital players at reduced costs. According to an online magazine for soccer, the total expenditure on the platform was $13 million in Ethereum.

Venly:

Venly is a peer-to-peer online marketplace for BFTs that currently has more than 200.000 gamers. The Peer-to-peer NFT marketplace in Venly lets it's the users that log in to create, buy and sell characters of the game, collectibles, and collectibles, without having to fear receiving cryptocurrency first. User accounts can be linked to their digital wallets so they are able to sell and buy assets via blockchain games.

Nifty Gateway:

Nifty Gateway is a centralized U.S. dollar marketplace. It has various artists and brands to create Nifties. Nifties is a term that is used for NFTs. Sales are structured around "drops," after a drop finishes or artwork is sold.

You can use a peer-to-peer marketplace through which Nifties can be sold again. It has Featured works of different artists and brands such as Beeple, BD White, Cam Hicks, Forbes, and Playboy.

Zora:

Zora is a decentralized auction house. It helps the artists capture the value that labels, galleries, and big brands have usually taken as a commission for service and distribution. Music, video, images, GIFs, and text NFTs can all be found for sale through linked Ethereum wallets like MetaMask, WalletConnect, and Coinbase by the buyers. Additionally, it serves as a marketplace. Zora is also an open-source protocol, built on one of the most commonly used standards for NFTs, known as ERC-721. It allows the creators to purchase and resell NFTs anywhere that assimilates with the protocol and specify royalty percentages for resales on secondary platforms.

Decentraland:

Decentraland is one of the first-ever virtual worlds that is owned by users. Decentraland uses the concept of the metaverse, it lets the users discover casinos, kingdoms built underwater, and visions of space. They do so while using a builder tool to develop land holdings and accumulate power and influence. It can be played using a VR headset or through a web browser. In the last week, the site was able to make 306 sales which generated $1.2 million, as per the NFT sales database NonFungible.

Rarible:

Rarible and OpenSea are somewhat similar to each other. However here you have to pay a fee for each of the artwork that you create and then put on the blockchain. This is a great platform if you are looking to mint individual pieces. Your work may not go unnoticed here but the costs are pretty high.

Minting of each work can cost you $40 to $80. Rarible allows you to mint everything as an NFT. Rarible is on its way to becoming a decentralized independent organization. This means that Rarible will be administered by the Ethereum blockchain's rules. This would let the public, permissionless use. RARI is a token of governance that allows the buyers and sellers who are active the most to vote for platform upgrades and participate in moderation decisions.

The Sandbox:

It is a video game where the Ethereum blockchain is used by the players to monetize their experiences. SAND is a cryptocurrency that is used as a usage fee for the game. It is a kind of utility token. It is a web-based marketplace that allows the users to upload, publish and sell designs that are made using VoxEdit. VoxEdit is a 3D voxel modeling package like NFTs. Game mechanics can be easily changed using the scripted behaviors after the creations are published and purchased. An editor can be used to place on land parcels. These in turn make changes to the game mechanics.

MakersPlace:

MakersPlace is a gallery of digital artwork formalized around creations that are developed by the creator. Short films are featured on the home page of the website along, with images of lunar landscapes, heady motion graphics, and reimagined statues and mythic gods. Whenever a piece is sold, it is issued and signed by its creator. It is logged onto the blockchain network permanently. The blockchain also verifies it. You can use tags that are searchable in order to find the ownership rights. It makes the site informative and easy to work with. On this site, the work that is presented can be purchased through auctions that happen digitally. Ether or a credit card can be sued to make payments.

GROW.HOUSE:

GROW.HOUSE is said to be one of the first metaverses for lovers of cannabis, crypto, and decentralized finance. GROW.HOUSE is designed using the Polygon network and lets users grow digital cannabis, earn $GROW tokens, buy NFTs as well as gain information regarding yield farming. Once it goes live, the marketplace of GROW.HOUSE will allow users to purchase cannabis flowers as NFTs.

Zeptagram:

Zeptagram was founded in Stockholm by Christina Löwenström and Johan Forsman Löwenström. This marketplace lets musicians create tokens of their tracks and then sell them as NFTs. Then they sell a fraction of their ownership rights to their fans or to the investors. Musicians receive incentives due to the royalty agreement whenever a resale happens. Zeptagram has created its own currency which goes by the name Zeptacoin. Zeptacoin is used in payments of royalties and buying and selling of music rights on the platform.

Valuables:

Valuables allow users to auction their tweets for money. The money is in the form of ether. Entering the URL of the tweet or typing the user handle in the search bar enables people to place their bids. Offers begin at a minimum of $1. That only happens if the seller has decided on a reserve price. After the bid is placed, the buyer is directed to the tweet of the seller. There they let the user know that an offer is made by them. Valuables were the site where the CEO of Twitter Jack Dorsey sold his autographed first tweet. It was sold for $2.9 million.

CHAPTER NO 14

HOW TO GET BACK YOUR FUNDS?

Founders Fund backs Royal, a music marketplace planning to sell song rights as NFTs

An investment in a platform aiming to unite music rights with NFTs is being led by Founders Fund and Paradigm, which will let users purchase songs' shares through the marketplace of the company, earning royalties as the music financed in garners fame.

The scheme, "Royal", is run by Justin Blau, an EDM artist whose stage names are 3LAU, and JD Ross, runs a co-founder of home-buying startup Opendoor. One of the more active and noticeable figures in the NFT community includes Blau who has launched a number of upstart efforts aimed at exploring how monetization of music through crypto markets could be possible. Blau says that NFTs caught his full-time attention when COVID changed his plans for the tour, he aimed to find a way to change the power dynamics on "platforms that were extracting all the value from creators."

Blau set his own record, in March, weeks before many heard about NFTs after the $69 million Beeple sales at Christies, and for a collective $11.7 million worth of cryptocurrency sold a lot of custom songs and artwork.

Just as a broader bull run for the NFT market the royal's investment declaration comes which appears to reach a fever pitch, hundreds of millions of dollars worth of cryptocurrencies are dumped by investors into community NFT projects like CryptoPunks and Bored Apes. A number of platforms have been seen emerged and matured in recent months by visual artists who are interested in putting their digital works on the blockchain simplifying the process of monetization of their art, fewer efforts have been focused on musicians.

A $16 million seed round in Royal is being steered by Paradigm and Founders Fund, with involvement from Atomic — where Ross was a general partner recently. The deal for Founders Fund was led by Ross's fellow Opendoor co-founder Keith Rabois.

Not a lot is being shared by the company about their launch or product plans, including the time when the platform will really begin selling fractionalized assets, but it's pretty clear that Blau's music will be profoundly leveraged by the company to bring early fans/investors to the platform. For early access on the site, the users can sign up presently.

Aiming to help creators share their success with fans the NFT startups pursuit more intricate ownership splits, tons of speculation is taking off around how they will eventually be treated by regulators. While the ICO thrive of 2017 led to a copious amount of founders receiving SEC letters asserting securities scam, entrepreneurs in this upsurge are working a little harder to avoid that consequence. According to Blau the startup's team is diligently working with legal counsel to guarantee the startup is being entirely compliant.

Given the extensive landscape of crypto investors looking to expand, guaranteeing that democratizing admittance to purchasing music rights truly welfares the fans of those artists or creates new fans for them may be the company's greater challenge. That being mentioned, Blau records there's abundant room for improvement amidst the existing possession spread of music royalties, largely spread among labels, private equity groups, and hedge funds.

Blau says "A true fan might want to own something way earlier than a speculator would even get wind of it,". "Democratizing access to asset classes is a huge part of crypto's future."

CHAPTER NO 15

HOW TO CREATE NFTS ART WITH NO CODING EXPERIENCE?

Despite having a long history dating back to 2012, because the topic has only recently gained attention from many people, especially investors, you've probably read about NFT for the umpteenth time. Consequently, we will not be boring you with unnecessary bluffs and instead focus on the main topic that being "how to create NFT art with zero coding experience."

However, we will not move right into the discussion without briefly explaining what NFT means. At least for those who may just be stumbling on the topic for the first time. So what does NFT stand for?

Understanding NFT

Non-fungible Token is abbreviated as NFTs and is termed by experts as a type of cryptographic token on a blockchain representing a single asset. In this context, assets essentially do not denote any type of cryptocurrency as expected; rather, they refer to real-world possessions such as art, music, in-game items, and movies, among other art collections.

The word "Non-fungible" may sound bizarre, and one may wonder what it is in this context. Firstly, in finance fungibility describes the property of a good or a commodity with interchangeable individual units and each of whose parts are almost identical to another part.

According to the context, fungibility is when two different assets—for example, a unit of $200 bills, and another unit of $200 bills or maybe 5 units of $40 bills—with the same value can be switched and still retain their actual value. Likewise, in the crypto world, 1 Bitcoin is the same as 1 Bitcoin, same as 1Etherum if substituted with another.

Whereas, a "Non-fungible" asset, is distinctive and its value is separate from another NFT of equal or similar value. To rephrase it, each NFT is distinctive in terms of its qualities, and its worth is variable. In contrast, comparisons of NFTs to precious stones like Diamond, gold, and their likes can be made.

How to make NFT Art with No coding experience

Moving ahead to the main discussion, how are NFT arts created? Firstly, many individuals and potential investors are promoted to seek information on how to create digital assets due to the recent increase in market demand for NFTs.

For example, in one of its publications, Coindesk reported that dealing volume at OpenSea, which is a famous NFT marketplace, amplified from $1 million in August of 2020 up to $8 million in January of 2021. It reached up to $50 million in February of the year 2021.

What is even more exciting, a $23 million seed round was also unveiled by the startup managed by Andreessen Horowitz. This all totals up to corroboration of how unsettling NFT is in the crypto space. Now it's time to dive into the "how". Let's begin!

Initially, opposing to as commonly believed, a skill in coding or program development is not essentially needed to make an NFT; although, having it is a huge advantage since it escalates your chances of getting sales with higher bids. So is it done as a beginner?

Honestly, there are numerous ways to develop an NFT, while some of which need a lot of time and energy, others do not need a lot of skills and a lot of time. And they all end up selling anyway.

Markedly, you may be required to have a creative skill as NFT influences art in any form or medium. In this case, graphic arts can be engaged as a case study to show the demands of the process.

For instance, working with graphic editing tools like Photoshop, MS Paint, or CorelDraw and their likes will be mandatory for a graphic artist. Later on, you will have to transpire a unique and different idea from the abundance of art that's on your ideal choice of the marketplace at the present.

Alternative ways such as 3D modeling could also be tried, which is a harder path for beginners. Designing animated graphics or characters would entice potential clients' a 3D modeling tool would be used.

You may list your art piece on a reputable NFT marketplace, once it is created, where proving ownership of the work is obligatory before it's set up for sale. We'll shortly get into how to join an NFT.

How to enlist and sell NFTs

The process of registering NFT arts mostly has to do with the individual blockchain protocol of different sites and differs from site to site. You may be needed to apply to create a project for it to be sold as an NFT, for some marketplaces.

Whereas in other scenarios, all that needs to be done is create a MetaMask wallet on the marketplace. Before proceeding, we need to know what the alliteration word stands for?

According to Yahoo Finance, a wallet that exists exclusively on your computer and offers you full control of your funds is described as a Metamask. As described by Wikipedia, it is a software cryptocurrency wallet used to interact with the Ethereum blockchain.

Wikipedia further explains that users can gain access to their digital wallets via a browser extension. Also, the users can access the wallet through a mobile app. You can use that in order to interact with the dApps.

Precisely, despite having the ability to be held on other blockchains, NFTs are frequently kept on the Ethereum blockchain.

Moving further, a user becomes a probable trader by creating a MetaMask wallet, enabling him to upload his NFT art on the marketplace, wait for the collection to be approved and accredited, and then tolerantly wait for a customer to approach.

Since NFT art sales are profitable that enables the artists to monetize their works, which causes a rise in their fortune, eradicates mediators, and avoids traditional market forces, its disadvantage is the very high gas fee the artists are charged. At the completion of every successful transaction a high commission is charged, this may cause artists to make less money than they should.

Also, tokens are not possessed by most projects with a marketplace where NFTs are handled. However, some such as AFEN tokens owned by AFEN exist hence constructing a dispersed NFT marketplace for African art. As they have a lot of improvements to make in terms of market valuation, the majority of these tokens are promising. The NFT industry is still expanding and will grow more as mass implementation becomes a reality.

Generally, NFT still is a very worthwhile business, and to begin you might want to know more about the AFEN NFT market.

CHAPTER NO 16

HOW DO NFTS WORK?

Paintings which are traditional works of art are treasured because they are unique. In contrast, digital files can be easily and endlessly replicated.

You see, with NFTs, we can "tokenize" artwork to create a digital certificate of ownership of assets" that can be bought and sold.

In cryptocurrency, a public archive known as the blockchain stores a record of what is owned by whom. Since the blockchain is maintained by thousands of computers around the world the records cannot be forged.

NFTs can also comprise keen contracts that might, for instance, give the artist a cut of the token's future sale.

At a very high level, the Ethereum blockchain consists of most of the NFTs. Native cryptocurrency token called ether (ETH) is present in Ethereum. The Ethereum blockchain network is powered by Ether, which also supports these NFTs. This is a distinguishing aspect to the likes of bitcoin or Litecoin which offer blockchains that are almost only used for transferring value. Notably, other blockchains – like Cardano, Polkadot, EOS, and Tron – which are comparable to Ethereum and have smart contract functionality can implement their own versions of NFTs.

Whatever is happening in the tangible world?

An NFT sensation is the NBA Top Shots which arose from a licensing agreement made by the NBA and its players' union with Dapper Labs in 2019.

Short highlighting reels of NBA players are created and turned into NFTs by Top Shots, that can be bought and sold by collectors.

These digital assets are sold in 'packs' which are organized in such a manner so as each pack has a certain number of 'moments' (digital highlights), which ranges in price from $9 to $99.

These packs are of different types– with costlier packs comprising of highlights from bigger players, or more momentous games. Since the blockchain records its ownership, each pack is verifiably limited, consequently, demand these digital assets increases. Each pack has sold out since the first pack "dropped" in 2020. As a matter of fact, the Top Shot product according to CNBC has produced over $230 million in gross sales, which is an astonishing amount given the product being sold.

CHAPTER NO 17

WHAT MAKES NFTS VALUABLE?

The number of times a digital file can be copied is unlimited, counting the art included with an NFT.

But NFTs are intended to provide you with ownership of the work which is something that can't be copied even though just like with physical artwork the copyright and reproduction rights can still be reserved by the artist.

In terms of collecting physical art: a Monet print could be bought by anyone but the original is owned by one person only.

$69 million was made at Christie's when Mark Winkelman, the artist commonly known as Beeple, was able to sell a digital art piece as an NFT. According to the auction house, this puts him among the top three most treasured living artists.

So what makes NFTs so exciting?

To provide ownership for users to validate their ownership rights one can use NFTs.

This would permit the far more easy international transfer of digital assets than any set of collectibles seen before.

Moreover, NFTs give buyers assurance when they buy their assets because they offer legitimacy.

The consideration of use cases for NFTs has just begun. For instance, online news articles may be bought by someone as NFTs, there are more practical uses on their way apart from this appearing like an uncivilized indulgence of the elite.

So far, the thorough concentration of the crypto market has been on fungible digital assets like bitcoin and Ethereum.

Since NFTs provide a marketplace for assets such as digital art, game items, concert tickets, real estate, and more, this has been changed.

Digital artists are allowed for monetization of their work due to these new tokens by giving ownership proof, regardless of the number of people downloading and using the images.

How to invest in NFTs?

Since NFTs are not like openly transacted liquid tokens that can just be bought and sold, that creates a problem. Due to the diversity of NFTs, they are thinly traded and have various value drivers. People new to the market can't simply indulge themselves and start purchasing stuff.

What seems like a more practical tactic is Investing in the blockchain infrastructure supporting the NFT.

Investing in Ethereum or the Smart Contract Bundle, which can both be found on Revix's digital platform, is the shortest path to get an experience of the fundamental decentralized blockchain technology.

Revix customers can begin investing with an amount as meager as R500. No sign-up, monthly account, or subscription fees, are charged by fintech, but instead, a simple 1% transaction fee is made for both buying and selling.

Ethereum

The Ethereum blockchain creates and records most NFTs, hence providing a comprehensive record of the NFT ownership chain and custody. Ethereum like blockchains is fundamentally tamper-resistant and hackproof massive spreadsheets.

The blockchain will keep a precise archive of the transaction trail, as people will buy and sell NFTs in this rapidly improving marketplace, and the prices of rare collectibles will likely be increased.

According to Sanders, there has been a lot of discussion regarding decentralized finance, or DeFi. Also, the changes that it is going to bring about in the finance world. This would make the whole investment, lending, borrowing, trading process a lot easier for people. They will also be able to generate revenue as an interest outside of the banking system. NFTs have lately become really prominent and are a good example of how these innovative technologies can be incorporated in order to come up with a new marketplace for artists, real estate owners and owners of collectibles, etc.

For the majority, it may be hard to comprehend how a single tweet from Jack Dorsey can be sold for millions of dollars, and few people would be in the market for this kind of thing. It is assumed that this newly developing market depends particularly on Ethereum blockchain technology, but other cryptocurrencies such as Cardano and Polkadot will probably also take advantage of this new technology.

Smart contract cryptocurrencies permit creators for installing NFTs and build applications on top of the blockchain, which works in a similar way the Android and iOS operating systems work with mobile applications. These applications enable users in trading goods, cryptos, lend, borrowing and perform multiple financial transactions without a stock exchange or a back as an intermediate.

It is still not decided who will win the race to take over the DeFi space, however as of present Ethereum has a solid head start. Cardano and Polkadot also house smart contracts, are close behind Ethereum.

Ethereum, Cardano, NEM, EOS, and Polkadot are the five cryptocurrencies that comprise The Revix Smart Contract.

Your investment is correspondingly distributed over these five cryptocurrencies, and its portfolio is mechanically rebalanced each month hence ensuring that each cryptocurrency reaches a 20% allowance in the portfolio.

An astounding 200% have valued The Revix Smart Contract Bundle since January 1 this year.

Other ways to intelligently invest in cryptocurrencies

Two more crypto bundles that are fixated on precise investment themes are offered by Revix.

Revix's Payment Bundle delivers to make digital payments inexpensive, quicker and to provide more universal exposure to the major five payment-focused cryptocurrencies looking to contest with government-issued fiat currencies. Bitcoin (BTC), Ripple (XRP), Litecoin (LTC), Bitcoin Cash (BCH), and Stellar (XLM) are included in these cryptocurrencies.

Top 10 Bundle, which distributes your investment over the top 10 biggest cryptocurrencies as measured by market cap, is the third bundle presented by Revix. Ensuring that every crypto is provided a premium of exactly 10%, the portfolio is rebalanced each month.

Through Revix's online platform you can also buy and sell USDC which is a 'stablecoin'. Stablecoin is completely sponsored by the US dollar and a physical gold-backed token called PAX gold. This token allows the legal ownership of an ounce of gold

WHAT ARE NFTS ROYALTY SHARES?

Even after selling their NFTs, artists and content creators find that these tokens can be very advantageous for them since NFTs are in the glare of publicity. This feature is principally thought-provoking; they're called NFT royalties. You may want to know what NFT royalties are if you are new to this field. Let's find out!

What are NFT royalties?

All those times when you are able to sell your NFT creations on a marketplace, you will get a percentage of the sale price, this is due to NFT royalties. Smart contracts automatically execute continuous royalty NFT payments. You can choose your royalty percentage in most marketplaces. A standard royalty is about 5-10%.

There are numerous differences between NFTs and other traditional royalty payments.

When an author makes resales, some incentive is given back to the author and that is known as the royalty payout. Royalty payouts are recorded into the smart contract on a blockchain. Whenever a resale happens, the smart contract is responsible for making sure that the terms that were set by the NFT are achieved. In royalty specifications, a certain amount of money is sent over to the original artist from the revenue generated from the resale.

Royalties are not yielded by every NFT; this is something that should be kept in mind. If you wish to receive royalties from your NFTs, you have to mention that in the terms and conditions. Those terms and conditions are recorded in the Ethereum blockchain network and the rest of the process is all done automatically. It is not necessary to have intermediaries and also it does not depend upon the wishes and demands of the person who is transacting. This is something great for digital content, gaming accessories, physical items, etc. NFT royalties are a never-before-opportunity to increase the revenue that is generated by the artists and content creators. This is a benefit for the artists they get from these NFTs after they have created or produced something repeatedly. As more and more these artists become popular, they may end up getting an increase in the returns that they receive from their work.

This is a great scheme that is offered by the NFTs. This makes the artists and digital content creators work with more motivation and enthusiasm. This is also motivating them to become a part of the NFT industry. The system of royalties may be different for each of the marketplaces. Many new marketplaces are coming up with other techniques and ways to help artists receive enough money for their production.

Before the royalties' concept began on the NFT marketplaces, the artists would not be paid enough. They would only be paid for the time they sold their work as an NFT on the marketplaces. The artists after selling their work online would not have any track of other subsequent transactions that occurred after that. The only time they made a profit was for selling it the first time and then the buyer would gain profit after reselling. That was not something that motivated and inspired these artists and digital creators.

The people who would buy their work would wait for the right time and then sell that at tremendous prices. This system only benefitted the buyer and not the artist who created the art originally. The artist got no penny from his artwork and all that profit would go to the pockets of those who bought. Hence the common concept of artists as penurious or the starving artist.

NFTs have changed this whole concept from the grass-root level. Artists will be given a justified share every time their creations are sold. This will be forever.

How do NFT royalties work?

Here, the question arises that how does the royalty system work? So basically what happens is that at the time of minting the NFT for an original piece of artwork, the artist can decide over a certain amount that he would get after any other subsequent sales made by the buyer. Whenever the buyer sold the artwork of an artist, he would get the pre-determined amount of money from the revenue the buyer would generate from the sales. All the marketplaces do not allow you to have royalties claimed while minting the NFT However, Rarible does give you the option of royalties at the time of minting the NFT.

For example, you have an NFT artwork created on Rarible. Somebody buys that NFT for let supposes 8 ETH. This means that you have earned 8 ETH from your artwork. While minting your NFT, you have clearly stated that you would get a 10% revenue that is generated anytime this artwork is sold again. That means whenever the buyer sells that artwork, you will get 10% of the money generated.

Now let suppose, the buyer waits for the right time for a resale. Your popularity has grown by now and the buyer sells your artwork for supposing 200 ETH. That means that the buyer made a lot of money whereas you being the original creator could not earn that much. But as you have stated in the terms and conditions already that you would get a 10%incentive, which means you would get 20 ETH from the sale that was just made.

Now let's imagine that the new owner also might sell your artwork, you would get 10% proceeds from that sale as well. This means that every time your artwork is sold, you will get some revenue out of it. You will repeatedly be paid for your sold artwork. With the NFT royalties, you are at an advantage. This is a great way for the authors and original creators of the art to get paid for as long as their artwork is sold.

This means that no artist will have to suffer now. No content creator will struggle financially. There will be no fake or counterfeit products available in the market or even if they are they would not be worth the original product. Identification of what is original and what not has certainly become easy.

All these great things are a result of blockchain technology. Blockchain technology works on a distributed ledger that records the data of all the transactions that happen over the blockchain network. This makes the whole transaction process transparent and decentralized.

This digital ledger which records the data of transactions makes the work more authentic. Whatever conditions are set in the smart contract are to be fulfilled at all costs and that is possible due to the automated protocols of the network. You do not need an intermediary to process any transaction or dealing. All that is done automatically with great transparency.

Blockchain technology works in close connection to smart contracts. The two of them together make sure that the real author is known and the royalty payments are made as soon as a resale happens and transactions are recorded into the blockchain network. Due to this, any irregularities that may take place are eliminated.

Who gains from an NFT royalty?

Musicians creators, content creators, and artists gain from NFTs royalties. This is not again for the artists only but also the buyer. The buyer cannot be cheated as he would know what is authentic and what is a replica. He would not be cheated to buy something that is not original. This lets the buyers show off their digital collectibles and assets that they bought but also have an option to resell them at higher prices. It's a win-win situation for both parties!

Electronic musician Jaques Green had his track from 2011 has gained almost $27,000 in royalties. Mike Winkelmann who was in the news for selling his artwork for thousands of dollars, has designed the NFT of his artwork to produce 10% royalty from every consequent sale.

Artists like Steve Aoki, Ozuna, Kings of Leon, etc. are making full use of the royalty system. They are generating revenue from each sale of their art. This has the potential to be a great and considerable source of revenue for the creator and buyer as well.

Why use NFT royalties?

If you want to keep earning from the artwork you produced with a lot of hard work, you can do so by the NFT royalty system. It is a great way to earn from what you produced. This system is an excellent way for the artists and developers to gain profit from the resales. Before the NFT royalty system, they could not earn from their work in this way.

An artist can generate revenue with ease as a sports superstar, it all comes down to how popular they are. It is merely fair that they also gain an advantage from resales of their work.

Another amazing thing about the NFTs is that even though the original creator might sell the artwork as an NFT, he will still have ownership over the underlying copyrights. This is another way for them to profit. They still have an option of selling a fraction of their rights to somebody else.

The people who buy from these artists can also receive incentives from the royalties that are earned because of their ownership rights over the artwork. This may not be a common practice on the other marketplaces, but the new ones are launching and coming up with such ways to benefit the creators. For example, Bluebox has recently come up with such facilities.

Some aspects of thoughtfulness do exist as possible cases of intellectual property are yet to be clearly formulated on such transactions.

It is highly likely for the NFTs to become eligible as estate assets. The day is not far when these NFTs could be transferred as assets including the royalties through wills, trusts, and legal instruments. These activities are supposed to be done with utmost care.

NFTs are a great way for the artist to gain some profit after they sell their artwork to buyers. They may still earn even if they are no longer in ownership of their NFT tokens.

Secondary sales or resales are possible for generating revenue through the tokenization of assets. Also, distributing the royalties with those wanting to invest in the rights. Before this system, the intermediaries would keep earning from that asset and the artist would not earn a penny after he would sell his artwork. This practice has been completely eliminated now on these marketplaces.

Physical goods and assets can also take advantage of the freedom and prospects that these NFTs provide. This is so that the owner of the physical goods can also benefit just as the digital ones.

This is a great way for the artist and content creators to make enough money so they keep on producing work of top-notch quality. This is also a way to pay back these artists what they truly deserve. They would keep earning from their artwork as long as the buyers of their art resell it.

CHAPTER NO 19

HOW NFT CAN BENEFIT THE CREATOR?

The non-fungible tokens or the NFTs may not be as hyped as they were at some point in time but one thing is certain and that is that they are here to stay. These tokens provide a number of benefits to both the buyers and sellers. These NFTs are an outstanding solution to guarantee the uniqueness and source of physical and digital assets in a protected and transparent way.

The users of Algorand benefit from both the robust and flexible NFT infrastructure, they are also able to incorporate NFT royalties through a combination of Layer-1 features. These features allow them to generate their work. It can be about music, art, fashion items, patents, or other assets. In this way, Algorand's technology can refurbish the entire industries and support the creator economy as well.

Blockchain Can Help Creators Monetize Their Work

NFTs are becoming popular with every passing day. Well, that is because these NFTs guarantee ownership rights over the assets that are unique and uncommon. Not just that but some of the blockchain networks give the creators these advantages that they can keep on earning from the artworks or digital assets that they sell once. They get the opportunity to generate revenue from their assets every time they are sold to someone new. This is the royalty system introduced which helps the original creator of the assets a great deal.

Due to Algorand, the creators are given an opportunity to monetize their creations in a simple and hassle-free manner. Not just that but they can also contact their fans directly. The royalty scheme can be altered as per the wishes of the original creator to precisely reflect their relationship with their audience.

These royalties are the best way to help these creators. The majority of the artists are unable to collect royalties of their work, especially musicians. A huge number of musicians are unable to collect royalties for the work that they produce. The key factors that contribute to this issue are many. Most of the time they are unable to collect the royalties due to the vague nature of the royalty process. Another reason they are unable to collect royalties is that either they don't have their songs registered properly or because there is no one to claim for the rights when they go to the companies for publishing. They are known as unallocated royalties, and it was predicted that artists lose hundreds of millions of US dollars because of these payments that go missing. Blockchains are a great way to make sure that these artists are receiving their payments on a regular basis and are not cheated out of them. The best blockchain infrastructure is provided by Algorand. It can be used to build the ideal monetization scheme.

How to Construct an NFT with Royalty Features Provided by Algorand?

Algorand permits NFTs to fit in royalties through an amalgamation of features, which makes it simple to mint NFTs as well as integrate royalty policies.

Algorand Standard Assets (ASA) framework is used to create the NFTs. It also provides sustenance to the fungible and non-fungible tokens. Your tokens would gain an advantage from the Algorand's Layer-1. Algorand's Layer-1 is a quick, decentralized, and forkless network.

If you look at the minting process of a standard NFT on Algorand, it is really easy. The reason for that is that

Algorand sets a lot of emphasis on user experience. Developers can create the ASA-based NFT through the programming language that they prefer. It can be any programming language, Java, Go, JavaScript, and Python SDKs and REST APIs via a command-line utility. It can even be the one that is available publically for the creation of NFT apps. They are required to set up the immutable and mutable parameters for that reason. The "Total" needs to be set to 1. "Decimals" on the other hand needs to go with 0 while programming NFT.

NFT policies for royalties can be created by the developers. These can be created as per their needs and wishes.

AlgoRealm can be put to use in order to check the blockchain royalties. The royalty game for NFT was to test how all this process works.

AlgoRealm – the NFT Royalty Game that allows you to put the Test Layer-1 features to use

The AlgoRealm game works on a simple concept. It has two majesties.

- The Random Majesty of Algorand, who happens to have the Crown of Entropy NFT.
- The Verifiable Majesty of Algorand, who happens to be the Sceptre of Proof NFT.

If a user donates some ALGO tokens to the rewards pool, he will have the right of entitlement to one or both the titles. Higher donations would make it harder to dethrone other users.

The AlgoRealm NFT royalties that are donated to the Rewards Pool are controlled by a combination of ASAs, Algorand smart contracts, and atomic transfers. The goal is to connect ASA's manager addresses to a mix of Stateless and Stateful Smart Contracts that impose the royalty policy over the two NFTs. Here are the main elements:

1. ASA

The framework that is used to create AlgoRealm's artifacts is signified by NFTs. ASC1 is responsible for controlling ASC1 via the ASA clawback address.

2. Atomic Transfers

Atomic transfers execute collections of transactions that activate the concurrent interactions between the game's components that are Stateful and Stateless.

3. Stateful Algorand Smart Contract

Stateful Algorand Smart Contract is responsible for implementing the AlgoRealm Application that manages ASC1 global state. It keeps a track of the donations' amounts and current Majesties' nicknames.

4. Stateless Algorand Smart Contract

Stateless Algorand Smart Contract is responsible for implementing the AlgoRealm Law as a Contract Account. It approves NFTs clawback transactions based on the royalties' policy.

The interactions between the features listed above need to tail a specific sequence for deployment:

- Stateful Application deployment
- NFTs creation
- Stateless Contract Account deployment
- NFTs configuration
- Stateful Application configuration.

Mentioned below are some benefits of using non-fungible tokens. These advantages may end up providing the basis for their value.

Ownership

The leading and primary advantage of non-fungible tokens is obvious in the proof of ownership. Blockchain networks make it easy to associate the ownership to one account. NFTs cannot be divided and hence could not be distributed among multiple owners. This also makes sure that the ownership belongs to only one person. It helps protect from counterfeits and replicas.

NFT critics have indicated that people could just take pictures of NFTs and sell them or even give them away free of cost. It is possible that someone can have an image of the NFT. However, it is significant to inquire if you are the one who owns the asset. For instance, copying a picture of the Mona Lisa from the internet would not make you its real owner.

If you have an NFT for as an asset that makes you the real owner and appreciates the value of your NFT because it is legit. In simple words, NFTs can transform the orthodox customs of validating and handling the ownership of assets. Transferring ownership of an NFT is relatively easy as the whole information is recorded on the blockchain. You can discover the benefit of the easy changeover of asset ownership with NFTs in many everyday situations.

Authenticity

One of the biggest benefits of non-fungible tokens is that they are unique. Due to uniqueness, they are also scarce. The NFTs have unique records stored on the blockchain as well. Due to their unique nature, they are of great value. Scarcity of the NFT supply is ensured by issuing a limited number of NFTs by the NFT creators.

Considering the ticket case, some of the creators of the NFTs do create a number of copies. Alternatively, the immutability of the blockchain on which NFTs are stored makes sure that it is authentic. Immutability in blockchain-based NFTs makes sure that they are insusceptible to any changes, removal, or replacement. The authenticity of the NFTs can very easily be represented and that makes it its worthiest quality.

Transferability

NFTs are transferrable. NFTs can be easily bought or sold. You can freely trade these NFTs in a number of marketplaces without any issue. For instance, NFTs can be of great help in resolving the issue of 'walled gardens' in regards to online games.

Majority of the games, issue in-game items. These items are bought by the players so they are able to enhance their overall gaming experience. These items may improve the gaming experience but they are only specific to that one game and cannot be used elsewhere. This means that if the player no longer plays the game or it goes out of fashion, the player would lose his investment.

If you consider the NFTs, you would see the people who develop these games issue NFTs as the in-game items. These NFTs could be stored by the players in their digital wallets. These NFTs are not specific to one game only, they can also be used outside the game. Not just that but the player can sell them for profit too. Since smart contracts provide a base for NFTs, transferring ownership rights become easy by integrating the use of smart contracts. Ownership transfers can be facilitated by fulfillment of the terms and conditions that are set by both the trading parties.

Creation of Economic Opportunity

If you look at the advantages of the NFTs, you will see them directing you to the fundamental traits possessed by them. In today's world, there are wide applications of NFTs in the digital content domain. One of the main and strategic reasons for the likelihood of using NFTs in the world of digital content denotes the disjointed nature that this industry has.

There have been many instances where the content creators have voiced their concerns regarding platforms tossing down the profits that they are making. Let's consider an example here, a digital artist publishes their content on social networks. These social networking sites would also make money for the platform selling ads to the fans of the artist whose work has been published. The only benefit that it provides the artist is his exposure and not any financial gain from the platform.

These NFTs are one of the main factors that are leading to the development and growth of the artists' financial conditions. The creator economy would result in the artists focusing on the quality of work that they are producing. Not just that but also help the content creators elude the necessity for transferring ownership to platforms used by them for sharing their content publically.

CHAPTER NO 20

HOW TO BE A CRYPTO ARTIST?

There are a number of artists that work with NFTs and are known as NFT artists. This is not a new concept. NFT artists began selling their digital art as NFTs back in 2015. Now the majority of the auction houses have entered this business as well and with their entrance, NFTs have become more mainstream as they are selling the NFTs in millions of dollars.

Not just that but it has also come up with multiple opportunities for the people who deal with digital art and poster designing. Now the artists can showcase their works without any galleries. They can do so all online. Additionally, whenever any resale of the digital art happens, the artists are provided with a certain percentage of incentive so they can keep earning from the art that they produced.

Art collectors have also started to take interest in this field and they have started looking for artists on these platforms. The majority of art collectors can be found on these platforms nowadays. If you are also interested in collecting art pieces, you can start from these platforms and build your collection.

Below is an explanation of how you can get yourself involved if you are someone who loves to collect such art.

What is an NFT Digital Artist?

What basically is an NFT digital artist? Those artists that sell their digital artworks in the form of non-fungible tokens are said to be the NFT digital artists. Their specialty is the creation of digital art and then selling them as NFTs.

It is important to know what an NFT or a non-fungible token is?

The non-fungible token is a token of unique nature that signifies ownership rights of a digital art piece. Cryptocurrencies and all the units associated with them can be used interchangeably as they all have the same value. However, in the case of the NFTs, you cannot use them interchangeably. That is because the NFTs are unique and this uniqueness contributes to the authenticity factor of the digital art or any other asset.

Each of the NFT is unique and one of its kind. It can be traded for objects (tangible or digital) of dissimilar nature. You can think of them as digital files which are used to prove the authenticity or ownership of any digital asset. NFTs are listed and recorded on a public, and secured digital ledger known as a blockchain.

You can find numerous types of NFTs but the most famous ones are the ones that belong to the Ethereum blockchain.

NFTs can not only be used for digital art but they can be used for other purposes as well. But they have proved to be more worthy in the field of digital art.

Now, why is that so?

Well, that is because there have been instances of counterfeit products. For example, there are a lot of copies of the Mona Lisa painting available but there is only one original painting that is owned by the French republic. We cannot say something similar regarding the digital artwork.

The artists who own the art can keep the copyrights, reproduction rights, and a percentage of royalties to himself but NFTs have made the transfer of ownership of the artworks possible.

Being a digital artist or a creator and you want to sell your artwork on these platforms, you need to make some initial investment. You need to make that investment in order to mine the NFTs so you are able to sell them to the one who bids the highest.

You also have to pay the gas fee. This is important because this helps record your information concerning the ownership rights and authenticity on an Ethereum blockchain network.

There may be multiple copies of the Mona Lisa painting available and that may look exactly similar to the original one but still, they are not as worthy as the original painting. That is because the original painting has a historical value. The digital copies may be similar to the original but still, they are not original and don't have the same worth.

Now you might be thinking that why would you want to make a copy that is expensive when you can do that for free. Also, you might think at this point that why would someone go all the way to buy that expensive copy from you. Well, some of the reasons for that are mentioned below.

Selling digital art is hard

It has been acknowledged that selling digital art can be pretty challenging. In order to make themselves known, these digital artists upload their work on social media platforms to create a fan base and advertise their work as well.

The art that they post cannot be sold as it is available online and these artists know already that people would grab screenshots of their work and use them for different purposes.

There are two types of artists. The first ones only want to solve the problem with the art commissions while the other type wants creative liberty. These non-fungible tokens are a great way for these artists to keep generating revenue from their work.

If you are looking to generate revenue from the NFTs and that is your sole motive of getting involved in the business here is how you can do so.

A second reason

You must have dealt with such annoying and frustrating situations where you can only make money by selling your artwork once. On the other hand, the person who purchases the art can resell it for higher profits. They can share and reproduce it as many times as they want and keep earning from it.

The one who buys the NFT has the authority to further sell it. The good thing about the NFTs is that you will get a percentage of the proceeds that come from the resale of the artworks.

Dishonesty protection

NFT industry is working tirelessly for the protection of its clients from dishonest and fraudulent buyers. This also helps the clients that are dedicated to supporting the art.

Many fans react emotionally to certain artworks and would appreciate the opportunity to help the maker get some financial assistance for it.

Internet is a great way through which you can help the people who are looking to earn some money. It's a great way to invest your money in.

Previously, this was done by making a donation to the artist without getting anything in return. But now, a donation to the artist lets them get their hands on an

NFT that they legally own and have the right to use for non-commercial purposes.

Collecting art is investment & supremacy.

In the case of the collection of art, it's both about cultural appreciation and power.

Formerly, if you desired to build wealth out of theory and chance. You were only limited to either investing in the stock market or gambling.

Nowadays people are investing in various kinds of cryptocurrencies and NFTs as well.

New digital art markets such as Rarible, Nifty Gateway, OpenSea, super rare, or Foundation are so exhilarating that many people are actually becoming a part of it to make more money.

It is something that is the future.

People are becoming a part of the industry because this industry is getting bigger and bigger.

You will get to hear the success stories of creators that have been working all around the globe. The artists were first deprived of public acknowledgment and appreciation without financial payback. They made an effort in getting involved in the NFT space without assuring if it is legitimate and fair.

They now have the opportunity of earning in dollars. Those who work in the art world understand how hard it is to make money out of efforts driven by passion.

After long there is a piece of happy news for the creators that they will finally see a steady source of income in their creative future.

NFT's have made it is possible for everyone to have an equal chance of becoming successful as a digital NFT artist.

Ok, so how do I become one?

If you are questioning yourself regarding this, know that this is the right time. The market is hot and people are making money as well. Different blockchain technologies are working in the industry and continuously trying to reach the top by offering the best services to the users.

There are various platforms available that you can use. You need to do a little research regarding everything and then jump onto the bandwagon. Research well about the platforms and blockchain technologies available.

super rare focuses on digital artwork. Rarible on the other hand proposes digital collectible items and OpeanSea declares that CryptoKitties are sold by them.

You need to make a choice if you are a chic and classy artist who wants to get involved or just a casual illustrator who is looking for clients. Or just a creator who wants to work together on some random trend?

You may create any type of art, there is an NFT market that would be a perfect fit for your art profile.

Platform picking

The process of registration on each platform is different from the other. The changes might be very small but they do exist. Foundation allows you to discover a complete guide to becoming a creator on the platform. To be able to sell a project as an NFT in Nifty Gateway, it is required for you to apply. In KnownOrigin, you can connect in three different ways initially.

Regardless of whatever platform you choose for yourself, the process is pretty simple and hassle-free. The creation of NFT is a simple process too.

The art piece that you need to adapt into an NFT can be anything from an illustration to a video, an animation, a comic, a meme, a sticker, etc.

You need to think of what is your first NFT going to be. Once you are done with that you have to move on to the creation of your crypto wallet. You can use your crypto wallet to store your currency but also use it for registration on different marketplaces for NFT.

In the real world markets, you use dollars to purchase and trade stuff whereas these are digital markets and for trading, you will be using digital money or cryptocurrencies.

Again, there are various crypto wallets that you can choose from such as MetaMask, Atomic, Rainbow, etc.

The majority of them are free of cost. They work well with blockchain apps too.

Before starting, do some research on which crypto wallet will prove useful for you. For example, MetaMask is considered to be a better option for OpenSea and Rarible, while CoinBase is suggested for KnownOrigin or SuperRare.

Afterward, purchase a digital wallet and add some cryptocurrency to it.

Ethereum blockchain does not host all the NFTs but it is easy to work with. If you have just stepped into this space, beginning with Ethereum is a good choice.

There is a lot of variation in the price of Ethereum. You can start with dollars and then move to Ethereum and purchase some.

You don't have to make huge investments initially. The creation of NFTs doesn't usually cost a lot. It should take up to 200 dollars for you to create an NFT.

You need to make a few choices first. You need to choose your marketplace, purchase a crypto wallet and some cryptocurrency. Once you are done with this, you will be able to create an account on the platform and link your digital wallet.

You need to attain membership in a platform or a marketplace so you are able to sell your artwork as an NFT. You will have to remunerate the gas fee.

You can have the common files such as JPG, PNG, MP3, and GIF as NFTs as well. It is up to you if your NFT will be an individual piece. You have the right to choose whatever price you wish.

NFTs can be sold by bidding. After publishing, people would be able to see your work and then bid for it. If you are lucky enough the original price will be less than the final one.

If your art is listed on the platform that certainly does not guarantee somebody would purchase it. In order to make your artwork sell, you have to advertise your work in a way that people buy from you. You have to ensure that you have groomed yourself enough and have ample marketing skills to better advertise your product. Join groups that are about the NFTs on social media to have better insights.

CHAPTER NO 21

INVESTING IN ART AND LUXURY COLLECTIBLES

The digital art market is growing big with every passing day. The investments have gone up to 300% last year. Here are the details that are crucial for you to know about the NFT market.

NFTs are soon going to turn over the art system similar to how Bitcoin and Ethereum are going to change the financial landscape.

Mike Winkelman in the March of 2021, was able to sell his digital artwork, "First 5,000 Days" through an online Christie's auction for $69.3 million. This amount is regarded as the highest amount that has ever been paid for an artwork by any artist.

This sale was recorded after the months of maximizing the digital art auctions. In October, Winkelmann was able to sell the first series of NFTs, with a pair going for $66,666.66 each. In December, he sold some of his work for $3.5 million total. An NFT that was originally sold for $66,666.66 was sold again for $6.6 million.

Beeples work has become of great value and there are certain factors that contribute to it. The reason for his work becoming so valuable is his increasing fan base. He has around 2.5 million followers on his social media platforms. Winkelmann is one creative individual and he is able to create and publish one artwork on a daily basis. His project that goes by the name "Everyday's" has now over 5000 art pieces and this number is increasing with every passing day.

Beeple is not solely exploring the digital field, there are others too. Damien Hirst is another one who was able to sell a time-based open edition series of prints for $22.4 million. He also disclosed that he was about to launch a secret NFT art project called Currency that has been working on.

He said that this project has been in the works for the past five years. It has completely surprised him and helped him explore the concept of value via money and art. Now for the last three years, he has been trying to expand the project into the blockchain and NFTs.

"It involves 10,000 original works of art on paper, which I call "The Currency". I made them all five years ago, and they are in a vault but about to come to life through their launch on the blockchain. They also exist as NFTs and related cryptocurrencies. The whole project is an artwork, and anyone who buys "The Currency" will participate in this work, it's not just about owning it. It is the most exciting project I have ever worked on by far."

The NFT market is growing with every passing day. A big reason for this is the support it is getting from serious buyers and the money they are investing. It is important to know that what are NFTs and are really going to stay and shall be taken seriously?

NFTs are used to display the ownership of unique digital assets. The track of these tracks is recorded onto a blockchain network. All the details of ownership and authentication are stored on a blockchain. NFT stands for 'non-fungible token', and it can comprise anything digital, drawings, animated GIFs, songs, or items in video games. NFT can be unique or they can be copies like that in the print editions. Blockchain keeps a track of who owns the artwork. In quintessence, an NFT proves that the digital artwork you bought is unique or from a short run. That makes it scarce.

NFTs are the talk of the town as there have been some sales that have been happening. The sales that have been happening are worth millions of dollars. Notorious memes such as Nyan Cat and the "deal with it" sunglasses are being put up for auction. Another reason these NFTs making headlines is that the memes and art that have been sold for millions of dollars have been viewed by people free of cost. NFT is not about the liking of something that no one else has access to but about owning a version that is unique to something already enjoyed by many.

So why now is everyone talking about now?

The market is flourishing already but there are other things to consider as well. Covid-19 has made it essential for collectors to view the physical art online on the websites of top galleries. This setting doesn't excite me anymore.

This happens due to a reason and that is because it was not meant to be on this medium. That art was meant to be displayed in the gallery setting. What this occurrence has done is that by taking help of the publicists from galleries, art fairs, and auction houses, is to legitimize the purchase of expensive, high-level art online.

The number of active bidders in the Beeple auction was 33. 20 of these 33 never bid at Christie's prior to that. Most people have their wealth in the form of cryptocurrency and they still making more in the cryptocurrency market. The NFT market has created new opportunities in the world of art for many artists who spurned it in its more old-fashioned appearance. Trust is also a very important factor. There is a constant struggle by the industry people to get acknowledgment from famous galleries and auction houses as a way to inculcate trust in potential buyers.

It has already taken place. We have been told to purchase art online by these famous galleries and auction houses. We have also seen that art that has been created for some medium is better than art that hasn't been created for it. A lot of people have started to purchase art online. If you look at the NFT technology, you would understand that it is something that ensures individuality, scarcity, and worth.

Are NFTs something worthy to invest in?

Keld Van Schreven is an art collector and co-founder of KR1 Europe. It is considered to be one of the leading digital assets investment companies. A quote by Keld Van Schreven states that "NFTs are a very interesting option for art collectors as you are buying and investing in a new revolution as well as the art itself. NFTs are going to topple the art system as much as Bitcoin and Ethereum are going to change the financial landscape.

"Once you have bought an NFT, reselling the work you have bought couldn't be easier. There are several markets that you can buy and sell NFTs on and they have good liquidity. NFTs completely disintermediate the gallery system. NFTs are a game-changer for artists as well as collectors as they give artists new liquidity as well as a tamper-proof storage medium with automatic royalties on future sales."

Van Schreven states that one of the issues with the prevailing art world is the struggle of selling your art. Selling the art quickly is something that is not considered a good thing as artists don't get a cut of the resale price majority of the time.

Research for the right platforms is essential before you make investments in the market. Know that all the platforms do not allow to sell NFTs and also they not all of them are reliable. Commission rates differ too. Some of them have high commission rates. There also have been cases where frauds are selling the art of others as their own. Also, there have been multiple instances of the theft of the crypto wallets that store your NFTs and cryptocurrencies.

There are few platforms that are well-known and managed in a better way. Investors should not feel discouraged. Nifty Gateway, Super Rare, and Foundation, etc. are among the best platforms for NFT trading. You should be able to cover a lot of potential problems and challenges through this. Everything on the market is pretty transparent and you can see all the data and records of the previous ownerships. If you are still confused regarding this whole concept you can invest in Ethereum. It is the cryptocurrency that is used to mint these NFTs.

CHAPTER NO 22

AS NFTS ARTIST HOW TO MAKE SALES?

The strategies used to sell digital artwork have been shared by artists.

The world of digital artwork has been reformed by the NFTS, in a short amount of time, enabling the artists to sell their artwork for a large sum of money. When the worth of Ether which is the cryptocurrency bought and sold in this market increased tenfold, in January, it was said that this is only the beginning.

Many artists have followed suit in the NFTs market since the figures sales are appealing to very enticing sums. Not only has this new endeavor created many opportunities but it also provides with news tasks, such as self-promotion. You might be speculating what needs to be done to make a sale, If you have been allowed admittance to an If marketplaces such as Foundation, Opensea, Superrare, Rarible, or Makers Place, have allowed you admittance and your works have been tokenized you are probably wondering what you need to do to make a sale.

A person who earns through a creative job online cannot ignore the topic of NFTs, he is encouraged to understand a concept that is totally stuck in the terminology of cryptocurrency and blockchain technology. Some people strongly believe the NFTs to be a part of a digital upheaval that will grant creators control over their fates.

Others worry about the environmental impact and unrealistic expectations set by, say, the news that digital artist Beeple had sold a JPG of his collected works for $69 million in a Christie's auction.

While this endeavor is running on what is thought to be "treasured" digital art, however, it is also causing the same old complications that have beset artists for the longest of times: unclear publicity, the notions of elite collectors, and burglary. There are scammers stealing artwork and selling it as retail, for example, on ad-funded T-shirt shops, whom digital artists have to encounter. NFTs are now added to the list that digital artists have to keep an eye on.

If beginners are interested in joining the skirmish before this present level of enthusiasm lowers they must separate practical, logistical, and ethical challenges. As some artists profit from their digital artworks presented for a new audience of approachable, keen buyers, there still remains a question: Are digital artists benefitted by the NFT enthusiasm, or is it just helping to make affluent cryptocurrency holders even wealthier?

The top ten marketing strategies for endorsing digital artwork include:

1. Transfer to Twitter

Since you can add links on Instagram only if you have more than 10 thousand followers, this creates a problem for artists using this application to sell their artwork. Twitter is the new go-to platform for spreading links for selling crypto art because it enables you to share links. Instagram is not constructive enough because sales are contingent on the links to the auctions and the Instagram "link in bio" does not suffice, because it sends users directly to the gallery.

Earlier, Twitter was not thought to be a graphic platform by the arty world, but now people have understood that it offers a better way to exhibit work than Instagram. According to an artist who has sold seven out of the eight works put up for sale on Foundation, identifies that Twitter works wonders for presenting a series, a setup that seems to be acknowledged in the current market.

Twitter also offers feedback by sharing and retweeting the work of other artists.

2. Don't neglect Instagram

All social media play an important role in the promotion of your artwork. It is agreed that Twitter is indeed the finest stage for sharing links, but if you have an Instagram following, no matter how unassertive, let it not be ignored. You can use Instagram to not only display your portfolio and present your recent projects but also your past work. The progression and development of an artist's work can be pivotal for collectors.

3. Use hashtags correctly

The best way to build a circle in a world with millions of conversations and images occurring at the same time is by following the right hashtags. This will increase the chances of your artwork being spread and seen by many creators.

#nft   #nftart   #nftartist   #nfts   #nftcollector #nftcommunity   #cryptoart   #cryptoartist #nftphotography #nftanimation #nftvideo #digitalart are the twelve most used hashtags.

Using these hashtags in your profile description can be really useful. These tags can be used on Twitter as well as Instagram.

4. Share more than just work

As observed by the 3D illustrator Zigor Samaniego, who says that when you display the whole process of creativity, the ideas, and inspiration behind your work, people seem to take more interest in that. Out of all the Spanish artists who entered into the NFT world Zigor was one of the first ones. Zigor participated in an auction organized by Nifty Gateway gallery in October 2020 which earned him 10 thousand dollars. From that time on, his focus has been on the several ways to self-promote. As explained by him, "I understand that it helps to generate interest during the weeks leading up to an auction,".

You might wonder what the superlative way to do this would be? Well, it could be done through time-lapses, sharing bits of a piece and previews of details. Lots of thrill is created by images of artists working in their studios, so does an artist sharing and admiring the artworks by other artists.

5. Seeking out collectors... or not

Creative Gabriel Suchowolski explains that in the world of Twitter, there are a lot of people who say that they have lots of money that they wish to spend on crypto art but at the same time also want convincing. They may be authentic but the majority of the time they are not. This results in many artists being drawn to go out unambiguously search down collectors, guiding them to their artworks and messaging them privately. Do you wish to know if it is a good idea? The people interviewed have unanimously refused. Llorens says that he approaches only those people who have bid at his auctions or bought his earlier artworks.

6. Discord forums

Apps such as Discord allow users to create chat rooms for various purposes. It is referred to as the slack for gamers and presently crypto users too. Discord not only allows chatting but also provides more proficient features that include the sharing and storing of documents. To share your work, you can join the chatrooms specifically for crypto galleries.

To the private, you can be invited by other users. There are separate chatrooms for major legendary collectors in the NFT art world. Those who succeed in entering these chatrooms are considered elite since they have restricted access.

7. Promotion on Reddit

Reddit, a content aggregator, whose users have voting powers. A post rises in Reddit rankings and reaches a larger audience, if it gains more votes, Its visibility is lowered by the downvotes. Not only can you investigate what you don't understand in forums that share educational articles, but you can also showcase your arts in community threads like reddit.com/r/CryptoArt, which has nearly 8 million users. There is a special group dedicated to Ethereum exclusively.

8. Newsletters about NFTs

The artworks with maximum retailing possibilities are being sought out by trend hunters, including NFT hunters. A newsletter of top works is directed to the subscriber's email or Telegram accounts once or twice a week. In the case of breaking news or a sudden trend, an extra email with all the details is sent to the subscribers which make pitching your artworks for these trend hunters' contemplation very easy: all you need to do is send an email to the address that appears on their website.

9. Collaborations

Both in the significant and the not-so-significant groups, collaborations are an emergent fashion, because in the world of NFTs together is better. Only just, when the German DJ Boys Noize worked with visual artists Art Camp, Danae Gosset, and Danica they create a clip that ended up selling for $25,000.

A comparable sum amount of money was generated when Taiwanese singer Eric Chou collaborated with a visual artist and filmmaker, from Hong Kong, Wing Shea. In the smaller groups, similar methods can be observed: for instance, very recently a joint project of 100 unfamiliar artists, brought together by Loopify, an artist and writer sold for $89k, seven times the price initially put on Rarible.

10. Represent yourself in the truest way possible as an artist:

The existing economic crisis makes it fathomable as to why numerous artists are implementing NFTs. It can feel especially addictive particularly to the people who have previously profited from this development. Lloréns states that it's all this is so impulsive and random that you often get to feel that it is temporary and all you have to do is to take the maximum advantage from it.

You should definitely not do what everyone else is doing or what is demanded in the market, rather create art that represents you, that reflects your personality. This is a great chance given to the artist and content creators by the NFTs. This is so you focus on your art more and the demands of the clients less.

CONCLUSION

A distributed software network that is used as a digital ledger, as well as a secure way of transferring assets, is known as a blockchain. Blockchain technology initially emerged in the year 2009. The bitcoin blockchain first appeared as a bitcoin blockchain. The bitcoin blockchain is considered to be one of the most secure and resistant to censorship electronic cash systems. Nowadays, there are a number of blockchain technologies. Ethereum blockchain is powered by ether (ETH). The non-fungible token is a new concept the popularity of which is increasing with every passing day. The digital assets are traded peer-to-peer. That is so no one is able to change or alter any transactions that have been happening over the network.

Non-fungible tokens or NFTs are used to represent the ownership rights over a digital asset. All the information regarding the ownership of these assets is recorded on the Ethereum blockchain. You can interchange cryptocurrencies with each other but you cannot interchange the NFTs with each other. That is because the NFTs are unique and this uniqueness is a factor that makes them scarce as well. If you compare the cryptocurrencies and the NFTs you may conclude that cryptocurrencies and the NFTs may work on the same blockchain technology but if you look at their uses and purposes, you will find out that they are completely different from one another. Although the marketplaces where you can buy and sell the NFTs may accept payment in the cryptocurrencies. But creation and uses of the two are completely different from one another.

The NFT royalty scheme is a good way for the artists who create digital art to generate revenues after selling their artwork. Previously the artists suffered a lot financially because they were not able to earn enough from their art. This was something that jeopardized their art careers but through the NFT royalty scheme, the artists are able to earn a percentage of the total revenue generated with every resale. Whenever a buyer sells the NFT on a secondary platform and makes sales, the original artist will get the predetermined amount of incentives from the resale. This has helped the artists a lot with their financial issues and they are able to come up with more creative content.

NFT industries and markets are relatively new and the markets are highly volatile. Before you make any investment in the NFT market you need to do all the background research. You need to understand the market well because you never know how would the market be in the coming years. It is growing big and flourishing nowadays but there is no certainty that it would do so in the coming years. NFT markets may be a great way to generate revenue online but it comes with its risks which you cannot ignore.

There have been instances where people earned millions of dollars through the NFTs but you have to keep in mind that this may not always be the case. It is not necessary that you would earn so much through the NFTs. There are certain factors that contribute to earning millions of dollars through NFTs. However, you can generate revenue through the NFTs and people nowadays are doing so. Do all your relevant research and then select a marketplace for the NFT trading. It is important that you choose a marketplace that is popular and commonly used. You need to trust the marketplace that you are choosing because there have been multiple cases of fraud and theft on unreliable marketplaces. There have been a number of instances recorded where the cryptocurrencies were stolen from the crypto wallets of the users. In order to protect your digital wallets, you need to have a strong password and a secret phrase that you can use to protect them.

Experts say that NFTs have come to stay and are not going any time soon and we have been seeing that as well. The momentous growth that has been seen in these markets is proof that NFTs could indeed be the future if you like it or not!

Made in the USA
Middletown, DE
26 December 2021

57054885R00215